ADVANCE PRAISE FOR

PEDAGOGY OF HUMANIZATION: PREPARING TEACHERS FOR CULTURALLY SUSTAINING CLASSROOMS

"Culturally relevant pedagogy is not just an instructional method grounded in sound evidence and research; it's an approach to life and learning rooted in humanity—one that embraces how we best learn, how we best grow, and how we best realize our full potential as individuals and as a collective. But in a time of sociopolitical tension, where even the mere utterance of "culture" in education can draw ire or censure, teachers need not only guidance on how to teach in culturally relevant ways, but also assurance that we should. In *Pedagogy of Humanization*, Smith shares what culturally sustaining classrooms can look and sound like across multiple content areas, demonstrating how they shape minds, change hearts, and uplift our shared humanity."

Takeru "TK" Nagayoshi, 2020 Massachusetts Teacher of the Year and recipient of the 2021 Horace Mann Award for Teaching Excellence

"High praise for the *Pedagogy of Humanization: Preparing Teachers for Culturally Sustaining Classrooms* by Chelda Smith Kondo where one journeys through and with culture to the heart of a humanistic pedagogy that embraces youth as complex individuals worthy of dignity and respect. It insists that all teaching is political and how, at its best, leads to both individual and collective empowerment."

Angela Valenzuela, Ph.D., College of Education, University of Texas at Austin

PEDAGOGY OF HUMANIZATION

EDUCATIONAL PSYCHOLOGY: MEANING MAKING FOR TEACHERS AND LEARNERS

EDITED BY CATHRENE CONNERY, PHD, GREG S. GOODMAN, PHD, AND ALTHEA J. PENNERMAN, PHD

Inspired by the contributions of Vygotsky, Freire, and a host of post-modern, feminist, and critical educators, *Educational Psychology: Meaning Making for Teachers and Learners* is a collection of books dedicated to individual learners and seeking to create a collective, egalitarian enlightenment. This educational psychology series strives to involve the best of today's researchers and practitioners in a dialogue dedicated a mutual educational and cultural advantage for both teachers and learners. Looking to stimulate and promote positive changes in the pedagogy and practice of learning, *Educational Psychology: Meaning Making for Teachers and Learners* seeks contributions from writers who are both proffering solutions and are proud to have their voices heard.

As a field of inquiry, educational psychology has continued to evolve by responding to changes in our understanding of the importance of cultural diversity, individual learner propensities, and the collective need to find relevance and purpose. In pursuit of these goals, we invite authors to submit proposals for texts designed to enlighten teachers and students on topics that inspire today's learners: equity, creativity, experiential learning, cultural diversity, STEM, interdisciplinary study, international education, authentic assessment, peace education, second language acquisition, outdoor education, and other new and novel approaches.

If you share our passion for promoting educational change, we invite you to consider Myers Educational Press for your publishing project. To assist you in the process, we are available to provide you with resources to support the development of your project all along the continuum from concept development through publication. Please contact us for further assistance concerning your proposal.

M. Cathrene Connery
General Editor
cconnery@salisbury.edu

Greg S. Goodman
General Editor
gsgoodman17@gmail.com

Althea Pennerman
General Editor
ajpennerman@salisbury.edu

Books in the Series:

Children and Trauma:
Critical Perspectives for Meeting the Needs of Diverse Educational Communities
by Brianne Kramer & Jennifer McKenzie (2022)

Pedagogy of Humanization:
Preparing Teachers for Culturally Sustaining Classrooms
by Chelda Smith Kondo (2024)

PEDAGOGY OF HUMANIZATION

Preparing Teachers for Culturally Sustaining Classrooms

BY CHELDA SMITH KONDO

Myers Education Press

Gorham, Maine

Myers Education Press

Published by Myers Education Press, LLC
P.O. Box 424
Gorham, ME 04038

Myers Education Press is an academic publisher specializing in books, e-books and digital content in the field of education. All of our books are subjected to a rigorous peer review process and produced in compliance with the standards of the Council on Library and Information Resources.

Library of Congress Cataloging-in-Publication Data available from Library of Congress.

13-digit ISBN 978-1-9755-0509-7 (paperback)
13-digit ISBN 978-1-9755-0510-3 (library networkable e-edition)
13-digit ISBN 978-1-9755-0511-0 (consumer e-edition)

Printed in the United States of America.

All first editions printed on acid-free paper that meets the American National Standards Institute Z39-48 standard.

Books published by Myers Education Press may be purchased at special quantity discount rates for groups, workshops, training organizations and classroom usage. Please call our customer service department at 1-800-232-0223 for details.

Cover design by Teresa Lagrange.

Visit us on the web at **www.myersedpress.com** to browse our complete list of titles.

Contents

Acknowledgments

All praises to God, because for so much of this project, there was only one set of footprints.

Thank you Illenin, Elijah, and Izzy, Behrmann, and Tashiba. It's humbling how you humanize me so that I might learn and teach how to humanize others. Thank you to the director and staff at the Loman Art House Café in Dakar, Senegal for giving me a refuge to write and reflect. Special thanks to Babacar for adopting me and the kids and Mr. Daniel for mentoring Elijah who created original illustrations for this book.

Being a Visiting Scholar at the Opportunity & Inclusive Growth Institute (OIGI) set the foundation and space for this project to unfold. I'm grateful to Abigail Wozniak, the institute's director, who trusted a sociologist of education to have valuable insights to offer economists working to pursue an economy that works for ALL—especially those perpetually marginalized and disenfranchised. Pairing me with Monique E. Davis, an incredible human and talented graduate assistant, facilitated completion of the book's first draft. Monique, your investment in the project, your collaborative approach, and skillful editing enhanced the breadth and depth of the book.

Shakia Asamoah, you took the lead on a crucial part of this journey. With incredible dedication and a black feminist lens, you reviewed the first draft of the book for missteps in humanization. You critiqued whether the activities were doable and the insights and theories, accurate. With grace, you humbled us. Thank you.

Thank you, Katie Brkich, my work wife; despite incontrovertible evidence to the contrary, you ALWAYS believe in me.

You said I should I write a book and we did it! Thank you.

Thank you to all the contributors of each individual chapter:

Alesia Moldavan

Alexandra J. Reyes

Anne Valauri

Ariel Cornett
Deborah Garrahy
Erin Piedmont
Kara Taylor
Katie Brkich
LaPortia Mosley
Laura Vines
Montana Smithey
Sam Rhodes
Tameka Ardrey

Thank you, Bruce Field, for being an incredible mentor and department chair.

To Greg Goodman, my mentor, editor, and cheerleader extraordinaire.

Finally, the generous support of Georgia Southern University's College of Education made this book possible. Specifically, I'd like to thank Tracy Linderholm and Dean Sharon Subreenduth for your grace and grant funds to hire a thoughtful, kind, and meticulous copyeditor, Julie McLaughlin. Thank you, Greg Chamblee, for loaning me the absolute best graduate assistant.

Ready for it? Rebecca Martini, girl! I'd consider becoming a Swifty just for us to shake it off. When I was at my wits' end, trying to figure out how to license images or format chapters—you stepped in to fill in the blank space. Greg must have known that you belong with me because you carried the logistics of this project and did so with impeccable style. Without your help, I'm certain I would have given up, so thank you for saying "you need to calm down". Most importantly, thank you for having an unmatched work ethic. You are an inspiration, and this is me trying.

Preface

Chelda Smith Kondo

THIS IS A BOOK WRITTEN to make critical pedagogy (Freire, 1968) and one of its most celebrated iterations—culturally relevant pedagogy—practical and applicable for students and teachers. It aims to bridge a persistent theory to practice gap by answering the question, "How do we do it?"

Theoretical Summary

Paulo Freire once shared that his childhood experiences of hunger taught him about the relationship between social class and knowledge. He learned that when his basic needs and humanization were not addressed, his education was compromised. Freire is the father of critical pedagogy, a type of teaching and practice that centers the lives of students and makes their learning relevant for empowerment and liberation. As a teacher, he taught 300 Brazilian farmworkers to read and write in 45 days so that they could advocate for themselves and participate in the decision-making that affected their daily lives. The connection between education as opportunity for liberation and improving one's quality of life was explicit and actualized. Critical pedagogy, in its simplest terms, is an educational philosophy that encourages educators and learners to analyze and critique power dynamics while also challenging inequality and inequity. Freire's revolutionary book *Pedagogy of the Oppressed*, which outlines the theoretical frameworks of his approach, has sold nearly 1,000,000 copies worldwide and fundamentally changed the course of education when we consider those who are socially marginalized (Freire, 1968).

Teachers report that their favorite aspect of being an educator is the capacity to be oneself, to form authentic relationships with students, and to empower others—especially those who are marginalized. Culturally relevant pedagogy (CRP) is an educational philosophy partially inspired by critical pedagogy (Ladson-Billings, 1994). CRP is a way of teaching that has three tenets—academic rigor, cultural competence, and critical consciousness—and it was originally conceived to highlight effective ways of teaching African American children. This book aims to expand and actualize Freire's mission of education for liberation by applying CRP across subject areas and with varying forms of intersectional identities. Practicing CRP facilitates the opportunity to be oneself, to form authentic relationships with students, and to empower others—especially those who are marginalized.

The "rigor" in "academic rigor" is consistent with the way we think about rigor in any other context. "Rigor" could be substituted for "challenging" and "growth oriented." Academic rigor means that any child who is being taught in a culturally relevant way should be growing academically because they are being challenged. Inherent in that approach is an understanding of what the child already knows and can do. The role of the teacher is to figure out what the child must know and be able to do to grow academically and determine the most effective ways to transfer those knowledges and skills. For the prekindergarten level, this could mean taking the child from letter recognition to letter sound association. At the fifth-grade level, it could mean helping a child grow from writing a paragraph consisting of three simple sentences to composing a five- to seven-sentence paragraph that includes a thesis statement. Even if you're a homeschooling parent, academic rigor is essential because it allows for the child to consistently grow; it also provides opportunities to address any gaps in a child's learning while enhancing their interests or exceptionalities. Academic rigor meets the learning goals of those who are working below benchmark or grade level, as well as those at and above benchmark or grade level. It is teaching that considers, first and foremost, the knowledges and skills that the student has already mastered.

The second tenet, cultural competence, is a journey without a final destination. In other words, one can never arrive at being culturally competent, but one can practice cultural competency and continue to evolve and grow in that area. Cultural competence considers one's intrapersonal (personal) culture and interpersonal (social) cultures. The intrapersonal is the initial place to start when one is building cultural competencies. This means that we acknowledge that every individual has lifeways to unpack—cultural practices, skills, knowledge, values, norms, beliefs, motives, and objectives. There is not a single person without culture and knowing this is the first step in establishing an active cultural competence. Thereafter, there is knowledge of others (interpersonal culture). The number of cultural and subcultural groups that people can belong to, access, be aware of, or consider is limitless. There is an equally limitless number of cultures and subcultures that you and I may never be aware of. The goal of practicing cultural competency is to understand the self (the intrapersonal), understand the cultures of the students you interact with and the communities they belong to (the interpersonal), and, because we live in a larger society, understand the culture(s) of the society that we live in.

Having the cultural competencies just mentioned is critical to the establishment, development, and expansion of one's critical consciousness, the last tenet of CRP. Critical, in the context of both critical pedagogy and critical consciousness, refers to systems of power and oppression. Having a critical consciousness about those systems allows one to orient themselves relative to those systems to determine how one might begin to address and dismantle oppression. If you are worried that it's too intense for children, say, in a second-grade classroom, to process, I invite you to consider how much the students in that classroom experience marginalization on a daily basis. Marginalization means treating someone, a group of people, or something as lesser than, insignificant, or peripheral to what is centered and important. If children of color are old enough to experience racism, then their peers are of the age to learn about racism. If any child is old enough to experience bullying, then their peers are old enough to learn about bullying and how to recognize and counter it.

If you have ever walked into an elementary classroom and seen a child who is separated from their peers, that child usually has a distinguishable identity marker that society has deemed less worthy. Perhaps the child is a multilingual learner, is bigger than everyone else, has a visible skin condition, or has an observable physical disability. Regardless of the reason, that child's experience of belonging has been compromised because of marginalization. A classroom that fosters critical consciousness would empower not only that child but also the others in the classroom to notice when marginalization is occurring and then to counteract it. Many of you have raised your children or have been raised yourselves to be inclusive of those who are marginalized. If you were also raised to notice, understand, and challenge the systems that allowed marginalization in the first place, you were raised with critical consciousness. That is counter-oppressive. Consequently, a classroom that takes up CRP is a safe space that will allow *all* children to experience academic growth, personal and social appreciation of culture, and an increased awareness of inequities, along with the empowerment to address them.

Another extension of critical pedagogy that this book unpacks is culturally sustaining pedagogy (CSP; Paris, 2012). Now, before you say, "What?!? Another iteration?" let me be clear that in this book, these three educational theories are interwoven with one another. Critical pedagogy inspired CRP, which inspired CSP. Much like evolution of culture, it is imperative that the ways that we understand, and practice teaching and learning evolve and advance over time. Ladson-Billings (2014) herself recognized that CSP was the remix 2.0 of CRP. What CSP adds to our practice of critical pedagogy is a meaningful way to address aspects of culture that are counterproductive to our collective liberation. For example, CSP allows us to challenge misogyny in hip-hop culture without dismissing the value of hip-hop. CSP is inherently asset- and growth-oriented; therefore, one's practice of academic rigor, cultural competencies, and critical consciousness is enhanced by the ability to do an inward reflection, analysis, and potential modification. Beautifully, CSP returns to two of critical pedagogy's most foundational tenets: dialogue and knowledge co-creation. Through dialogue, cultural and educational competencies can be unpacked, negotiated, and transformed.

Within each of the asset-based pedagogies is a dismantling of the hierarchy between teacher and student. The teacher is not the holder of all knowledge, and the student is not devoid of any knowledge. Instead, there is a recognition that the teacher has some specialized knowledges and skills, as well as an amalgamation of cultural values, beliefs, and practices that they bring with them into a classroom. Likewise, students come to the classroom with an amalgamation of cultural values, beliefs, and practices, as well as competencies and skills that they have learned through previous educational experiences and within their respective communities. The classroom is a site for knowledge exchange and co-creation.

Through an authentic application of critical pedagogy, CRP, and CSP, classrooms can become a site for personal and collective transformation. Intellectual and social assumptions of what is "normal" can be questioned, addressed, and reoriented. All children—especially those who are historically marginalized and underserved (read: oppressed)—can belong. Belonging is the opposite of marginalization. Curriculum in these classrooms can include and amplify perspectives and counternarratives beyond the demographic majority. Essentially, classrooms that take up these practices can be more humanizing, both individually and collectively. This book offers examples and explanations of how several teacher educators, future teachers, and some classroom teachers learn about and practice culturally relevant and sustaining pedagogy.

Positionality Statement

The primary author of this text, Chelda Smith Kondo, is a Black, straight, cisgender, newly middle-class Haitian American woman. *I am she/her*. I am so much more than those identity markers listed; however, through critical pedagogy, I have come to understand that those markers inform how people view or read me and inform how I read and experience the world. I'm not shy about my biases, both implicit and explicit, because part of my intrapersonal cultural competence is knowing that each of us has implicit and explicit biases, and the best thing I can do for myself is gain greater awareness of them so that I might exist more intentionally in my pursuit of maximum critical humanization.

Positionality statements about the other contributors to this text are included in each chapter to contextualize the perspectives, experiences, and identities that inform and shape the information being shared. Positionality statements help us be more transparent about who we are, the experiences we've had, and the assumptions, values, and objectives we hold. They disrupt the false notion of objectivity and allow us to be vulnerable about our subjectivities. Positionality statements allow us to explicitly deny neutrality and instead contextualize how our personal, social, and professional identities and experiences impact how we show up in the classroom and, by extension, how we teach.

Throughout this text, readers will sense and observe many instances where I diverge from, challenge, and stretch a colleague's thinking, being, and doing. At times, you may notice tension and synergy among coauthors of a specific chapter. In this, we intend to offer an example (not a model) of what it has meant for us to live our critical pedagogies in and through relationships.

Book Origin Story

My primary contribution in the early stages of this collaborative effort was to insist on an infusion of critical pedagogy throughout the program. At the time, I was the only faculty member in my department who had expertise in critical pedagogy, so I became versed in many facets of a teacher preparation program—from policies and field placements to accreditation and the curriculum across the core subject areas. My goal was to understand what the standard practice was, and then meaningfully figure out how to satisfy the minimum while offering both students and faculty an opportunity to create learning experiences that were academically rigorous, extended cultural competencies, and empowered all actors to be critically conscious. In 2018, I became the director of the program and was institutionally given more power to actualize my objectives.

This book, *Pedagogy of Humanization*, is an amalgamation of that effort. A chapter dedicated to each subject area—whether it's physical education, mathematics, science, literacy, or social studies—demonstrates how to practice culturally relevant and sustaining pedagogy. Those chapters are written by faculty members with subject matter expertise who have also had training in critical pedagogy, CRP, and CSP. Therefore, the faculty writing these chapters and teaching these courses aspire to model the beliefs, attitudes, and practices of critical pedagogy, CRP, and CSP.

Importantly, preservice teachers must have ample opportunities to observe, practice, and evaluate the merits of CRP tenets with culturally and linguistically diverse learners. Although it is an evolving endeavor, every course in the program embeds critical pedagogy content while supporting candidates toward instruction that is inclusive and culturally sustaining. Methods courses expose candidates to, and help them develop, evidence-based practical strategies designed to enhance instruction for *all* learners, especially those who are historically marginalized. Intentional work on critical awareness, sensitivity, and professional dispositions is also embedded throughout the program.

Guide to Reading This Book

This book has been designed and constructed as a companion text to guide undergraduate-level (e.g., Bachelor of Arts) or graduate-level (e.g., Master of Teaching) preservice and in-service teacher professional development. Preservice teachers (PSTs) will read this book to connect the material they study in teacher education courses to the daily work of being an educator who aims to be justice oriented. However, this is not a foolproof guide or a "how-to" manual that can be completed without direct support from mentors and colleagues. Instead, readers will practice the sort of engagement in individual and community growth that ignites the possibility of teaching as a force for social change. In many ways, chapters of the text could be used through a flipped classroom approach whereby faculty assign students readings and activities ahead of class and use instructional time to connect, clarify, remediate, or extend rather than teach. By inverting the typical cycle of content acquisition and application, this book invites PSTs to study and practice critical pedagogy ahead of and during direct and guided instruction.

PSTs, in-service teachers, and teacher educators alike want to teach in ways that support critical consciousness, and yet it appears unattainable (Smith Kondo, 2022). It does not have to be this way, and this book offers teachers and teacher educators a theoretical and practical guide to face this problem directly. When the book is adopted program wide, it can encourage cohesion across subjects, courses, and experiences, *and* it can encourage PSTs' development of more integrated identities as critical pedagogues, complete with model lessons, exercises, and assessments. I hope that all readers will have two primary experiences: They will feel validation and guidance in their struggles to apply theory into practice, and they will do the tangible work required to build a community of education scholars and practitioners who are committed to trying, failing, and trying again as they do the work of critical pedagogy in elementary teacher preparation.

Each section is broken into subsections and chapters designed to complement a class or experience included in typical teacher education programs. After readers begin with the introduction and Section 1 (Essential Foundations), they may read the remaining chapters out of order—all the other chapters connect back to Section 1 (Chapters 1–3). The text is designed to be iterative, so readers can encounter the content areas in any order. For example, PSTs might read and complete the science chapter (Chapter 10) as part of the requirements for their science methods course regardless of whether they have already completed the math chapters (Chapters 8 and 9) or their math methods course. When this text is adopted by a teacher education program, all instructors, field experience supervisors, and even cooperating teachers will be working with it to support PST and in-service teacher development, so there will be common language and experiences across contexts. PSTs will have repeated opportunities to practice critical pedagogy within each chapter, thus growing in their capacity to integrate critical pedagogies into their ways of knowing, reflecting, and acting across all aspects of their work as educators. Artifacts and exercises completed throughout the text could even contribute to a portfolio assessment of PSTs' growth as critical pedagogues. Additionally, some exercises could be adapted to accommodate the specific contexts of given elementary classrooms.

Reflective vignettes written by practicing teachers and alumni of the courses on which each chapter is based appear at the end of each section. They highlight three important features of this text: (1) Alumni reflect on how curriculum and pedagogy have been *received* by students, not just how faculty designed and conceived of them; (2) alumni illustrate the importance of faculty humility and the need to offer a range of opportunities for student feedback in order to design teacher education programs that are attuned to student needs; and (3) these alumni contributors also serve as "voices from the field," speaking back to their preservice experiences after having spent several years as teachers of record in their own elementary classrooms.

The following supportive resources are included in each chapter:

- Positionality statements of the chapter author(s)
- Praxis-oriented introduction with discussion of the relationship between content and critical pedagogy
- Key terms
- Key ideas
- Activities, disclaimers, exercises, and reflection prompts

As you read the book, consider, what does it look like to teach academic rigor and cultural competence, and promote critical (sociopolitical) consciousness? We, the authors, attempt to practice the pedagogy we're promoting, so you're invited to be an active reader and participant. It is our hope that you'll be transformed in your reading and doing as much as, or even more than, we were in our writing.

References

Freire, P. (1968). *Pedagogy of the oppressed.* Continuum.

Kondo, C. S. (2022). Walking the talk: Employing culturally relevant pedagogy in teacher education. *Teachers College Record, 124*(4), 65–94.

Ladson-Billings, G. (1994). What we can learn from multicultural education research. *Educational Leadership, 51*(8), 22–26.

Ladson-Billings, G. (2014). Culturally relevant pedagogy 2.0: aka the remix. *Harvard Educational Review, 84*(1), 74–84.

Paris, D. (2012). Culturally sustaining pedagogy: A needed change in stance, terminology, and practice. *Educational Researcher, 41*(3), 93–97.

SECTION I

ESSENTIAL FOUNDATIONS

ONE

Social and Cultural Foundations (Historical Grounding: From Multicultural Education to Culturally Sustaining Pedagogy)

Chelda Smith Kondo

Overview

More than any other aspect of schooling, teachers make the greatest impact on student achievement (Andrew & Jelmberg, 2010). That said, education researchers, leaders, policy makers, and even some parents are deeply invested in quests for "best practices" and panaceas to respond to the pervasive achievement gaps across ethnic and racial, class, ability, and language groups. Power and privilege are distributed inequitably in our society, and those who are socially located at the margins of gender, citizenship, skin color, ability, sexuality, neurodiversity, mental health, body size, housing, wealth, and language consistently and increasingly underperform on standardized measures of academic progress. This is not to imply that persons who are gender expansive, undocumented, darker hued, significantly disabled, LGBTTTQQIAA+ identifying, significantly neurodivergent, who have a vulnerable and unstable mental health condition, and who are larger, homeless, under sourced (poor), and/or English learning are inherently inferior or incapable. Contrastingly, they are equally capable, but they exist in a society that associates life's advantages and disadvantages with one's social location and status. Dangerously, teachers and others often associate these marginalized social groups with limited intellectual capacity and talent, and deflated overall human worth and potential. However, social locations and human worth are not related. One does not have to be White, wealthy, able-bodied, heterosexual, neurotypical, slim, rich, and/or a native speaker of English to "earn" worth and have potential. One's very existence validates their intrinsic value. Teachers would do well to adopt that mindset for themselves and Others.

Although scholars and educators widely accept that teacher education has the greatest potential to shape quality teachers, there is considerable doubt about its effectiveness. Over 60% of educated school alumni felt underprepared to address the reality of modern day classrooms (Levine, 2006). According to a 2021 report, White students made up only 47% of the public school student population in 2018 (Schaeffer, 2021). This is in stark contrast to the overrepresentation of White middle-class monolingual women in the teaching labor force, teacher education programs (TEPs), and teacher education. In essence, the field of education and teacher preparation continues to center a culturally dominant perspective in its policies, curriculum, and practices. This does not imply that White teachers and teacher educators cannot successfully teach Black, Indigenous, and People of Color (BIPOC) students. Rather, it means that ongoing and critical commitments must be made to abate the cultural differences associated with race.

To structurally reform teacher education considering these demographic disproportions, specifically in the interest of the least served in P–12 spaces, accreditation agencies have created various standards that hold TEPs accountable for preparing all teachers for a culturally and linguistically diverse classroom. Furthermore, TEPs are encouraged to increase BIPOC student enrollment in a TEP and to recruit and retain BIPOC faculty. In essence, those teaching and preparing teachers would do well to be culturally representative of the nation's demographic population. Accreditors even review programs on how well they address asset-based pedagogies. While some TEPs take a comprehensive approach to multicultural teacher education—whereby licensure courses infuse aspects of multiculturalism—others have designed individual courses that center cultural competency development.

In this chapter, I trace the roots and extensions of asset pedagogies, from multicultural education to culturally sustaining pedagogy. To begin, I survey public education and its peripheral treatment of minoritized youth, including an exploration of the many controversial, yet fluid, understandings of the term "culture." Thereafter, I focus on the history, definition, and goals of multicultural education, including transformative approaches. I describe how TEPs address multiculturalism and the national discussion for diversifying the teaching labor force. I then discuss teacher candidates of color in multicultural education courses. Throughout, I explore the potential of culturally relevant pedagogy to enhance the capacity of teacher candidates to be effective with diverse populations, as well as the limitations of multicultural education to address issues of culture and schooling.

Education Context and Culture

National compulsory education laws require all children of a minimum age to attend school. Although this concept has been crystallizing since the Massachusetts Act of 1642, rigorous consideration of how to effectively teach children who represent marginalized identities has only emerged within the last 80 years. Schools that were once considered merely spaces to prepare children for the workforce began responding to their fundamental role as socializing entities operating in an increasingly diverse and dynamic society. The most pressing concern in understanding and contextualizing the state of BIPOC students in the U.S. education system is the educational outcomes disparities across social groups. This means that children whose identities are structurally marginalized in society (e.g., students from single-parent homes, students from under-resourced homes, multilingual learners, Black and Brown children, LGBTTTQQIAA+ youth) experience academic underachievement related to access and quality, just as their adult counterparts experience marginalization across varied social determinants of health (i.e., economic stability, social and community context, neighborhood and built environment, and healthcare access and quality). Unfortunately, there is also a disciplinary parity that translates into adulthood, wherein students from marginalized communities are disproportionately punished in schools, and, consequently, their adult equivalents are overpoliced and incarcerated—hence, the school-to-prison nexus (Love, 2016).

Teachers, like all human beings, have attitudes and biases that impact the educational experiences of their students. Multicultural education aims to acknowledge the context in which marginalization happens, and to whom, while unearthing what educators can do to mitigate and disrupt those oppressions (Goodman, 1999). The lack of preparedness of teachers in underachieving schools causes and sustains academic underperformance and social displacement. The problem of underachievement is never the fault of a child. They are whole people able to have potential realized if they encounter circumstances that humanize them and make learning engaging. In schools where the teachers have low expectations, exhibit impatience, lack creativity, and disrespect or dismiss students' home and community cultures, children will underachieve. Multicultural education can help educators recognize the systemic inequities in our society and their role in it, and then work through the process of undoing harm while also transforming educator mindsets (Goodman, 1999). When teachers underestimate students, they also underserve them.

The Demographic Imperative

Of the many issues facing public education, the demographic imperative—"the disjunction between the sociocultural characteristics and previous experiences of the typical teacher candidate and those of many of our K-12 students" (Lowenstein, 2009, p. 166)—is a foundational dynamic that affects the schooling experience. The demographic imperative is the backdrop against which many of these sociocultural issues materialize. As the nation's students become increasingly ethnically diverse, its educators remain largely monocultural. According to the National Center for Education Statistics, in 2017–2018, about 79% of public school teachers were White, 9% were Hispanic, 7% were Black, 2% were Asian, 2% were of two or more races, and 1% were American Indian/Alaska Native (Schaeffer, 2021). In addition, in 2017–2018, about 76% of public school teachers were female, and 24% were male, with a lower percentage of male teachers (11%) at the elementary school level (National Center for Education Statistics, 2022). These disproportions exacerbate challenges with equitable and quality instruction for students. Myriad intersecting cultural differences can facilitate misunderstandings in classroom spaces, ranging from ethnicity to social class, gender biases, or religious practices, among others. These distinctions too often create barriers for instruction, relationship-building, and humanizing interactions.

Together, the previously stated "gaps" intersect to "divest youth of important social and cultural resources, leaving them progressively vulnerable to academic failure" (Valenzuela, 2010, p. 3). School failures, academic and cultural, often further marginalize disadvantaged communities. While the culture gap between teachers and students cannot remain static, the idealized notion of every student instructed by an individual with a comparable culture is problematic because it promotes segregated education in which students learn in superficially homogenous classrooms. That said, there must be an intermediary resolution where culture and education can intersect to benefit *all* students and transform educational experiences while considering social inequalities that mediate schooling journeys. Multicultural education attempts to work against schooling-related injustices and works to empower those students historically disenfranchised by education.

The Ambiguity of Culture

Given that this book is replete with mention of, and emphasis on, the term "culture," it is worth taking a moment to clarify the term. Edward B. Tylor (1871), founder of cultural anthropology, stated, "Culture, or civilization, taken in its broad, ethnographic sense, is that complex whole which includes knowledge, belief, art, morals, law, custom, and any other capabilities and habits acquired by man [sic] as a member of society" (p. 1). Since then, the field has expanded to refine, contradict, or validate Tylor's definition, but its core principles of knowledge, belief, art, morals, law, custom, and habits have widely persisted.

As culture interacts with people, it evolves. Hoffman (1996) criticized the field of multicultural education as an entity that reduces the innate complexity of culture. While she acknowledged culture as "the heart of multiculturalism," she condemned its co-optation by educators and scholars who limited culture to "recipe" (that which "does things" to people), "essentialized difference" (difference is diluted and stabilized), or "culture as category" (that which is stereotyped). For example, teachers, often well intended, who take up multicultural education do often co-opt culture in these reductive ways. For too many, blackness is a recipe for academic underachievement, essentialized as hip-hop and stereotyped as behaviorally challenging. Bennett (2003) concurred with Hoffman's critique of culture portrayed as a deterministic set of social behaviors. These dispositions undermine any efforts to establish authentic rapport and to appreciate the cultural assets (see Table 1.1).

Table 1.1. Ambiguity of Culture

Culture as	**Example of co-optation**	**Explanation**
Recipe: "does things" to people	Asians are good at math.	The cultural "recipe" here is that someone is Asian, and their "Asian-ness" makes them good at math.

Culture as	Example of co-optation	Explanation
Essentialized difference: diluted and stabilized	Boys are strong.	Boys are essentialized as "strong" and reduced to their physical attributes.
Category: stereotype	All Latinos are Mexican.	Latinos, people who come from many different Latin American countries, are all nationalized as Mexicans, which erases other nationalities.

Others in multicultural education advocate for an understanding of the term that encompasses all forms of existence (e.g., learning, interacting, performing, translating) to transform and transcend the personal and the contextual (Nieto & Bode, 2012). The complexity of culture and the inevitability of two or more cultures meeting—and sometimes blending or competing—within one person is what Anzaldúa (1987) described as borderlands that resist fragmentation and thrive in the consciousness of the "both-and" nature of human existence. In this book, culture can be both collective and individual and, most times, a negotiation between the two. That said, active and existing culture is inaccessible, and as scholars, we work with the residue of lived realities when we attempt to frame it. The perpetual evolution of culture undermines our capacity to comprehensively understand and, even while reading this book, know that culture is actively shifting.

What Is Multicultural Education?

At its core, multicultural education addresses the diversity of humanity as it relates to our varying social demographic groups and our learning experiences. Because we live in a patriarchal, capitalist, racist, and heteronormative society, the primary demographic groups centered are gender, class, race and ethnicity, and sexuality. However, we acknowledge intersectionality, and we reason that no one demographic group can capture one's lived experiences, be it oppressive or privileged. In this book, we will often focus on race and ethnicity as a dominant form of multicultural identity that mediates schooling experiences; this is partly due to the available statistical data across ethnic and racial lines.

According to United States Census Bureau (2020) reports, people of color make up 39.9% of the U.S. population. Hispanic or Latino are the largest minority group, representing 18.5% of the population, followed by Black or African American (13.4%), Asians/Pacific Islanders (5.9%), Two or More Races (2.8%), and American Indians/Alaska Natives (1.3%). Given that schools reflect national demographic transformations, equity in schooling experiences remains a public issue. Given the history of chronic scholastic underachievement among students of color in public education, the need to find alternative approaches to the "one size fits all" assimilation model is as critical as ever.

History and Definition

During the civil rights movement of the 1950s and 1960s, Black Americans struggled for and demanded social justice, which included voting rights, fair housing, equal employment rights, and quality education. Much like the uprisings of 2020, Black Americans mobilized across the United States to challenge state-sanctioned discrimination, violence, and oppression against their community. These grassroots efforts led to the Civil Rights Act of 1957, the Civil Rights Act of 1964, the Voting Rights Act of 1965, and the Fair Housing Act of 1968. Importantly, in 1954, the Supreme Court, in *Brown v. Board of Education*, overturned the landmark *1896 Plessy v. Ferguson* ruling that authorized segregation. *Brown v. Board of Education* declared that racially separate schools are "inherently unequal." These legislative and judicial changes aimed to suspend and prohibit further racial discrimination against Black Americans, but we know that effort did not materialize as Black Americans had hoped. Virtually six decades after the Supreme Court professed that "separate but equal" schools are unconstitutional, schools in the United States remain heavily segregated by race and ethnicity at the intersection of socioeconomic status (Bai et al., 2021). In other words, schools with a high concentration (over 51%) of BIPOC students tend to also be high-poverty schools where more than 51% of students receive free or reduced lunch (National Center for Education Statistics, 2022). Moreover, those inequities are widespread and are evidenced by the systemic marginalization of Black Americans across every social determinant of health (criminal justice, employment, housing, health care, and education).

"Institutional racism," also known as systemic racism, is a term that refers to a form of racism that is embedded in the laws and regulations of a society or an organization. It manifests as discrimination in areas such as criminal justice, employment, housing, health care, education, and political representation. *Plessy v. Ferguson* was one form of legal institutional racism that authorized racial oppression, creating insurmountable obstacles for Black people to be self-determined and experience a decent quality of life. You may think that all of this is in the past, but standardized testing is an instrument of racism and a biased system. High-stakes testing, such as mandated statewide testing of K–12 students, the SAT, the ACT, and even your teacher certification tests, such as the Praxis, are designed from a White, middle-class framework. These biased standardized tests marginalize Black, Latin(o/a/x), and Native students, as well as students from some Asian groups, by inauthentically assessing their knowledge and skills and further contributing to the replication of racial and economic inequality.

During the civil rights movement, educational scholars became increasingly invested in understanding why Black students underperformed on standardized tests as compared with their White counterparts. Even given the acknowledged implicit biases within standardized assessments, the reality of their pathologizing effects is undeniable. In other words, even as civil rights activists understood the tests were unfair and designed to further marginalize Black students, just like the literacy tests for voting access during Jim Crow, Black people took on the extra burden of navigating those tests because underperforming on them meant denial of access to a quality education and an overall quality of life. With assessments serving as the primary marker of achievement and, consequently, the primary evaluator of teacher quality, multicultural education emerged as a teaching intervention.

Banks (1995) outlined four phases of multicultural education and its evolution to becoming a major component of addressing diversity and the academic performance gap: (1) the Ethnic Studies Movement; (2) the Multiethnic Education Era; (3) the Victims of Society Enlightenment Period; and (4) the Relationship Development Period. The first phase emerged during the civil rights movement of the 1960s, addressing the social justice needs of historically oppressed people. Scholars like Carl Grant, Geneva Gay, and James Banks transitioned from a singular focus of ethnic studies into an interdisciplinary effort that encompassed teacher education and schooling. The Multiethnic Education Era aimed to motivate institutional and cultural shifts to improve equity (Banks, 1995). The third phase occurred as other marginalized groups, such as women and people with disabilities, joined the collective voice for equity in schooling. The extension caused a shift from multiethnic education to multicultural education (Banks, 2012). The fourth iteration of multicultural education expanded complex theory and praxis through research-based considerations of various identity markers, like language, ability, and gender (Banks, 1995). In 1996, Sleeter argued that multicultural education should shift toward a social movement that manifests theory into practice. That is our objective with this book.

Multicultural education aims to revolutionize education in the interest of all people by imagining and practicing democratic human relations in and outside the classroom. As Nieto and Bode (2012) explained, multicultural education mediates unjust practices in schools that inhibit quality education for all students. Encircling all constituents of the schooling process, multicultural education aspires to function as a social change agent. Many educational theorists agree that themes of developing a more just society, eliminating oppression, and educating students for high academic achievement are the fundamentals of multicultural education. Nieto and Bode (2012) reminded us that "a multicultural approach values diversity and encourages critical thinking, reflection, and action. . . . Its opposite is what Freire (1972) calls 'domesticating education' that emphasizes passivity, acceptance, and submissiveness" (p. 219). This approach rejects teacher-centered pedagogy that assumes students are cognitively bankrupt and dependent on the teacher to deposit knowledge, resulting in stifled potential and the social reproduction of inequalities. Critical multiculturalism, an extension of multicultural education, "views teaching as a tool for establishing and maintaining social justice both in and out of schools by confronting and disrupting the issue of inequity" (Park, 2013, p. 105). Doing so involves "conscious reflections" during which teachers introspectively take stock of their biases, perspective, values, agendas, and influences (Castro et al., 2010). At its core, multicultural education is activism oriented.

Theorizing that multicultural education functions as platforms on which to enact multicultural practice, Bennett (2001) identified four principles of multicultural education: honoring cultural pluralism; working toward the ideals of social justice; affirming culture in the teaching and learning process; and envisioning educational equity and excellence in the education of all children and youth. Nieto and Bode's (2012) seven basic characteristics of multicultural education echo the social justice, cultural affirmations, and educational equity aspects highlighted in Bennett's analysis (2010). They also theorized that multicultural education is antiracist, fundamental for all students, comprehensive in its pedagogical reach, social justice–oriented, process-oriented, and critical. Nieto and Bode (2012), as well as Bennett (2001), reflected on what Dewey (1897) described regarding education as being both the process and the goal. This duality exemplifies the complexity interwoven in the concept of multicultural education.

While I could give you a history lesson on all the iterations of multicultural education that have emerged over the last 60 years, I think it would be most useful to discuss the more enduring aspects of multicultural education and the more contentious arms of the approach that are at the center of education debate today.

Transformative Approaches to Multicultural Education

Culturally Relevant Teaching

Transformative approaches recognize that people are both free individuals and members of social groups, integrated—whether they like it or not—into systems of power that shape them (Bruch et al., 2004). These approaches span from cultural inclusivity to critical pedagogy, using content to engage students in reading the word to read the world (Freire, 1972). Major approaches that fall into the spectrum of transformative teaching practices are culturally relevant pedagogy (Ladson-Billings, 1995b), culturally responsive teaching (Gay, 2000), empowering education (Shor, 1992), and culturally sustaining pedagogy (Paris, 2012). I describe the major tenets of these approaches because they are current and have been empirically proved to improve learning experiences and opportunities for marginalized youth. Although practitioners grapple with how to effectively implement these approaches—what Ladson-Billings (1995a) called "good teaching"—the fundamental approaches of these practices uphold the ideals of multicultural education.

Culturally relevant pedagogy (CRP) is defined as "pedagogy of opposition not unlike critical pedagogy but specifically committed to collective, not merely individual, empowerment" (Ladson-Billings, 1995a, p. 160). Ladson-Billings (1995a) sketched out three propositions for CRP. The first addresses the development of academic success for students. This means fruitfully working alongside students in the areas of literacy, mathematics, technology, and civics to best prepare them to be contributors and active participants in a democracy. CRP advocates for advancing the academic competence of marginalized youth through collaborative sharing, allowing students to be educationally competitive with their privileged peers. Second, CRP advocates a readiness to cultivate and maintain the cultural competence of each student in both home and school cultures. According to Ladson-Billings (1995a), "culturally relevant teachers utilize students' culture as a vehicle for learning" (p. 161). In other words, teachers must value and build on the knowledge and skills that students bring from their home cultures. Rather than discounting the lived experiences of individual students, which often leads to a sense of rejection and exclusion (Valenzuela, 1999), educators are encouraged to embrace home cultures as foundational and connected to classroom learning. The final criterion for CRP is that "students must develop a critical consciousness through which they challenge the status quo of the current social order" (Ladson-Billings, 1995a, p. 160). This principle extends the achievement of students beyond academia and into sociopolitical arenas that investigate power differentials and critique injustice. Educators facilitate the expansion of students' critical consciousness by helping them to identify, analyze, and transform social inequities. Critical teacher reflection is central to enacting culturally relevant teaching practices. Culturally relevant pedagogues are internally reflexive while outwardly working to empower their students.

Culturally Responsive Teaching

Another approach of multicultural education is culturally responsive teaching (CRT). Much like CRP practitioners, culturally responsive teachers commit to educating the whole child (Gay, 2000). When defining the "whole child," it is imperative that we not confuse the term with popular educational methods that often generalize education, promote assimilation, and impose monocultural, monolinguistic, White middle-class ways of existing and learning. Gay (2013) stated, "I define culturally responsive teaching as 'using the cultural knowledge, prior experiences, frames of reference, and performance styles of ethnically diverse students to make learning encounters more relevant to and effective for them" (pp. 49–50). Culturally responsive teachers are cognizant of and intentional about maintaining and developing cultural identity and traditions in addition to promoting academic achievement (Gay, 2000). Essentially, Gay, like Ladson-Billings, modified the constraints of culturally responsive education to move beyond language. Gay (2000) characterized CRT as a method to bring to light "the higher learning potentials of ethnically diverse students, simultaneously cultivating their academic and psychosocial abilities" (p. 20). She, like Ladson-Billings, echoed the call for educators to cultivate the relational competencies of every student in an endeavor to help students shape and pursue self-determination. Gay (2000) urged teachers to incorporate the cultural knowledge, past experiences, academic and social strengths, frames of reference, and performance styles of ethnically diverse students to successfully instruct and co-construct knowledge in learning environments.

Gay (2000) described CRT as having numerous distinctions. Among them is the validation of individual cultural heritages both as legacies that influence students' outlooks, mannerisms, and approaches to learning, and as valuable content embedded in the formal curriculum. CRT also requires educators to identify individual pupils' learning styles to aid in differentiated instruction that will lead to academic achievement. Finally, CRT infuses multiethnic and multicultural information in all standard areas of study to promote a globalized educational experience. Echoing a major component of CRP, CRT bridges home and school life to best facilitate academic instruction in the context of sociocultural realities. Perhaps the most notable difference between CRT and CRP is CRT's roots in a wider range of culturally and linguistically diverse students. When Ladson-Billings (1994) conceived of CRP, she was doing research with teachers who were successful with African American students. Meanwhile, Gay's work had a more diverse student consideration from its inception. In her own words, Gay (2002) stated,

> The more variance that there is between students' cultural, racial, ethnic, and intellectual characteristics and the normative standards of schools, the greater are the chances their school achievement will be compromised by low or negative teacher expectations. Children of color, poverty, and disability are highly variant on these criteria of normalcy, and are subjected to greater unfair teacher attitudes, expectations, and actions. (p. 614)

This attention to demographic differences impacting teacher disposition, which often frame historically marginalized students in the deficit, is at the heart of the demographic imperative. CRT centers the intersectional identities of students in classrooms where multiple marginalized identities can exist, thereby requiring differing approaches to cultural responsiveness.

Empowering Education

Empowering Education (Shor, 1992) resists traditional schooling methods as an iteration of critical pedagogy. With emancipation (read freedom) as his agenda, Shor (1992) aimed to disrupt the traditional teacher/student, "expert/incompetence" dynamic for a more equitable and balanced power distribution. This emphasizes dialogic learning processes between students and teachers. It encourages participatory problem-posing pedagogy that minimizes teacher-talk and orients "students to democratic transformation of society by their active citizenship" (Shor, 1992, p. 29). The late Black feminism theorist bell hooks (1994), in her conception of feminist pedagogy, imagined a radically transformed schooling space that resembles Shor's collaborative model and balances the voices in the classroom to arrive at co-constructed knowledge. This echoes CRT's advocacy for co-creation of knowledge between all participants in the schooling process.

Heavily influenced by Marxist theory, Empowering Education is intentional about addressing political oppression in the classroom. Transmitting liberatory theory into liberated practice, Shor (1992) outlined an "agenda of values of empowerment" (p. 17) in which education insists on involving active participation on the part of the learner. He avowed that all learning is value-laden and that the learner is always dealing with knowledge in the affective realms. Much like Gay (2000) and Ladson-Billings (1995a), Shor (1992) emphasized the significance of relevancy grounded in the community as well as in students' past, present, and future lives. Shor (1992) situated Empowering Education as multicultural, dialogic, desocializing, and democratic; its values are interdisciplinary, highly researchable, and based on activism. He defined empowered education as "the exploration of subject matter in its social context with critical themes and bodies of knowledge integrated into student language and experience" (p. 144). The teacher in the classroom is the facilitator responsible for guiding students toward empowerment, but she herself cannot grant freedom.

Culturally Sustaining Pedagogy

Culturally sustaining pedagogy (CSP) is an amalgamation of the mentioned transformative approaches to multicultural education. It honors the three tenets of CRP by maintaining academic rigor, cultural competence, and critical consciousness as critical elements for a quality education. Like CRT, CSP embraces the home life of students in a way that more authentically reflects what they most need to belong and thrive beyond the school setting. Like Shor's Empowering Education, CSP is radical in its efforts to liberate through education. Like its predecessors, CSP emphasizes teaching that is tailored to the cultural and linguistic pluralism of students while resisting a Eurocentric standard for student worth.

More than two decades after the introduction of the most prominent transformative iterations of multicultural education, CSP has emerged as the most contemporary way to take up asset-based pedagogies because it lovingly critiques its predecessors while also embracing their merits. Thus, it is not framed in competition to CRP, CRT, and Empowering Education. Rather, it distinguishes itself by challenging one of the most enduring problems in American education: the White gaze (Paris & Alim, 2014). CSP is keen to acknowledge that developing one's cultural competence and critical consciousness should not be for the sole purpose of mastering academic achievement or academic assessments that are inherently Eurocentric and biased. It is not enough to embrace, center, and amplify the culture and forms of knowledge of historically marginalized groups only as a vehicle for them to succeed in a White world. CSP invites critique and evolution of culture and forms of knowledge of historically marginalized groups. Thus, CSP can embody the merits of critical pedagogy as Freire envisioned it, where education is liberatory.

CSP reintroduces an element of choice and self-determination in schooling a child or a community culture; it is not just a pedagogical tool and shouldn't be reduced to such. Culture is validated and valued without the child ever mastering the performance tools of an institution designed for the child to fail. CSP is concerned with cultural competence from the perspective of valuing the students' culture for culture's sake and not "correcting," "whitening," "sanitizing," or "whitewashing" student culture for White consumption and approval. At the same time, one of the most novel aspects of CSP is its inclusion of reflexive analysis of one's culture. Paris and Alim (2014) explained that educators "must work with students to critique regressive practices (e.g., homophobia, misogyny, racism) and raise critical consciousness" (p. 92). This means that, as students learn their histories and learn to make sense of their culture in conjunction with learning about the "isms" of the world—such as ableism, sexism, or classism—their education will allow them to unpack, analyze, and critique problematic aspects of their culture. For example, if a student gains the consciousness to understand that capitalism is dependent on the exploitation of labor and the mass consumption of people, they may come to analyze their participation in fast fashion. Arriving at that decision would not negate the value in fashion as a form of expression, but rather would empower the student to live more intentionally within their cultural practices. This might lead to a student participating in more thrift shopping, clothing swaps, upcycled fashion, or learning to sew, as opposed to constantly buying poorly made clothes.

Another interesting development in CSP is the introduction of possibilities for how one identifies. Historically, Black, Asian, and Latinx groups were constructed in very limiting and deterministic ways that failed to capture the complexity of intersectional identities and narratives. CSP aims to complicate those demographic groups and the associated understandings attached to them. Blackness and every other social identity is not monolithic. There are Black children from lower income households who are Multilingual learners and academically achieve. Perhaps more simplistically, there are Black children who are not African American and therefore have a wide array of cultural differences and practices that do not map onto the racialized constructions of Blackness that had been made popular and accepted in our understandings of diverse identities. Much like the definition of culture, culture itself is evolving, and "youth continue to inhabit a world where cultural and linguistic recombinations flow with purpose" (Paris & Alim, 2014, p. 92). Perhaps the biggest reason why educators cannot instruct from a teacher-centered approach is that it is the youth/students who are up to date on their culture, for they are the ones capable of guiding culturally sustaining teaching. Even the most diligent pedagogue who has done the work of studying the culture of their students at best would be working from students' traditional practices, or what Paris (2012) may refer to as "heritage practices." Paris and Alim (2014) encouraged educators to be led by the question, "What is it we're seeking to sustain through classroom learning?"; the response to that question cannot be solely determined by a teacher, a curriculum, or a school district. Culture is "dynamic, shifting, and ever-changing" (Paris, 2012, p. 95); thus, for teaching and learning to be worthwhile, youth/student culture should be at the heart of what is being sustained and extended (Paris, 2012).

Ladson-Billings (2014) noted,

> In developing this theory, culturally sustaining pedagogy . . . these authors use culturally relevant pedagogy as the place where the "beat drops" and then layer the multiple ways that this notion of pedagogy shifts, changes, adapts, recycles, and recreates instructional spaces to ensure that consistently marginalized students are repositioned into a place of normativity—that is, that they become subjects in the instructional process, not mere objects. (p. 76)

The endorsement of CSP by its most admired and validated predecessor, the creator of CRP, is salient for the advancement of multicultural education and our overall conception of those who are historically and systemically marginalized in education and society. According to Bruch et al. (2004), "celebratory," "critical," and "transformative" approaches to multicultural education often overlap, but "it is useful to conceptually distinguish them for purposes of highlighting the important contribution each can make to a vision of meaningful access through multicultural developmental education" (p. 13). CRP, CRT, Empowering Education, and CSP are all transformative approaches, but they also embed elements of the critical and celebratory categories. Their goal of empowering students and teachers as change agents and their emphasis on activism facilitate critical consciousness that analyzes the isms that oppress students. As each approach demonstrated, "critical consciousness is brought about not through intellectual effort alone but through praxis—through the authentic union of action and reflection" (Freire, 1970, p. 48). Materialization of critical consciousness in classroom spaces is largely the responsibility of teachers, with consideration of their capacity and willingness to work toward social justice.

Quality of Teacher Education

The academic achievement gap is the landscape on which new teachers must prove themselves effective, and therefore well prepared by their TEPs. Criticism of the ineffectiveness of TEPs emanates from scholars, parents, politicians, policy makers, and teachers themselves (Korthagen et al., 2006). Thus, in their national evaluation of TEPs, the National Council for the Accreditation of Teaching Education's (2010) Blue Ribbon Committee recommended "a dramatic overhaul of how teachers are prepared" (p. 2) to meet the needs of public education's most disenfranchised groups. The National Education Association (2022), in conceptualizing strategies for closing the achievement gap, argued for improved teacher education programs that recruit, develop, and retain qualified teachers and paraeducators. Amid debates regarding empirically based versus practically oriented reforms in TEPs, there is consensus that candidate predispositions toward culturally diverse populations are largely unacceptable.

Council for the Accreditation of Educator Preparation

You want to make sure the TEP you're enrolled in is accredited, just like you want the brands that you buy, or the home or car that you purchase, to be inspected so you know they meet a certain quality standard. Accreditation means that the program or institution has been monitored and reviewed by people outside that institution who have the professional knowledge and skills to determine whether high standards are being met and exceeded. The Council for the Accreditation of Educator Preparation (CAEP) is the gold standard evaluating teacher education programs in the United States. According to the CAEP website, its mission is to "advance equity and excellence in educator preparation through evidence-based accreditation that assures quality and supports continuous improvement to strengthen P-12 student learning." You'll note here that the emphasis is still on the P–12 students, but the accountability is on the TEP to prepare its graduates to meet the needs of those P–12 students, given the various disparities we discussed earlier.

CAEP uses seven standards to measure the quality of a program, and they range from content and pedagogical knowledge to candidate recruitment progression. I want to highlight just a few elements from some of the standards, but I highly recommend that you familiarize yourself with all seven so that you too can determine whether your teacher education program is up to par. CAEP had a committee of 21 representatives from the field of education, including P–12, higher education, state education departments, and nonprofit education organizations convene to revise what is now the 2022 CAEP standards (see Table 1.2). Social justice measures were amplified in the revisions.

Table 1.2. 2022 CAEP standards

Standard Title	**Content**
R1.2 Content	"... candidates know central concepts of their content area and are able to apply the content in developing equitable and inclusive learning experiences for diverse P-12 students." (CAEP, 2022)
R2.2 Clinical Educators	"... who demonstrate a positive impact on candidates' development and diverse P-12 student learning and development." (CAEP, 2022)
R3.3 Competency at Completion	"... candidates possess academic competency to teach effectively with positive impacts on diverse P-12 student learning and development . . ." (CAEP, 2022)
R4.2 Satisfaction of Employers	"... employers are satisfied with the completers' preparation for their assigned responsibilities in working with diverse P-12 students and their families." (CAEP, 2022)

In the mentioned standards, you are the candidate or completer being referenced. As you can see, quite a few competencies are required of the candidate, mainly on being knowledgeable, flexible, and having the appropriate dispositions to positively impact the learning and development of diverse P–12 students. Discussion of clinical educators refers to classroom teachers you work under or schools where you are assigned to complete your practicums, internships, student teaching, or whatever term is used in your TEP. Remember, there are seven standards, and I'm only highlighting snippets of four. The others, while continuing to require high levels of dispositional shift and competency on the part of the candidate, are also structurally looking for the TEPs, their faculty and staff, and administrators to be continually mindful of, and active in helping improve the academic experiences of, diverse P–12 students and their families. It is precisely because of historical marginalization in schools that we would now have accrediting bodies that would make schools and teacher preparation programs accountable to marginalized youth whose ancestors were disenfranchised in and by P–12 schooling.

Multicultural Teacher Education

In keeping with CAEP's spotlighting of candidate preparedness for diverse populations, pedagogical knowledge requires preservice teachers (PSTs) to take up the ideals of multicultural education by critically examining their predispositions and the implications of bigoted perspectives. The standards position teachers as adapters to learners' needs, according to students' cultural identities, which reflects practices of CRP. The designated space to critically reflect on one's prejudices and develop competencies to enact transformative approaches to multicultural education in TEPs is the diversity course, but it shouldn't be the only course. PSTs should have the opportunity to learn how to practice transformative approaches to multicultural education in every single preparation course. Effective multicultural education is integrated across the curriculum because no subject area is isolated or objective. When multicultural education is not siloed to a random class that one must take, but instead is integrated into other subject areas such as math, science, social studies, art, music, health, and PE, the opportunities to practice transformative and humanizing pedagogy abound.

In many TEPs, a multicultural education course is a prerequisite for licensure. That said, one might conclude that an "A" average in a course about diversity and multicultural education reflects a degree of intercultural competency, as deemed appropriate by authorities in a TEP (e.g., the department chair, teacher educators, college dean, accreditation agency). Many students rely on the grade they receive in a course as a sufficient measure of achievement, even if they have not grown, changed, shifted, or been transformed. I implore you to not be that person. You must be committed to growing through your TEP, and whatever professional development opportunities you experience, because it makes such a significant difference in the lives of the students you encounter. The achievement disparities persist and widen precisely because the adults are not changing.

Born in response to systemic inequities, multicultural education is inherently resistive to injustice. As teachers are challenged to meet the needs of all learners, multicultural education must and will evolve. One of the most difficult and persistent problems to address is what some researchers have identified as fundamental gaps between theory and practice in multicultural education. As an approach to multicultural education, CRP is plausibly the most pervasive in P–12 classrooms (Morrison et al., 2008). Through the approach, Ladson-Billings (1995b) declared, "not only must teachers encourage academic success and cultural competence, they must help students to recognize, understand, and critique current social inequities" (p. 476). Originally conceived for the education of African American children, CRP has been appropriated to address the needs of all learners, specifically those who are traditionally marginalized. Shifting demographics in public education and the widening of the achievement gap have popularized the approach. Operationalizing CRP has been an objective of practitioners, and its effectiveness has been well documented. Given the urgency of preparing more qualified teachers, it seems fitting that this book would explore CRP across the curriculum—still, it will do so while incorporating the fundamentals and values of CSP.

A Note on Critical Race Theory and Schools

Given the time of this book's publication, it is relevant to address the theoretical elephant in the room: critical race theory (CRT). CRT is a theoretical framework developed out of legal studies. Ladson Billings's (1998) and many other educational theories take up aspects of CRT to explain systemic inequities in education; however, CRT is not commonly part of teacher preparation or K–12 curriculum. It is a set of theoretical tenets that explain that although race is socially constructed, racism is normalized and pervasive in American life. With such a long history of people denying "seeing color," or the impact of race and racism in the pervasive marginalization of BIPOC, CRT has become a useful framework for illustrating the experiences of BIPOC.

CRT consists of five tenets: the notion that racism is an ordinary aspect of life; interest convergence; the social construction of race; storytelling and counter-storytelling; and Whiteness as property. Together, these major components are useful for explaining and framing what American society has long denied. Because CRT is not central to multicultural education, nor is it a traditional part of multicultural teacher preparation, I encourage you to do some research on it for yourself before deciding its merits.

But one core aspect of CRT I would be remiss not to unpack is the argument that racism is systemic—meaning that existing policies, practices, laws, and rules inherently marginalize people of color. Now, this does not mean that racism cannot be perpetuated by an individual or that it cannot be internalized; those are realities as well. However, racism that is embedded within structures, systems, and institutions is a lot more insidious and difficult both to notice and to dismantle. One only needs to look at patterns of racism as it relates to educational funding, discipline, or curriculum, whereby BIPOC are misrepresented or underrepresented, to see that racism affects education in schooling in systemic ways.

This understanding of racism as being systemic contradicts what most of us have come to believe is just a person-to-person or an interpersonal problem. Racism can in fact be systemic, interpersonal, internalized, and ideological. When racism that is interpersonal, meaning between individuals, is limited to a few "bad apples" who carry outdated biases that lead to racist acts, then it is easier for us not to acknowledge the ways we benefit from systemic privilege as well as the ways that we ourselves can be oppressive to others. It easily becomes a matter of perspective, as opposed to a matter of fact. Racism that is internalized can be useful for those who want to maintain a system of hierarchy. When a person internalizes racism, they believe they are inherently inferior to White people, and then they work to mask, abandon, or apologize for their racial group and its supposedly inherent inadequacies. Internalized racism fuels White supremacy. Interpersonal racism means that most of us don't have to be accountable because we believe we are inherently good and therefore cannot be racist. Ideological racism occurs when data or science is misused to justify hierarchy of human beings, with BIPOC framed as inferior. Ideological racism has its roots in eugenics, and, as previously discussed, this is evident in standardized testing.

Systemic racism is the umbrella that protects these other three iterations and allows them to persist in such a way that we don't notice the rainstorm. It is not surprising that we are having a national conversation about whether we should teach CRT in schools, when most teachers, parents, and students have never studied CRT, don't understand its concepts, and believe the discussion of race itself is racist. I empathize. You, as a person and teacher, will have to decide if you accept that racism is embedded within systems and institutions, and whether that will affect your teaching.

References

Andrew, M. D., & Jelmberg, J. R. (2010). *How teachers learn: An educational psychology of teacher preparation* (Vol. 8). Peter Lang.

Anzaldúa, G. (1987). *Borderlands = la frontera: The new mestiza*. Spinsters/Aunt Lute.

Bai, Y., Straus, S., & Broer, M. (2021). *U.S. national and state trends in educational inequality due to socioeconomic status: Evidence from the 2003–17 NAEP* (AIR-NAEP Working Paper No. 2021-01). American Institutes for Research.

Banks, J. A. (1995). The historical reconstruction of knowledge about race: Implications for transformative teaching. *Educational Researcher, 24*(2), 15–25.

Banks, J. A. (Ed.). (2012). *Encyclopedia of diversity in education*. SAGE.

Bennett, C. (2001). Genres of research in multicultural education. *Review of Educational Research, 71*(2), 171–217.

Bennett, J. (2003). *Teaching and learning science: A guide to recent research and its applications*. Continuum.

Bennett, C. (2010). *Comprehensive multicultural education: Theory and practice* (7th ed.). Allyn and Bacon.

Bruch, P. L., Jehangir, R. R., Jacobs, W. R., & Ghere, D. L. (2004). Enabling access: Toward multicultural developmental curricula. *Journal of Developmental Education, 27*(3), 12–19.

Castro, A. J., Kelly, J., & Shih, M. (2010). Resilience strategies for new teachers in high-needs areas. *Teaching and Teacher Education, 26*(3), 622–629.

Council for the Accreditation of Educator Preparation (CAEP). (2022). *2022 CAEP standards*. https://caepnet.org/standards/2022-itp/introduction

Dewey, J. (1897). The psychology of effort. *The Philosophical Review, 6*(1), 43–56.

Freire, P. (1970). *Cultural Action for Freedom*. Harvard Educational Review.

Freire, P. (1972). Education: Domestication or liberation? *Prospects, 2*(2), 173–181.

Gay, G. (2000). *Culturally responsive teaching: Theory, research, and practice*. Teachers College Press.

Gay, G. (2002). Preparing for culturally responsive teaching. *Journal of Teacher Education, 53*(2), 106–116.

Gay, G. (2013). Teaching to and through cultural diversity. *Curriculum Inquiry, 43*(1), 48–70.

Goodman, G. S. (1999). *Alternatives in education: Critical pedagogy for disaffected youth*. Peter Lang Pub Incorporated.

Hoffman, D. M. (1996). Culture, self, and multicultural education: Reflections on discourse, text, and practice. *American Educational Research Journal, 33*(3), 545–569.

hooks, b. (1994). Confronting class in the classroom. *The critical pedagogy reader*, 142–150.

Korthagen, F., Loughran, J., & Russell, T. (2006). Developing fundamental principles for teacher education programs and practices. *Teaching and Teacher Education, 22*(8), 1020–1041.

Ladson-Billings, G. (1994). What we can learn from multicultural education research. *Educational Leadership, 51*(8), 22–26.

Ladson-Billings, G. (1995a). But that's just good teaching! The case for culturally relevant pedagogy. *Theory Into Practice, 34*(3), 159–165. http://www.jstor.org/stable/1476635

Ladson-Billings, G. (1995b). Toward a theory of culturally relevant pedagogy. *American Educational Research Journal, 32*(3), 465–491. doi:10.3102/00028312032003465

Ladson-Billings, G. (1998). Just what is critical race theory and what's it doing in a nice field like education? *International Journal of Qualitative Studies in Education, 11*(1), 7–24.

Ladson-Billings, G. (2014). Culturally relevant pedagogy 2.0: a.k.a. the remix. *Harvard Educational Review, 84*(1), 74–84.

Levine, A. (2006). Educating school teachers. *Education Schools Project*.

Love, B. L. (2016). Anti-Black state violence, classroom edition: The spirit murdering of Black children. *Journal of Curriculum and Pedagogy, 13*(1), 22–25.

Lowenstein, K. L. (2009). The work of multicultural teacher education: Reconceptualizing white teacher candidates as learners. *Review of Educational Research, 79*(1), 163–196.

Morrison, K. A., Robbins, H. H., & Rose, D. G. (2008). Operationalizing culturally relevant pedagogy: A synthesis of classroom-based research. *Equity & Excellence in Education, 41*(4), 433–452.

National Center for Education Statistics. (2022). Concentration of public school students eligible for free or reduced-price lunch. *Condition of Education.* U.S. Department of Education, Institute of Education Sciences. https://nces.ed.gov/programs/coe/indicator/clb

National Council for the Accreditation of Teaching Education. (2010). *Transforming teacher education through clinical practice: A national strategy to prepare effective teachers.* http://caepnet.org/~/media/Files/caep/accreditation-resources/blue-ribbon-panel.pdf

National Education Association. (2022). *Solutions to the educator shortage crisis.* https://www.nea.org/student-success/recruit-and-retain-educators

Nieto, S., & Bode, P. (2012). *Affirming diversity: The sociopolitical context of multicultural education.* Pearson.

Paris, D. (2012). Culturally sustaining pedagogy: A needed change in stance, terminology, and practice. *Educational Researcher, 41*(3), 93–97.

Paris, D., & Alim, H. S. (2014). What are we seeking to sustain through culturally sustaining pedagogy? A loving critique forward. *Harvard Educational Review, 84*(1), 85–100.

Park, G. C. (2013). Critical multiculturalism for immigrants of color. *Anthropology and Education Quarterly, 17*(1), 101–108.

Schaeffer, K. (2021, December 10). *America's public school teachers are far less racially & ethnically diverse than their students.* Pew Research Center. https://www.pewresearch.org/fact-tank/2021/12/10/americas-public-school-teachers-are-far-less-racially-and-ethnically-diverse-than-their-students/

Shor, I. (1992). *Culture wars: School and society in the conservative restoration.* University of Chicago Press.

Sleeter, C. E. (1996). *Multicultural education as social activism.* State University of New York Press.

Tylor, E. B. (1871). *Primitive culture: Researches into the development of mythology, philosophy, religion, art and custom* (Vol. 2). J. Murray.

United States Census Bureau. (2020). *QuickFacts.* https://www.census.gov/quickfacts/fact/table/US#

Valenzuela, A., Jr. (1999). Gender roles and settlement activities among children and their immigrant families. *American Behavioral Scientist, 42*(4), 720–742.

Valenzuela, A. (2010). *Subtractive schooling: US-Mexican youth and the politics of caring.* State University of New York Press.

TWO

Personal Identity: Positionality, Intersectionality, Biases, Triggers

Chelda Smith Kondo

Positionality Statement

Chelda Smith (she/her)

I AM A BLACK WOMAN BORN and partly raised in Haiti. Although I grew up far below the poverty line, in my adult life, I've been mostly middle to upper class. I identify as heterosexual, yet I recognize that sexuality and gender are fluid. I have cisgender and able-bodied privilege. I was naturalized as a United States citizen shortly after completing my undergraduate degree, and since then, I have had the privilege of a United States passport and an American identity. Having lived in the United States since elementary school, I have had the opportunity to develop English proficiency that, in most cases, allows me to pass as a native English speaker. I begin this chapter by naming some of my demographic identities, and especially my privileges, because as a Black woman, I exist at the intersection of racism and sexism (i.e., misogynoir). My racial and gender identities dominate how I understand myself and how I am perceived by others. Moreover, being both Black and a woman in a patriarchal, White supremacist society, I am rarely discussed with assumed privileges. "Privilege" has become synonymous with whiteness, and while we will eventually address White privilege, this book (and chapter) is specifically concerned with the complexities of our individual and collective identities (e.g., religion, ability, language, gender, sexual orientation, citizenship, socioeconomic class) and how they might impact experiences of privilege, power, and/or discrimination. Furthermore, we explore how the intersection of these various social identities can compound one's privileges, as well as how identities can collide and interlock to exacerbate one's oppressions (see Disclaimer 2.1).

Disclaimer 2.1

> One can be privileged **and** oppressed simultaneously. I am not saying that one identity can cancel out another. Instead, I am saying that the lattice of social identities that make up our individual and collective identities mean that sometimes one or two identities are more dominant than others, and dominant in favorable or unfavorable ways. Context matters.

Nevertheless, because of structural and systemic oppressions (i.e., societal rules, "norms," laws, policies, and practices), those of us in marginalized groups and as marginalized individuals have very little control over how we are perceived in a world that is structured by those committed to exclusion. Thus, my Black Haitian woman person conjures varied, often deficit-based, perceptions before I even enter a room. It is subject to racism (Black), sexism (woman), xenophobia (Haitian—read: sh*thole). Still, I disclose my demographic identities as an act of resistance, a demonstration of solidarity, and a counternarrative. Considering what I just shared, some of you are struggling to take me or this book seriously but keep on reading. And don't worry, we'll unpack that . . .

Key Terms:

- **Deficit-based:** focused on difficulties and unmet needs of people.
- **Demographic identity:** a particular quality or characteristic that you share with a group of people (i.e., gender, social class, marital status, citizenship, nationality, religion, etc.).
- **Identity:** the conditions and/or characteristics that shape a person's being (i.e., bus driver, Māori, uncle).
- **Identity properties:** general aspects of one's identity, combined with their demographic identity in relation to social, political, and historical construction.
- **Social construct:** a notion or idea that exists because people in a society agree and/or accept that it exists based on shared experience or tradition (e.g., gender roles, value of money, rightness or wrongness). Constructs about identity properties exist, and they can be deficit based.

Key Ideas:

1. ***Cultural competence:*** There isn't one way to exist, but there is a dominant standard that we're measured against. We all have fundamental aspects of identity—size, neurodiversity and ability, citizenship status, language, education, gender, social class, age, location and place, sexuality, race and ethnicity or indigenous status, political orientation, religion. Identities are socially, politically, and historically constructed concepts that evolve and shift in value based on culturally dominant "norms" and power differentials.
2. ***Critical consciousness:*** These fundamental aspects of identity play significant roles in determining how we understand and experience the world and others. They mediate the types of privileges and/or oppressions we experience. We learn about our own identities, and the identities of others, through interactions with communities, family, friends/peers, organizations, institutions, systems, media, and other social connections. We also have agency and can think for ourselves; therefore, we're able to form perceptions and ideas about identities beyond dominant narratives.
3. ***Academic rigor and identity:*** You, a collection of various identities, are the center of your pedagogy. Therefore, you must know yourself to teach others in ways that are culturally relevant and sustaining and/or to work toward social justice. Your biases, strengths, growth areas, comforts, boundaries, triggers, interests, and so much more will explicitly and implicitly inform your planning, instruction, classroom management, pedagogical content knowledge, professionalism, and relationships (or lack thereof) with students, their families, and communities. Without knowledge of self, you're embarking on a reckless journey that will inevitably lead to harm (unintentional or otherwise). Teaching is deeply personal, social, and political. The ideals that form the basis of your personal and political identities influence and impact your teaching.

Academic Rigor and Identity

Extending from the work of Gloria Ladson-Billings (1994), which explains that culturally relevant pedagogies (CRPs) promote academic rigor, cultural competence, and critical consciousness, we'll first unpack what it looks like to teach about and explore identity in an academically rigorous way. Academic rigor traditionally references a certain level or standard of achievement. In an academically rigorous environment, high expectations are normalized. For example, this book assumes that you're capable of authentically engaging with its content, self-guided activities, rubrics, and exemplars. And while no aspect of this effort will be perfect or complete—that's the nature of identity development—there should be evidence of your growth and progress that bends toward intersectional justice. Academic rigor in relation to identity requires a thorough and complex understanding of oneself, others, and society. Likewise, it requires unremitting work (read: humility) to heal where needed, and to grow, learn, and constantly evolve. It is always seeing color and other marginalized identities and accommodating accordingly.

When it comes to our identity properties, we humans have very little control over our phenotype. A phenotype is a combination of physical and behavioral characteristics; essentially, it's how our DNA manifests itself. Phenotypes describe our observable characteristics, such as height, eye color, skin color, and hair color. These characteristics, laden with social value, are distributed through a genetic lottery because we did not select them for ourselves. For example, if you were born with your left hand as your dominant hand, that was not your choice. However, you were likely born into a world that centers right-handedness, and the pervasiveness of right-handed systems in our society can leave you feeling marginalized. From shaking hands to saluting or swearing-in, right-handedness is regarded as the "right" and standard way. Appliances, desks, notebooks, cars, and even guns are designed for the comfort and maximum usability of right-handers. Historically, children have been forced to assimilate into a right-handed world and mask their discomfort. If you were born right-handed, you were literally dealt a winning hand, and that was not of your choosing. In essence, you won that round of the genetic lottery and were born with right-handed privilege.

Our identities are fragmented and fluid, but also evolving. If it were static, you would not still surprise yourself with some of your decisions and behaviors. Who you were 10 years ago is not who you identify as today. By extension, who you are right now likely is not who you'll be after you read this chapter, and most certainly after you read this book. When it comes to being critical pedagogues, we need to address fundamental aspects of identity and the nature of their coexistence and intersectionality (e.g., body size, neurodiversity and ability, citizenship status, language, education, gender, social class, age, location and place, sexuality, race and ethnicity or Indigenous status, political orientation, or religion). Our identities are socially, politically, and historically constructed concepts that change and shift in value based on culturally dominant norms, power differentials, and cultural context. For example, being Muslim in the United States may be negligible 364 days a year, but for sure, we can all empathize that on September 11 each year, having a Muslim identity presents unique challenges. Similar analogies could be drawn for any other identity—sometimes it's beneficial, other times it's a disadvantage. It is when identity interacts with systems of power that oppression occurs (see Figure 2.1).

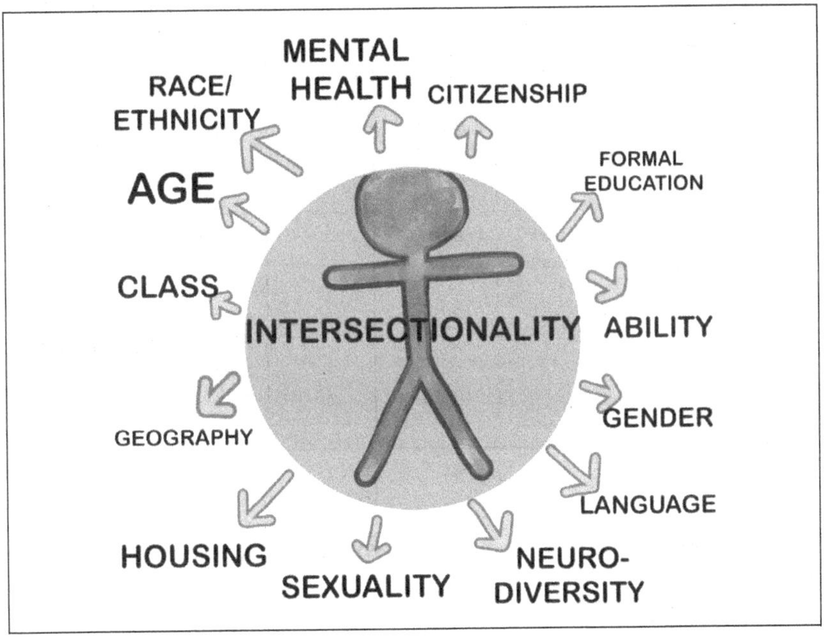

Figure 2.1. Intersectionality.

To begin making sense of your own identity properties, I'm going to ask you to complete a Funds of Knowledge (FOK) (Moll & Gonzalez, 1994) form (See Figure 2.3 on page 55 and in the Appendix). Seriously, complete each empty section of the form as though you're a student in my class. If you have school-age children in your communities, feel free to complete one for them, too. It's a great way for teachers to learn about the student and see them more appreciatively.

The knowledge that students (read: humans) embody can directly or indirectly connect to formal classroom learning. It encompasses the experiences, skills, and proficiencies acquired through historical and cultural interactions of an individual through their community, family, and culture. Essentially, through everyday living, *you* have Funds of Knowledge (see Appendix), and so do your students (see Table 2.1).

Table 2.1. Academic Rigor and Identity

Student #	1. Race/ Ethnicity	2. SES	3. Home Language	4. SPED (IEP)	5. Funds of Knowledge	6. Challenging Circumstances
	What to reflect in the curriculum and what to be mindful of to avoid acting on implicit biases:		*What to consider and accommodate:*	*What to legally address in learning:*	*What to celebrate and incorporate into teaching:*	*What to consider and accommodate in teaching:*
1. Dr. Smith	Nationality Haitian Black (B)	Lower income (LI)	Haitian Creole		Dancing, planning, organizing, extroverted, curious about justice, likes reading	Struggles with conjugations, raised by single dad, socially excluded
2. You						

Notes:

1. Race/ethnicity: Asian (A), Latinx (L), White (W), Black (B), Native American (NA), Middle Eastern (ME), Other (O)
2. Socioeconomic status: lower income (LI); lower middle (LM); middle (M); upper middle (UM); upper (U)
3. Language: Spanish, French, Tagalog, Korean, Vietnamese, Portuguese, Yoruba, Creole, etc.
4. SPED classification: autism, deafness, visual impairment, speech impairment, intellectual disability emotional disturbance, etc.
5. Funds of Knowledge example: hip-hop culture, activism, environmental injustice, going to the museum, recycling, exercising, visiting Grandma, barbecues, sports outings, holiday celebrations, religious beliefs, work ethic (pretty much your student's community- and family-based skills and knowledges, and anything they know or experience that affects their self-perception and self-determination)
6. Challenging circumstances: major stress-inducing experiences and circumstances (recent loss of family member, divorce, housing instability, anxiety, PTSD, etc.)

What Is Power?

Most of us are familiar with "power" in a mechanical or electrical engineering context. In critical pedagogy, power is social and institutional. Power is influence, authority, and capacity to do something as intended. Power impacts the lives of others with or without their cooperation and consent. Social media has an effective "influencer" population because of social power. As a society, as individuals, and as collective groups, we are influenced by the preferences, behaviors, choices, values, and narratives of others. In critical pedagogy terms, that notion of power is extended to having a capacity to influence the actions, beliefs, and behaviors of others. Moreover, one has an authority that legitimizes that influence. That capacity and that authority are based on our social norms and social affirmations. When it comes to who leaders are, societally, men are more socially approved as leaders than women. In teaching elementary school, women are more socially approved as educators than are men. Here, we have an example of how gender identity has varying social capital that depends on the context. We can associate this notion of pathology that because men are socially approved to be leaders, leaders are compensated at a higher rate, which fits into the larger narrative of patriarchy. Conversely, women are socially approved to be in education, an undercompensated field. And, in the rare instances in which men are engaged and employed in elementary education, they tend to have leadership-based roles, such as administrator. When reviewing the pay differences between administrators and faculty, we see that a compensation disparity maps onto gender disparities.

Power Distribution

Put more simply, we can think of power as a matter of whose voice is heard and whose isn't. By voice, we mean not only the voice of a person, but also their representation. The United States is a democracy, which should mean that we have a system of government in which individuals can speak for themselves to be heard, or they can choose a representative to speak on their behalf. Theoretically, there is an alignment of values, and citizens feel that they can be represented by their elected officials. In a democracy, the population majority would rule—that is, the values, priorities, needs, concerns, desires, visions, and goals of the majority would be privileged.

Figure 2.2. Power Distribution.

However, in the United States, this is not the case. Let's use the image in Figure 2.2 as an analogy for society. We see a family of seven operating as a democracy. There are two parents and five children. There's the eldest child and the youngest child. One might think that because the children outnumber the adults, the children's values, priorities, needs, and concerns would dominate how the family functions. Or one might figure that the middle children's voices would be heard more, because there are three middle children, and only one eldest and one youngest. Adults tend to have a minority-rule approach to their households, which allows them to be the primary decision-makers. Often this power distribution is tied to income—that is, the highest earners direct funds. So now we have the intersection of economics (income) and age (adult). In a patriarchal society, if we have a traditional heterosexual family, you can also assume that in most households, the man (because of the gender pay gap × socialized gender roles) determines the family's priorities.

Minority rule is not unique to families. Take, for instance, Syria, which has been ruled by the Alawis, or South Africa, which was ruled by the Afrikaners—or Iraq by the Sunni, or Zimbabwe by the Shona. In all these instances, the minority group ruled the entire population. With their socialized and institutional power, the priorities of the group or individuals in power dictated for everyone else what societal norms were, who was afforded privileges, and who was dealt disadvantages. If you're thinking, "Oh well, in the United States, we have not had this issue," I invite you to look at when a minority group of colonists arrived and decided to dominate the existing and majority population of Native Americans. Through colonialism, Indigenous communities were subject to minoritarianism and eventual genocide. Another example: When the enslavement of Africans was rampant in the United States, in many states, there were more enslaved people than enslavers. Yet, it was the enslaver who had the power and influence; it was the enslaver whose voice was heard. Consider that in your future classrooms, there will be power differentials. You will be the adult—the one with the most responsibility, authority, and influence in that space. Your postsecondary education credentials and teaching experiences will legitimate and validate your authority, but you will not be part of the majority. Ask yourself, Will your classroom be a democracy, or will you be an authoritarian?

When we discuss equality versus equity, I want to clarify that equality means the same "thing" for everybody, and equity means adjusting that "thing" to meet individual need. It's important to recognize that people have different needs, because those in power typically design a world, or a household, or a classroom, or a society that typically meets their own needs, to the disadvantage of those whose voices are not heard. Put differently, those who are disempowered are silenced or made voiceless. Critical pedagogues don't just ask the question, what are the needs of those who are marginalized? They also ask, why does this need exist? and What is my role in either exacerbating or dismantling the cause of these needs?

One example of how a classroom teacher might meet the needs of a minoritized group in their classroom—whether one person or a group of students—is through a preferred names policy. Preferred name policies allow each individual student, for whatever reason, to determine how they will be addressed. Those who are gender nonconforming stand to benefit from having a teacher who respects them enough to support self-identification. Likewise, having a teacher create a classroom environment that is safe for LGBTTTQQIAA+ youth to self-identify allows everybody else to understand how they identify. If a teacher can be proactive and implement this policy ahead of introductions—ahead of addressing anyone or making attempts to address anyone—they can avoid potentially misgendering or deadnaming students. Furthermore, a student who prefers a nickname over their formal name, or their middle name versus their first name, can also self-identify. Critical pedagogues understand that the classroom is a community and that respected self-identification, facilitated through humanizing dialogue, is one of the most effective ways to foster an equitable and inclusive classroom community.

Vulnerability and Power

To establish community and to be in community with others, teachers must be reflective, vulnerable, and humble. When I say that teachers must be reflective, I'm explicitly saying that teachers must come to know what their identity properties are and what privileges and disadvantages are associated with those identity properties. Moreover, how are those identity properties leveraged, and what implicit and explicit biases does the teacher have? Like you, and everyone else, I have biases, and they interact with my privileges and disadvantages. As a teacher educator, I have the power to impact each student's grade, and although I make efforts to reduce bias through rubrics and nameless grading, I cannot eliminate it. As teachers and teacher educators, we make judgment calls that are mediated by our biases and upheld by our power. My triggers surrounding sexism are activated when a student mistakes me for the teaching assistant and my White male students as the professor, or when they insist on calling me Mrs. Smith when I've identified myself as Dr. Smith. Still, in those situations, I must maintain professionalism and find teachable moments that aren't disenfranchising to students whose intent I must professionally trust.

If you are a woman-identifying teacher with unresolved trauma with men, implicit biases against Asian people, or triggers surrounding noise, it is imperative that you acknowledge and understand these qualities about yourself and address them so that your male, Asian, or expectedly noisy students don't trigger you by merely existing. For example, if you hold a stereotype that associates Latino boys with violence, you may be intimidated by a Latino third grader and see him as a threat. This would adversely impact your relationship, undermining not only his educational experience in your classroom, but also your classroom management. Notice that the negative experience that this young Latino might have in your classroom has absolutely nothing to do with anything he has done, or not done. The concept of Latino male-hood, and all its associated stereotypes, mediates how you will treat this child and how you will perceive Latinos. Therefore, because of these unresolved biases, Latino students who enter your classroom will arrive at a disadvantage.

Conversely, a teacher who has a positive bias toward Asian students might greatly benefit a Hmong student who has entered their classroom. That student might experience high expectations (i.e., teacher efficacy), which often lead to or correlate with high performance. However, that positive bias is associated with a stereotype: the *model minority*. In the United States, Asians are considered the minority group that best aligns with the cultural expectations and preferences of the dominant population group (White Americans). Therefore, Asians are considered the model among minority groups. This comparison of Asians against other Black, Indigenous, and People of Color (BIPOC) and culturally minoritized groups sets an expectation that Asian Americans will be exceptional students in science, technology, engineering, and math (STEM), and quiet, obedient, hardworking, and self-reliant. The stereotype of the high-achieving Asian student is a double-edged sword, however: If a Japanese student has unmet academic or social needs, they might be overlooked. The teacher might be operating from stereotype that Asian students do not need support.

Impacts of Identity on Vulnerability and Power

Mitigating power imbalances will not eradicate them, because that's nearly impossible. However, lessening them begins with vulnerability, and this happens through dialogue. At the beginning of this chapter, I listed some of my identity properties, and I explicitly talked about my privileges. I recognize that by virtue of even writing this book and having you as a reader, I am positioned as an authority figure. This is a position of power. My voice is being heard. However, I also know that there is a school of thought based on the idea that vulnerability undermines one's credibility. In other words, identifying myself as Black or as a woman or as Haitian could interact with your own implicit and explicit biases to my disadvantage, and you may not trust what I'm saying. You may dismiss my PhD, my 10+ years of teaching experience, my publications, my research, and my trainings, all because you only conceive of Black people, women, or Haitians within stereotypical deficit-based social constructions. The stereotypes of Black people as being lazy, undereducated affirmative action hires might be enough for you to dismiss anything that I have shared. Stereotypes of women being emotional and less rigorous may also work to my disadvantage. Stereotypes of Haitians being in a perpetual state of dire need and dependence may render me useless to you because I'm at the intersection of three identities that our society undervalues individually. Put together, these stereotypes form a trifecta, creating an intersectional identity that you may be unable to trust and respect. I understand. As a person who is still working through my own implicit and explicit biases, especially around age, I am having to constantly confront who it is I think are legitimized subject matter experts. As I examine the world through a critical lens, I must acknowledge my own internal contradictions. There are tensions between my internal and professional understandings and trainings, and my socialization. Media heavily relies on stereotypes based on negatives—some of which I've internalized, even about myself—so I'm making sense of this and negotiating an identity that I can sit with as I try to humanize individuals, regardless of whether I ever interact with them.

I'd be remiss not to acknowledge that this notion of keeping distance from, and keeping your identity from, your students is rooted in an extreme amount of privilege. Revealing too much of yourself as an educator might undermine your credibility, but this argument also assumes that everyone can mask any socially marginalized identities they might have. Thus, this perspective perpetuates whiteness as property and, thus, whiteness as norm. I am not White-passing. The moment you meet me, you'll see that I am Black—the dark-skinned, nappy-headed, big-nose and big-lipped kind. Add to that whatever dehumanizing image suits your stereotypes. I am not male-passing. The moment you see me, you'll likely identify me as a woman. Add to that whatever dehumanizing images come to mind. When we insist that educators and leaders—or anybody—mask or conceal their identity, we sustain systems of marginalization and stigmatization that purport whiteness and maleness as rightness, and proximity to whiteness as our best effort. It is exclusionary, demeaning, dehumanizing, and oppressive (see Disclaimer 2.2).

Disclaimer 2.2

> This doesn't mean that you ever out someone for their class, race, gender, sexuality, anything. We don't out other people. People choose what they share with us based on their comfort level. If you want a classroom where students can show up as their full self, create a safe environment for them to determine freely that your classroom is a place where they can thrive.

Doing this work is exhausting and inconvenient. It requires a commitment with no end in sight. At minimum, it will exhaust your time and your energy if you're doing it right, and at times it will also drain your resources. You'll experience internal conflict, tensions, embarrassment, failure, moments of joy, and growth and reflection. One way to measure if you're making progress in your development toward critical consciousness is to assess whether any of your growth has translated to your personal life. If you can enjoy all the same songs, shows, or movies; have the same conversations; hang out with all the same people; and do the exact things you did before you encountered and began the journey of developing critical consciousness, you are failing. By virtue of thinking critically, you should be questioning things; when we question things, it is disruptive and, at times, combative. Relationships will be severed. If you are fortunate, new relationships will emerge and thrive.

This is not specific to White people. If you are a male—whether Indigenous, Asian, Black, Latino, or other ethnic/racial group—and you're thinking critically about oppression, you should not be able to consume content that is sexist and be ok with that, and you certainly shouldn't be comfortable practicing socialized sexism. When I say, "socialized sexism," I mean the casual ways we expect the women in our lives to do thinking, planning, and executing of logistical matters that make our lives easier. Whether it's in a romantic sense (planning out an entire date) or in a professional sense (making copies, organizing schedules), it is sexist to burden women with what sociologists call the "mental load." If a Black man is doing the work of becoming critical, you should be taking note that while Black men and Black women, and all Black gender-nonconforming folks, experience racism, Black women, and gender-nonconforming folks also experience sexism and homophobia at the hands of all men—including Black men. That's how patriarchy functions. And because of proximity violence, Black women, and gender-nonconforming folks experience violence at the hands of Black men more than any other group, because that is who we are in closest proximity to. So, as I said, being a critical pedagogue requires continuous self-reflection, awareness, healing, and personal growth (read: humility and vulnerability).

Making Sense of Oppression

Becoming a critical pedagogue is not an intellectual or socialized sport. One cannot theorize, date, partner, procreate, volunteer, travel, teach, or "friend" their way to critical consciousness. Being critical affects how we vote, how we spend our money, what we enjoy, content we consume, where we live, whom we confront or defend, and every other facet of our being. Adopting a critical consciousness lens upends your life. If you're a Latinx person who is able-bodied, and you're thinking about Latinx-specific issues such as immigration or the opportunity gap, but you're not thinking about the higher murder rates of Latinx trans folks or folks with disabilities or the recent violent attacks on Asian Americans and Pacific Islanders, that's problematic. Your critical consciousness is not evolving. One is not critically conscious just because they belong to a minoritized group. One is not critically conscious because they can think about one minoritized group that they don't belong to. Critical consciousness acknowledges the very messy and complex nature of systemic oppression and intersectional injustice. We are not one identity, and oppression does not have one face. Structural oppression creates and sustains policies, practices, and norms that marginalize folks from one angle to another. Oppression overlays, and it compounds until nearly all of us are masking something, or just a few of us get to thrive and exist in a way that is self-determined. As a classroom teacher, you must understand these larger complexities, and your role in them, so that you're not perpetuating them.

One simple way that systemic oppression shows up in the school curriculum relates to the words "canon" and "classic." When we look up the definition of "canon," we see that it is a collection, or a list of sacred books accepted as genuine. In other words, books in the canon are the standard for literature. Similarly, the word "classic," as in classical music, refers to a work of art recognized as the highest quality, outstanding with inherent and established value. When a curriculum is built on the canon or the classics, and a teacher accepts that those works are the standard for highest quality, the teacher is accepting that White men who biasedly created these lists and standards are the authority on worth and value. They determine what should be normalized and what should influence everything else. There is nothing inherently superior or more genuine in literature written by White men versus any text produced by a nonwhite person or a non-man. However, because of power differentials, it is White men who determine the canon and the classics, but it's on all of us to decide whether we will continue to legitimize and validate that (see Activity 2.1).

Activity 2.1 Personal Privilege Self-Evaluation

Let's unpack one aspect of your identity proprieties (privilege) by completing a personal privilege chart to assess your degree of ability, nationality, and religious privilege. Below are six examples of demographic identity privileges. As you read through them, cross out those that don't apply to you.

1. When I apply for jobs, my legal right to work in this country probably will not be questioned.
2. People from my country are visible and positively represented in politics, business, and the media.
3. I can assume that I will not have to work or go to school on my religious holidays.
4. My religious views are shared by most people in power (teachers, leaders, government officials, and political candidates).
5. I can assume that I will easily have physical access to any building.
6. I can hear what's going on around me without using an assistive device.

Reflection: What was it like to focus on privilege that did not center race? Did you learn anything new about yourself and how you're experiencing the world? Did any advantages stand out to you?

Cultural Competence and Identity

Cultural competence requires that we understand the nuanced ways in which our society functions and the ways that our demographic identities are socially constructed, always mediating how we experience the world and how the world perceives us. Cultural competence requires an ongoing assessment of one's identity for the sake of understanding self and others. This understanding, when used intentionally, could lead to us leveraging our social capital to the benefit of those who are othered and marginalized. Cultural competence could also help us to avoid internalizing impostor syndrome because we understand that our oppression is not an indictment on our worth, but a thriving function of a broader system that thrives on exclusion and exploitation.

For example, many of us grew up with the idea that meritocracy is real because of the myth of the "American dream." This dream suggests that through hard work, determination, and perseverance, anyone and everyone can become middle class or even well-off economically. It does not account for systemic oppressions such as ableism, heterosexism, xenophobia, and other socially constructed hierarchies that culturally, institutionally, socially, and personally limit access and achievement of Others (Said, 1978). The concept of meritocracy has convinced us that the world is accessible in relatively equal ways to all of us—we just need to work hard enough to access what we desire, or think we deserve. However, when we understand that institutional structures are in place that are intended to marginalize many of us—whether because of neurodiversity, size, ability, hair texture, language, and all sorts of other social identities—we understand that meritocracy and the supposed American dream are myths. By design, these structures thrive or survive through suppression of others to sustain dominance. There are gross social inequities that limit our capacity to access or manifest a self-determined life. And those social inequities are directly linked to the value that is placed on social identities. For example, in the United States, although we do not have an official language, it is widely understood that English is the language of wider communication and therefore the language of power and access. Unfortunately, many of us translate that to mean that English is the language of intelligence. Therefore, if a person is an English learner or a native speaker of other languages, monolingual folks whose dominant language is English tend not to place value on the intelligence of that individual or, by extension, their language group. This is also true in the international business context (i.e., English is the international language of business), which contributes to huge swaths of global inequality because so many non-English-dominant countries and people are excluded from participating in international business. Critical pedagogy—and, by extension, the theory of consciousness—is born out of Brazil, where the dominant language is Portuguese. The same country that promotes meritocracy and the American dream also admits, "it's not what you know but who you know" (classism x racism); "money talks" (classism); "you can sleep your way to the top" (sexism and sexual exploitation); "it's survival of the fittest" (ableism), "the rich get richer, and the poor, poorer" (classism), and so on.

I'll explain cultural competence differently, using two 2021 pop culture occurrences. Let's take, for instance, the recent globalization of Afrobeat. When Justin Bieber (American pop) made the choice to collaborate with Wizkid (Afrobeat), he leveraged his social capital with a Western audience to elevate an already brilliant and talented artist—and, by extension, an African continental genre. Through cultural appreciation, and arguably some cultural appropriation, Justin Bieber was able to amplify the inherent value of Afrobeat. A reverse example of this is the global phenomenon of the show *Friends*. *Friends* is a completely American contextual piece of pop culture. The language and nuances of the show are rooted in its English-language and American cultural context. However, I have traveled to many non-English-speaking countries where people freely and excitedly let me know that they learned to speak English through the show. And although the show has been translated into more than 25 languages, a 2015 survey by the education publisher Pearson English found that of the English learners surveyed, nearly 60% used American movies and TV shows to improve their skills, with *Friends* at the top of the list (Hunt, 2019). YouTube channels exist that are dedicated to learning English using *Friends*—meaning that this source of entertainment, much like Afrobeat, has been adopted and then adapted as an educational tool for accessing a language and a culture. We as teachers can do the same for our students when we choose to see the value in their culture.

Cultural Competence and Identity Within the Classroom

As discussed earlier, students' Funds of Knowledge consist of everything they know and bring with them into schools (i.e., skills, language, geography, practices, role play, histories, behaviors, beliefs, values, etc.). When we see the value in that—the essence of their being and humanity—we can see their funds of knowledge as an opportunity for us to learn from, and with, them. This is the opposite of viewing their ways of being as obstacles to eliminate. The idea is that we can help mold and shape students who are culturally fluent so that when they hear the language of wider communication (English) in the United States, they can understand and participate in the activities surrounding that language; at the same time, they can maintain, and have a deeper appreciation of and embeddedness in, their own home language, practices, and culture.

One example of how I have used my cultural competence to help my preservice teachers is in the scheduling of assignment deadlines and my office hours. I recognized that most of my students were full-time employees with families, and eventually I understood that they were most available to focus on their schoolwork on weekends. Although it is not ideal for students to reserve only weekends to concentrate on their studies, I decided to meet them at their place of reality. I implemented Sunday 11:59 p.m. deadlines with a 24-hour grace period for assignment submission, and I had office hours every Sunday evening, when students could hop online and ask questions as they were preparing to submit their assignment. I knew that choosing to give up 2 hours of my weekend was beyond my work responsibilities, but I also realized that prioritizing my students' needs was the best pedagogical course of action.

Classrooms mirror the larger social structures and, therefore, the social stratification of our society. As the classroom teacher, you have an opportunity to leverage your privileges and power to directly confront, challenge, and dismantle some of those hierarchies. The very first step in approaching this audacious goal is to know that you (and I) have been socialized under the same social structures and stratifications, and we need to heal from the trauma that we have likely internalized. For example, many of us have been conditioned to believe that a person with a physical disability lacks intellectual capacities; the two are unrelated. The same stereotype of unintelligence applies for those who are fat-bodied, English learners, neurodivergent, lower income, nonwhite, religious minorities, or undocumented. Through media representations, including "the canon" and "the classics," these social groups have been perpetually framed as intellectually less capable. Because academic achievement is seen as the premier measure of one's worth in a schooling context, students with those identities suffer when teachers internalize deficit-based stereotypes. Even students without those identities suffer because they too are being socialized to view their fellow humans as deficit-based; thus, the cycle of oppression continues.

Cultural Imperialism and Cultural Competency

In a popular TikTok video, a person phones a call center, and the representative speaking has a non-Western accent. The caller asks, "Do you speak English?" The representative, speaking perfect English, replies, "No. Would you like to be transferred to someone who does?" The caller enthusiastically responds, "Yes!"

The exchange demonstrates how language and accent have been conflated to determine competence. When the representative answers the caller's question and asks if the caller wants to be transferred, they demonstrate their English proficiency. Still, the caller subconsciously cannot detach accent from language proficiency or competence. That TikTok discourse exchange encapsulates the notion of social stratification that says that even when you speak perfect English, if you do so with an accent, people will assume that you are less capable—and sometimes assume that you don't speak English at all. This is the impact of cultural imperialism (see Disclaimer 2.3).

Disclaimer 2.3

DOES NOT EXIST!!!!

So, what can you do? Begin by acknowledging that your view is not the worldview. There literally is no [one] worldview. Viewpoints are socially constructed. There isn't even a [single] U.S. view. We have an immeasurable amount of diversity—much of which we have limited access to because of notions of "America first" or Western dominance—that keeps us from having any singular view. Second, understand that your perspectives are not neutral. They are not "normal." Your perspectives, values, norms, behaviors, and knowledge (read: culture) are an amalgamation of your socialization. What you learned at temple or other places of worship, at home, in school, during holidays, on the playground, at the market, from that one random person who maybe yelled at you, from that traumatizing experience you might have had, from your life experiences, and from the books you read, the movies you watched, the music you listen to—all of that contributes to your perspective.

It does not mean that your perspective should be, or is, the premier or dominant perspective, nor is it right or wrong. The goal is for it to be more and more (and more) humanizing—especially toward the dehumanized.

If you, as a teacher, go into the classroom with the idea of what is "right" and "proper," and your mission is to socialize your students into mini versions of yourself or your ideals, you are essentially attempting to colonize your classroom and the minds of your students. Instead, I encourage you to think about how you can be in a partnership with your students—where you exist as a guide helping them to achieve grade-level academic achievements while also exploring and extending their cultural competence and critical consciousness. To do so, you must be willing to be vulnerable with your students. You must be willing to do the work of finding authentic resources that do not perpetuate stereotypes, most especially those that frame historically marginalized demographic groups in the deficit. Ideally, you would teach your students in a way that allows them to be culturally multiliterate. They would know that on a standardized test, they should select, "In 1492, Columbus sailed the ocean blue" on the multiple-choice part of the assessment, but then during the essay portion, they should debunk the fallacy that Christopher Columbus discovered America. They would argue that during four separate trips, which began in 1492, Columbus never set foot in North America. Yes, students would learn how to craft a well-researched position that would allow them to learn in the process of writing that critical essay—and the assessment reviewer might also walk away with questions of whether the curriculum is humanizing or accurate.

Ideally, before becoming a full-time teacher of record, you'll become familiar with the community in which you'll be teaching. Let me be clear: Regardless of the characteristics (i.e., funding, pollution, green and blue spaces) of the neighborhood—the people who live where you are teaching are living in a community. And like every other community, there are norms. These include traditions, practices, values, and ways of being, knowing, learning, communicating, and functioning. There are power dynamics. In some communities, the locus of power resides at the church, others with the school board. For other communities, power is found in government offices, local schools, or the neighborhood association. Either way, as a classroom teacher, you will be in a position of power—relative power, but power, nonetheless. If you are an outsider to that community, you don't just have the work of minimally learning the grade-level academic standards and content, the post-grade-level academic standards and content, and the academic standards and content for least two grade levels below (for differentiation purposes); you also have the responsibility of learning and appreciating the culture(s) of that community (see Disclaimer 2.4).

Disclaimer 2.4

> If the thought of entering the community where you will teach terrifies you, please don't teach there. Those people have inherent value, but you don't see it yet. That's okay, but they deserve better, so work on you—far away from them.

You know how when a person is looking to buy a house or rent an apartment, they're encouraged to check out the place at night? When you check out a community at night, it's like seeing the blueprints, or the subtext that you'd likely miss in the daytime. It's as though you get to see the backside or the underbelly of a community. The same could be said about being encouraged to test drive a car without the sales agent. So how do you get to see a community's underbelly? Well . . . be there. Attend the school board meetings and the PTO meetings and stay after for the informal meetings. Attend the parent–teacher conferences, neighborhood association meetings, and community events in the area. Attend the community Quaker meeting, the church service, or the mass, or visit the mosque, temple, or wherever folks are worshiping. If possible, stay after and see the meeting after the meeting. Be respectful and minimize your presence so you can better appreciate, not detract from, the experience. This is not the time for questions; you can conduct your independent research before and after.

Identity Lottery

Activity 2.2 allows us to theoretically simulate the distribution of various phenotypes and social identities that most people do not choose for themselves. I have selected some of the most hyper-marginalized identities, and I ask that you consider seriously what it might be like to exist with the chosen identity.

I recognize that for some of you, the identities may reflect your actual identity or that of someone you know. I do not mean to frame you or your identity in the deficit; rather, this activity aims to highlight how we are socially stratified in society and how something as incidental as one's phenotype can determine how they are treated, seen, and, in the case of students, taught and managed. My hope is not to yield guilt or shame. Guilt and shame do not sustain activism. Instead, I hope you gain awareness that can lead to you humanizing Others more and using your unearned privileges to advocate for equitable accommodations.

Activity 2.2 Identity Lottery

Instructions: Follow the steps, and do not look ahead.

Step 1: Pick a hand. Choose the one that feels luckiest or best, or that just attracts you. Write down your selection.

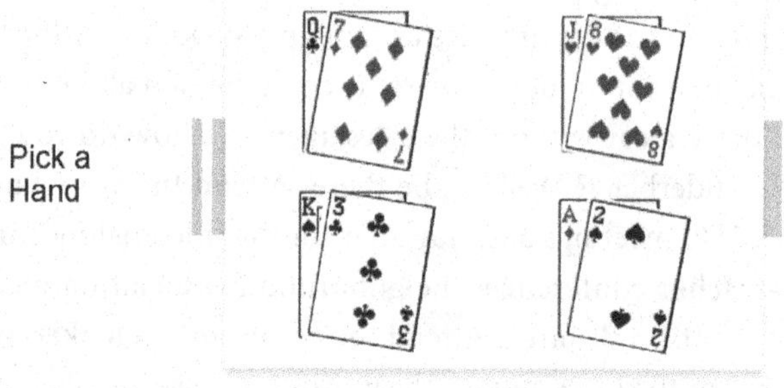

Step 2: Here I reveal demographic identities associated with the elements of each card.

Identity Lottery

- Ace: Houseless/Highly Mobile
- King: Visible Disability
- Queen: Neurodiverse
- Jack: Undocumented in USA
- Spade: Lower Socioeconomic/Under-Resourced
- Diamond: Black/African American
- Club: Latinx/Hispanic
- Heart: LGBTTTQQIAA+ Spectrum
- Odd Number: English Learner
- Even Number: Fat Bodied

Step 3: Your new social demographics correspond with the hand you chose. Are you still feeling lucky or like a winner? Why or why not?

Identity Lottery Results

Ace Diamonds + 2 Spades =
Houseless, Black, Fat Bodied, Visible Disability

King Spades + 3 Clubs =
Visible Disability, Low Socioeconomic Status, English Learner, Latinx

Queen Clubs + 7 Diamonds =
Neurodiverse, English Learner, Latinx, Black

Jack Hearts + 8 Hearts =
Fat Bodied, LGBTTTQQIAA+, Undocumented in USA

Debriefing after the activity

1. How does your personal identity compare with the identity you were randomly dealt?
2. How do you imagine that a person with those identities currently experiences schooling?
3. How are you prepared to humanize and embrace a student with those identities in your future classroom? Can you do so with the highest expectations?
4. What personal work, research, and activism might you need to engage in to support a student with those identities?

Activity 2.2 may be a trigger for many, especially those whose identities are used to represent social identities that are marginalized in society. To anyone who has any of the identities listed, I am sorry. Next, I share the hand that I was dealt, and I caution anyone from assuming meritocracy worked in my favor. I am the exception, not the norm, for people who are Black, English learning, from under-resourced communities, and neurodiverse. Until the norm is that everyone can access a decent quality of life and be self-determined, it is irresponsible and dishonest to assess the virtues of meritocracy and the American dream on outliers. So, to anyone who has any of the identities presented in this activity, I am sorry. As a mother of two children who have some of those identities, despite my privileges, I have zero assurance that their fate will not succumb to systemic oppression. So, selfishly, I'm trusting you to be a change agent that helps dismantle those structures that seek to invalidate and oppress them.

Critical (Sociopolitical) Consciousness and Identity

You can't be a good critical pedagogue if you stay in the comfort of conflict aversion masked as politeness, professionalism, or congeniality. This does not mean that you must be rude or aggressive; however, I especially encourage you to avoid being passive-aggressive. Rather, be informed. Learn the language of inequality and get very comfortable naming it. Each of us belongs to varying social demographic groups that use coded language to marginalize Others (i.e., those who are different). One way to show up as a critical pedagogue: When you are a witness to an oppressive act—be it a microaggression or active dehumanization—name it. Regardless of whether you choose to maintain a relationship with the offender, learn to manage your tone. Lovingly ask, "Were you intending to marginalize group XYZ?"; "Are you aware that such and such policy causes group XYZ to have particular experiences?"; and "Have you considered making a policy practice or behavioral change so that group XYZ could have a more positive experience and realize their potential in whatever context we're discussing?"

Asking questions with the right tone (and often the right skin tone) is incredibly disarming. Remember, the goal is to also humanize the person who has created an offense or has taken up oppressive behaviors, practices, and policies. They too are subject to socialization that encourages exclusion and oppression. More than likely, they too practice masking what makes them different from supposed norms. They too are subject to false hierarchies and binaries. Therefore, when we engage them, the goal is to eventually enlist them as co-conspirators in the mission to humanize everyone—including themselves. It is not useful to demonize anyone, because truly, the revolution will require the humanization of us all.

It is through your modeling of humanization of self and others—the way you are vulnerable and kind (again, not polite, and nice)—that you can invite that person to grow with you. Let them know that you are still struggling with specific demographic groups. *You are*. In spite my 10+ years of critical pedagogy education, research, teaching, and service, I too still have struggle groups. In the context of this book, struggle groups are the demographic groups we find challenging to humanize in a collective way. While we may make an exception for a friend, partner, or colleague of that group, we tend to struggle to have an asset-based view of the larger demographic group.

Next, I share one of the struggle groups that I'm still making sense of; I've made tremendous progress, and I'll describe how I did it. Afterward, I invite you to complete at least one iteration of this fill-in-the-blank template to make sense of your own struggle groups (Activity 2.3). I invite you to reflect on how it became a struggle group, and what you can do to humanize the humans in that group. Note: It doesn't matter if you have a "friend" or "neighbor," or if you like or care about someone, who belongs to this group (see Table 2.2 and Activity 2.3).

Table 2.2. Dr. Smith's Former Struggle Groups

Dr. Smith's Former Struggle Group (2001–2014)	Reflection
Mexicans are my "Struggle Group(s)" I am nervous/ afraid/ intimidated/ unsure about ___ *Mexicans*_______ I've heard they ___are *ruthlessly violent, and hate black people* _______ The media/world shows me they are ___*murderers and gang members*_______ My experiences tell me they are ___*not in my immediate communities*_______ The only thing(s) that could change my mind about them is/are *spend time with them, question the agenda of the media, visit their country, consume their media, learn to appreciate their culture, understand their history, read their stories, build genuine relationships with their community members, remember how it feels to be judged, become more humble, become more patient, etc.*	This is a shameful part of my past but one that also highlights my personal growth. Mexicans were once a struggle group of mine because during my late teens and early 20s, media representations I consumed about Mexicans were largely deficit based. Movies like *Training Day* and the news primarily demonstrated deficit and dangerous stereotypes (e.g., cartels and the drug war). Realizing the depths of my biases upon rejecting a scholarship to Fordham University, which is in a Latinx community in NYC, in 2006, I began the journey of addressing my deficit-based biases of Mexicans. I performed all the action items on the left, with a culminating trip to Ciudad Juarez in Chihuahua, Mexico, in 2012. At the time, this city had one of the highest murder rates in the world, but I still encountered humanity. I've since visited various states in Mexico countless times and continue to heal. Decolonizing the mind is lifelong work.

Dr. Smith's Current Struggle Group (~2010 to present)	**Reflection**
White Women are my "Struggle Group(s)" I am nervous/ afraid/ intimidated/ unsure about ___ *white women*_______ I've heard they are ___*liars. "Karens" manipulative, perpetual victims, sexually liberated and they hate Black women but love black men* _______ The media/world shows me they are ___*helpless, conservative, feminists, they cry a lot, are rich daddy's girls, judgmental, protected*_______ My experiences tell me they are ___*diverse in their lived experiences, they cry a lot, protected, exploitive, kind, heard working, dependent, superficial, entitled, believed*_______ The only thing(s) that could change my mind about them is *if I continue to explore my triggers with White women, work more to humanize each individual, find White women who are true allies that advocate for others in a way that doesn't explicitly benefit them, etc.*	Unlike Mexicans, who are a hypermarginalized group and removed from my immediate community, White women are a privileged group who have dominated my professional education and work environment since 2010. Having done all the **"thing(s) that could change my mind,"** I continue to struggle because I am often at the mercy of their institutional and socialized power. I can respect and appreciate the content and contributions of White women in media, but my lived reality is rife with entitlement, fragility, and exploitation. When I thought I made friends in the past, I was eventually exploited as the token Black friend and mistreated. I will continue the work of humanizing White women and find some solace in our shared struggle of sexism, but this journey is far from being completed.

Activity 2.3 Struggle Groups

________________________________ **are my "struggle group(s)."** I am nervous about/afraid of/intimidated by/unsure about_______________. I've heard they are ________________________________. The media/world shows me they are ________________________. My experiences tell me they are ___________________________. The only thing(s) that could change my mind about them is/are ____. **Reflection**

Changing the System

bell hooks says that we must embody a critical love that begins at the humanization of self, others, and, especially, Others (Said, 1978). In his 2006 show, *The Pimp Chronicles Pt. 1*, comedian Katt Williams says, as Americans, "we some goddamn bullies." He goes on to say,

> "You don't believe we gangsters, tell me what the Iraqi uniform look like? Don't worry—I'll wait, 'cuz you ain't never seen that mother*cker. [dramatic pause]. We ain't killing they army. . . . We killing them! We over there killing [humans] in sweatpants, tank tops, flip-flops, and a cowboy hat. . . . Our government pimps—they get on the news [and] they act like we ain't even over there killing real people. They don't never get on the news to say, 'Today we killed four men, three women, and two [children.] They use a word [average citizens] can't readily identify. 'Today we killed a group of insurgents.' . . . we at the house like 'I don't even know about the f*ck*ng insurgents. You can kill all them m*therf*ckers. I don't have not one insurgent friend!" (Williams & Binkow, 2006).

Disclaimer 2.5

> There are no people on earth who are not human.

I enjoy analyzing this piece of humor shared among local folk because it is central to how media manipulates our minds to the point where we fail to humanize human beings (see Disclaimer 2.5). Williams (2006) uses "friend" very intentionally to highlight who we readily identify as human and whose lives we deem valuable and worthy of humanization. If media uses the term "insurgent" to describe civilian men, women, and children, and we don't know what an insurgent is, we may think they're killing terrorists. This is how xenophobia and Islamophobia are cultivated. Decolonization ends otherness.

Next is a final activity to help your level of critical awareness (Activity 2.4).

Activity 2.4 Critical Awareness

Instructions: Read the following sentences and determine if there's an issue with any of them.

1. Sophia's son came out as a girl, and now his name is Savannah.
2. I think that mechanic tried to gyp me on the car repairs.
3. Eenie, meenie, miney, moe / Catch a tiger by the toe / If he hollers let him go / Eenie, meenie miney, moe.
4. When the principal reached her tipping point, she just spazzed out and started yelling at me.
5. Fuzzy Wuzzy was a bear.
6. I heard Andre went off the reservation.
7. I got a great deal off Facebook marketplace because I Jew downed the guy.
8. When Pedro asked for help with his report, I told him, "No can do."
9. Perhaps Brangelina reached its tipping point before splitting.
10. My daughter and I always Eskimo kiss before she leaves for daycare.

Conclusion

As you think about the tenets of CRP and how it relates to your identity development as a critical pedagogue, you can simply break it down like this: As clichéd as it may seem, changing the system begins with changing yourself. We are the system. We sustain its oppression—whether knowingly or unknowingly—and we have the power to alter that dynamic. We, you and I, must commit to learning the system to change it. We cannot remain complacent in it—especially if/when we start "succeeding" in it. What if all your kids pass the test because you've mastered teaching to the test, but none of them can think critically? Are you a good teacher because you're manipulating the system of hierarchy and social construction to achieve high test scores? We should be asking, are they ready to be change agents?

References

Hunt, E. (2019, August 9). How *Friends* taught the world to speak English: From Jürgen Klopp to Korean pop megastars. *The Guardian*. https://www.theguardian.com/tv-and-radio/shortcuts/2019/aug/09/friends-taught-world-speak-english-jurgen-klopp

Ladson-Billings, G. (1994). What we can learn from multicultural education research. *Educational Leadership, 51*(8), 22–26.

Moll, L. C., & Gonzalez, N. (1994). Lessons from research with language-minority children. *Journal of Reading Behavior, 26*(4), 439–456.

Said, E. (1978). *Orientalism*. Penguin.

Williams, K., & Binkow, G. (Directors). (2006). *Katt Williams: The Pimp Chronicles Pt. 1* [TV comedy special; DVD]. Home Box Office.

FOK Class Demographic Sheet

Grade________________________________Teacher________________________________

Funds of Knowledge: The competencies students embody that can directly or indirectly connect to formal classroom learning. It encompasses the knowledge, skills, and experiences acquired through historical and cultural interactions of an individual in their community, family life and culture.

Student #	**Gender**	**Race/ Ethnicity**[1]	**SES**[2]	**Home Language**	**SPED**[3]	**Funds of Knowledge** [4] Family values & tradition, caregiving, household chores, skills, knowledges, responsibilities, insights, experiences, family occupations, etc	**Challenging Circumstances** that *may* affect focus & learning
	What to reflect in the curriculum and be mindful to not act upon implicit biases			*What to consider & accommodate*		*What to celebrate & incorporate*	*What to consider and accommodate in teaching*
1.	F	Black	UM	Haitian Creole	Visual/spatial deficit	Of Haitian descent, strong faith, reading, recycles, loves historical fiction, running, speaks conversational Spanish	Recent immigrant, Learning English
2.	M	Other	LI	English		Mixed African American and Vietnamese, travels to Hanoi every summer, sketching, loves basketball	
3.	F	Black	LI	AAVE		African American, cooks well, recycles, social media, yoga	
4.	F	Latinx	LI	English		Peruvian, learning violin, loves sandboarding, yoga	Highly mobile
5.	M	Black	LI	French		Of Togolese descent, enjoys afro-beat music, loves math, has a YouTube channel	
6.	M	Latinx	LM	Portuguese		Brazilian, Afro Latino, meal prep, loves *America's Got Talent*, social media,	
7.	M	Latinx	M	English		Guatemalan, aspiring meteorologist, has a YouTube channel, likes long drives, yoga	Older sibling is undocumented
8.	M	Asian	LM	English	ADHD	Mainland China, calligraphy, painting cherry blossoms and other watercolors	From Wuhan
9.	F	Asian	LI	Hindi		Indian, wants to be a botanist, recycles, plays cricket, cooks well, social media, yoga	
10.	F	Middle Eastern	LI	English		Egyptian, Islam, dancing, hip-hop music, social media, Eid al-Fitr, and Eid al-Adha	Fasting at times
11.	M	Turkish	M	Turkish	Processing delays	Aspiring economist, loves musicals and sing-a-longs, loves the beach and nature walks, Eid al-Fitr and Eid al-Adha, Islam	Fasting at times
12.	M	Black	LI	English		Loves K-pop, Kemetic history, sketching, hip hop music, boxing, social media,	Mother, a boxer, recently passed away
13.	M	White	LI	English		Likes sketching, great story writer, loves theater, loves baseball & football, loves pizza	Parents divorcing
14.	F	White	UM	English	Dyscalculia	Elder care, hip hop music, likes hiking, likes teas, traveled to 6 countries in Europe	
15.	F	Native American	LI	Muscogee		Creek nation, social media, likes teas, loves autobiographies, types 40 wpm, recycles	

1. Race/Ethnicity: Asian (A), Latinx (L), White(W), Black (B), Native American (NA), Middle eastern (ME), Other (O)
2. Socioeconomic Status: Lower Income/Under-resourced (LI); Lower Middle (LM); Middle (M); Upper Middle (UM); Upper (U)
3. Language: Hmong, Somali, Tagalog, Swahili, Ewe, Portuguese, Yoruba, Creole
4. SPED Classification: Autism, Deafness, Visual Impairment, Speech Impairment, Intellectual Disability Emotional Disturbance, Etc.

Figure 2.3. FOK Class Demographic Sheet.

THREE

Critical Child Development

Tameka Ardrey

Introduction to Child Development

THE FIELD OF CHILD DEVELOPMENT seeks to examine and understand the growth and developmental changes of young children, from the womb through adolescence. It encompasses everything that helps shape us during the earliest stages of human life, including our biological, cultural, environmental, familial, educational, economic, and genetic experiences. Whenever you hear child development discussed, you'll typically hear it summarized according to three domains: (1) physical development, (2) cognitive development, and (3) social-emotional development (also known as psychosocial) (see Figure 3.1).

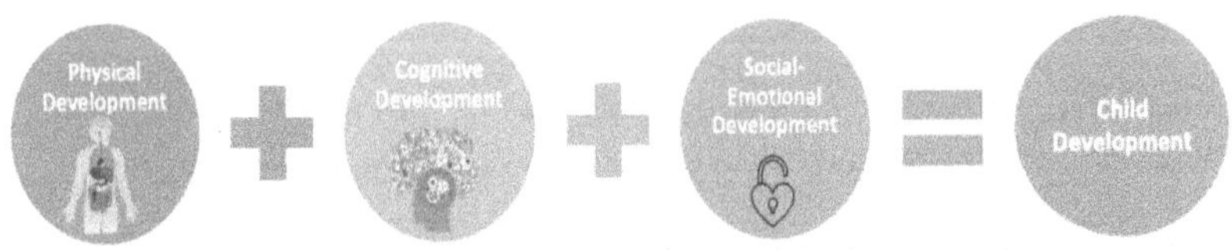

Figure 3.1. Child Development. These photos by Unknown Author are licensed under CC BY-NC.

Physical development refers to factors that pertain to the growth and overall health of the brain and the body. Cognitive development refers to changes in a child's intellectual abilities (e.g., memory, reasoning). Social-emotional development encompasses changes in a child's perception of self, in their ability to understand and regulate emotions, in the quality of their relationships with others, and in their understanding of morality. Although these three domains have very distinct focuses, they are heavily influenced by one another (see Pause & Reflect 3.1).

Pause & Reflect 3.1

As a teacher, you notice that one of the children in your classroom has started to sleep a lot. He has become a little aggressive with his friends, and his grades have started to decline. You reach out to the child's parent/guardian, and you find out the following:

1. The child's father is sick and has been in the hospital for the past few weeks.
2. The dad is the primary breadwinner, and his being out of work has put a financial strain on the family, and life has been stressful for everyone.

Based on what you have observed and the information you have received, what are some possible conclusions you might draw about the different domains of the child's development? Physical? Cognitive? Social-emotional? In what ways do these domains interact with one another?

Possible Response:

Physical: You have noted that the child may not be sleeping well out of concern for his father, and a change in the child's eating habits may be due to financial strain and stress.

Cognitive: You have noted that the child may be having a hard time paying attention and processing the class content because of everything going on.

Social-Emotional: You have noted that the child may be experiencing a lot of strong emotions as a result of the situation, and he might be having trouble identifying and regulating them.

Interactions: Lack of sleep and nutritional changes directly impact brain development, which may explain why the child is not performing as well as before. These circumstances may also be impacting the child's ability to regulate his emotions, hence the aggression.

It is important to note that although these domains are applicable to all of us, the lens through which they are applied is not. Unfortunately, pervasive understandings of the "science of child development" have consistently failed to acknowledge culture as a key factor in child development (Pence, 2011).

Instead, the process of development is often portrayed as black and white, with any shades of gray viewed as an abnormal. The one-size-fits-all approach portrays child development practices as being culturally neutral, when the truth is that it is rooted in Eurocentric assumptions about childhood. Don't believe me? Take a moment and think about your own schooling experiences. Think about the rules, the assessments, and the role your family was expected to play. I bet if you're honest, you can see an emphasis on valuing individualism, an upbringing in a responsive, two-parent household, and access to multiple resources—all of which are characteristic of white middle-class culture. Historically marginalized groups have been considered very little in the field of child development. In fact, the cultural specificity of normative standards of learning and development leaves little room for effectively addressing the needs of children from diverse cultures. This type of exclusionary practice ultimately undermines the importance of students' cultural experiences, and it can have detrimental implications for their learning and development. Hence, educators who understand the importance of implementing culturally relevant pedagogy are essential.

As highlighted in Chapter 1, culturally relevant pedagogy (CRP) consists of academic rigor, cultural competence, and critical consciousness to challenge the status quo. It is a powerful teaching strategy that creates a foundation of student strengths and cultures, makes core content engaging, and uses the children's funds of knowledge as a catalyst for all future learning. These approaches are child-centered and focused on strength and empowerment—a necessary combination to ensure that marginalized students are prepared to succeed in mainstream culture while still maintaining the integrity of their home culture. That said, the purpose of this chapter is to present a counter-narrative to the traditional approaches to addressing child development. I will provide a critical examination of the foundations of child development, including some of the key theorists and their theoretical contributions. Next, I will discuss how the tenets of CRP—academic rigor, cultural competence, and critical (sociopolitical) consciousness—can be intentionally merged with traditional understandings of child development to meet the needs of culturally and linguistically diverse students.

Positionality Statement

Tameka Ardrey (she/her)

I am a Black, cisgender, able-bodied woman who was born the only child of two amazing parents. I grew up in a lower-middle-class neighborhood, but my father always told me we were wealthy, and I believed it. My parents taught me that nothing in life is free. I must be a hard worker, self-confident, and diligent; operate with a spirit of excellence in all that I do; and, most important, remember that through my faith in Christ, nothing is impossible. These values have made me the woman I am today, and they have led me to accomplish great things—such as defying the odds of academic and career success for someone coming from my side of town, where children are traditionally labeled at risk for academic failure. Nevertheless, I don't take any of these things for granted because they have opened many doors for me and afforded me privileges to which many others around me are not privy; among these are employment opportunities with access to tremendous resources, acceptance into and completion of a competitive PhD program, and a platform to share my passion with others nationally and internationally. Just to name a few! However, despite all these accomplishments and the corresponding identities, my Blackness continues to be the one identity that I am constantly reminded of more than any other. I am reminded when I watch the news about police brutality, when I am reviewing research on academic achievement, and when my knowledge and expertise are often questioned by colleagues and others who do not look like me. It is for this reason that I am committed to using the privileges that have been afforded to me to advocate for equitable educational experiences for Black children and families. Banks (1992) asserted that there is a pervasive belief among African American scholars that "scholarship should be used to improve the conditions of their people and contribute to the formation of enlightened public and educational policies" (p. 278). It is in this spirit that I will be framing this chapter around CRP as a strategy to enhance the developmental outcomes of Black children. However, I want to be clear that many different intersecting identities that have a profound impact on child development could easily be incorporated into this chapter. Nevertheless, for the purposes of authenticity and transparency, I choose to focus on the one that I know best.

Key Terms:

- **Cognitive development:** all development related to the changes in a child's intellectual abilities (memory, reasoning, etc.).
- **Physical development:** all development pertaining to the growth and overall health of the brain and the body.
- **Social-emotional development:** all development related to the change in a child's perception of self, in their ability to understand and regulate emotions, in the quality of their relationships with others, and in their understanding of morality.
- **Zone of Proximal Development (ZPD):** the opportunity for growth between skills that children have already mastered and future skills that they can master with support from a more knowledgeable other.

Key Ideas:

1. ***Academic rigor:*** The key to incorporating academic rigor in meeting the developmental needs of culturally diverse students is to foster their scholarly identity by maintaining high expectations.
2. ***Cultural competence:*** To effectively meet the needs of culturally diverse students, you must be aware of how your own cultural experiences shape your teaching philosophy, instructional practices, and classroom interactions. You must also be intentional about building authentic relationships with students and their families to gain an understanding of their cultural norms.
3. ***Critical consciousness:*** You must be an advocate for the children and families you serve, understanding that learning and development cannot be simplified into just milestones and checklists.

Critically Examining the Foundations of Child Development

Although you may not be fully immersed in child development content, you've probably heard at least one or two of these names at some point in your life: Piaget, Vygotsky, Erikson, Bronfenbrenner. Each of these scholars was instrumental in establishing the foundations of child development. In fact, their work still informs many of the pedagogical practices that are still widely used today. However, there is a major problem: Let's see if you can identify what it is. Look at the images in Figure 3.2 and tell me what you notice.

Figure 3.2. Foundation of Child Development. These photos by Unknown Author are licensed under CC BY-NC-ND.

I'm pretty sure the first thing you noticed was their likeness among them—by likeness, I'm referring to the fact that they are all men of European descent. Now, although these four men are only a small representation of the field's contributors, they are an accurate cultural and gender representation of the child development field. Why is this problematic? The simple answer is that they represent very limited worldviews, particularly as related to the lived experiences and funds of knowledge of historically marginalized children and families. Consequently, their work alone is insufficient to thoroughly assess the developmental needs of children from nondominant cultures. There are two primary reasons for this. First, norms and practices are not interchangeable from one ethnic group to the next; rather, they are unique and rooted in the cultural understanding of a given group. Second, their research did not include participants representative of Black, Indigenous, or People of Color (BIPOC) (see Table 3.1). Therefore, it was impossible for these white men to understand the needs and experiences of children of color or to generalize from one population to the next.

Thus, continuing to use such value-laden assessment of white standards of learning and development as the norm can have detrimental effects on children of color; it not only undermines their culture but also alienates them and jeopardizes their security and sense of belonging. It must be noted traditional child development practices are shaped by the indigenous knowledge of a family's culture. Schafer et al. (2004) described indigenous knowledge as traditional, local knowledge developed in accordance with the specific conditions of a group of people indigenous to a particular geographic region. Consequently, the knowledge is contextualized by the experiences of the people and the conditions in which they live (see Pause & Reflect 3.2).

Table 3.1. Theoretical Limitations in Child Development

Theorist	Key Theories	Limitations
Piaget	**Four stages of cognitive development:** Children process new information through assimilation or accommodation. The goal is to achieve equilibrium (to be able to make sense of new information based on prior knowledge). Interaction is critical to cognitive development (Papalia & Martorell, 2021).	Stages of cognitive development are thought to be primarily universal. However, current research suggests that cognitive development may not be universal, nor does it occur in stages. On the contrary, it appears to vary depending on the lived experiences and cultural background of an individual (McDevitt & Ormrod, 2020).
Vygotsky	**Sociocultural theory:** Culture dictates the cognitive tools a child acquires to make meaning of the world around them. **Zone of Proximal Development:** Children can achieve more with the help of a more knowledgeable other, typically an adult. Adult guidance is imperative to cognitive development. Vygotsky believed that meaning is socially constructed, and he found culture to be a critical determinant in cognitive development because it determines styles. This ultimately means that there is no monolithic way of thinking (Papalia & Martorell, 2021).	Asserts that cognitive development is universal, and thus, his theory is applicable to and accurate for all children.
Erikson	**Theory of psychosocial development:** Psychosocial development results from conflict throughout an individual's life. We must resolve age-related "crises" that occur within eight key stages (Papalia & Martorell, 2021).	Research was based on men from Western cultures and underestimated the role of culture, given limited research participants (McDevitt & Ormrod, 2020). Culture affects how children navigate stages. Some stages last longer than others, depending on the positionality of the individual.

Theorist	Key Theories	Limitations
Bronfenbrenner	**Biecological systems model:** Relationships that children have with their families and others are impacted by local institutions and community (Papalia & Martorell, 2021).	Emphasis on culture is only in the macro-system, and even then, it is based on the *dominant* beliefs—white middle-class culture (McDevitt & Ormrod, 2020).

Pause & Reflect 3.2

Let's make it personal. Take a minute and think about the first time you realized you were a part of your racial group. How and when did this realization take place? What message did you receive about it? Were you taught any of the following?

- You have to work twice as hard to get half as much as others simply because of your skin color
- You have to speak and behave differently in public settings than at home to avoid being viewed as uneducated or undisciplined
- When any authority figure instructs you to do something, you do it immediately, without question.

Chances are, if you're not a member of a historically marginalized group, it may have been challenging to pinpoint when you first became aware of your racial identity and to realize that you probably did not receive any of these messages.

Wait—before you roll eyes and skip the rest of this activity, hear me out! I know that at first glance, this may appear to have nothing to do with child development, but it's actually a very important component. Racial socialization is an important part of child-rearing for BIPOC. African Americans use racial socialization as a parenting practice to equip their children with critical life skills so they can thrive amid the unjust social, political, economic, and cultural climates they will inevitably encounter as African Americans in the United States. Thus, the messages that African American children receive are a form of indigenous knowledge because they're based on lessons learned from past experiences.

The reality of the matter is that development is so much deeper than a child's performance according to age and stages; it is about their lived experiences and their ability to successfully navigate the circumstances they encounter daily, a practice that can be simply described as resilience. Masten (2001) defined resilience as "good outcomes in spite of serious threats to adaptation or development" (p. 228). Throughout history, resilience has been the nucleus of advancement and development for African Americans amid adversity. Despite societal barriers such as political, economic, and educational oppression, African Americans have still managed to survive in every area. In fact, research on resilience consistently emphasizes the role of culture. Consequently, to really capture the essence of child development for ethnically diverse children, culture must be placed at the center of the assessment. This would require child development theorists to look beyond their own cultural frame of reference to accommodate the needs and experiences of others. Ayers (2001) illuminated the importance of such awareness:

> We experience our own culture from the deepest levels toward the surface, and so our own culture can be largely invisible to us. The deep structures are the origins of everything, and they exert tremendous power and give meaning to the other levels of cultural experience. When we look at another culture, however, we tend to see the surface first, and we may fail to probe toward the deeper wellsprings of meaning. This, too, can cut us off, and make culture and other people invisible. (p. 76)

Now that we have established the importance of acknowledging the role of culture in child development, let's discuss how CRP can be used as an intentional pedagogical strategy.

Incorporating Academic Rigor to Meet the Developmental Needs of Culturally Diverse Students

The key to academic rigor is the ability to individualize instruction to position students for success and challenge them at the same time. The simplest way to think of academic rigor in terms of child development is through expectations. Expectations tend to be based on various ages and stages theories, such as those mentioned in Table 3.1. Accordingly, children's strengths and areas of improvement are determined by whether they meet a set of predetermined criteria. Don't get me wrong—there are some definitive insights about a child's current level development that can be drawn from such criteria, but they shouldn't be the end-all-be-all. There are always multiple factors that influence a child's rate and level of development. Let's explore language development to further illustrate this point.

Between 3 and 4 years of age, young children are expected to have a vocabulary of about 250–500 words, but research on language development indicates clear differences in vocabulary acquisition based on the socioeconomic status of their families. Children from high-income families typically experience 30 million more words within the first four years of life than those from low-income families (Hart & Risley, 2004). One reason is that high-income families tend to have more education, engage in more conversations with their children, and spend more time facilitating literacy activities, all of which put these children at a perceivably higher level of development than their peers. It's like giving one child a significant head start in a race against another child but still expecting them to reach the finish line at the same time. Thus, it is imperative for educators to understand that these milestones should be benchmarks to promote growth toward more equitable outcomes, as opposed to categorizing students as advanced or delayed. The focus should be on identifying culturally and developmentally appropriate strategies and resources to increase vocabulary exposure for children from lower income families.

Furthermore, it must be noted that optimal language development is based on the expectation that all students, regardless of ethnicity or home language, are expected to effectively communicate in Standard American English. Although accommodations are indeed made for some languages, such as Spanish, other languages are not valued or even respected as a "real" language, particularly other dialects of English. For example, studies have shown that teachers tend to rate the cognitive abilities, confidence, and academic success of African American students who speak African American English or Ebonics lower than those of students who speak standard English (Fogel & Ehri, 2006). Unfortunately, this is par for the course; throughout history, teachers have held students to lower standards, assuming them to be intellectually inferior and incapable of performing at a high level. This type of deficit thinking labels the children as failures before they even get the opportunity to demonstrate their knowledge and abilities, and often fosters a negative sense of self for the students.

Thus, it is imperative that educators truly believe that all students can achieve academic success and be intentional in communicating that belief to each and every child. One way educators can do this is through fostering the development of scholarly identity. Scholarly identity refers to the identification of oneself as an intelligent and competent learner in the schooling environment (Whiting, 2006). This is an important aspect of learning and development because it directly relates to an individual's belief in their ability to achieve and succeed. This is also a perfect place to implement Vygotsky's concept of the Zone of Proximal Development, which refers to the opportunity of growth between skills that children have already mastered, and future skills that they can master with support from a more knowledgeable other. By fostering scholarly identity in students, educators can not only meet them where they are, but also challenge them for even greater accomplishments (see Activity 3.1). Consider these recommendations:

- Encourage racial and academic pride through course content by exposing children to positive scholarly role models who are representative of their own racial and cultural backgrounds and with whom they can identify.
- Position each child for success by utilizing and placing more emphasis on their strengths and abilities, as opposed to taking a deficit-driven perspective that highlights what they can't do.

Activity 3.1 Seeing Development

This activity is a component of an assignment in my child development course. The assignment is designed to challenge students to begin to think critically about how we assess the development of young children in various education settings. Here's how it works:

1. Identify a child whom you can spend a few hours observing. I strongly encourage you to focus on a child whose culture is different from your own, if possible.
2. Observe and document the child's performance in all three developmental domains: physical, cognitive, and psychosocial. Don't overthink it—just document everything you see the child do as it relates to each domain in general.

3. Once you have data for each area, compare those with the theoretical principles or concepts that have been discussed in the course and in your textbook. Highlight any areas in the child that would be perceived as developmentally delayed.
4. Identify cultural factors that might contribute to any differences between the data you collected and what was presented in the textbook. This might require you to speak with the parents to gather additional information.
5. Identify some cultural and development strategies you could use to support the child in strengthening the developmental area.

Incorporating Cultural Competence as a Strategy to Meet the Developmental Needs of Culturally Diverse Students

Although cultural competence is imperative in all areas of development, it is particularly important to student social-emotional development. Research has found that teachers tend to rate behavior as positive or negative based primarily on ethnicity and socioeconomic status rather than on the actual behavior displayed (Humphries et al., 2012). To avoid such subjective approaches to assessing behavior, it is imperative that student behaviors be assessed in the context of their ability to navigate and negotiate the developmental situation in which they have been placed. This is where the role of the educator comes into play. There is a hierarchy of social and emotional skills that all children need to have to successfully thrive in a classroom environment, particularly if the culture of that environment contradicts their home culture. Thus, when the child's developmental capacities do not match the required skill set, behavioral problems may occur. Unfortunately, when it comes to children of color, mistaken behavior is often not viewed in terms of development at all, but as an act of willful disobedience.

There is a great misconception that appropriate behavior is common sense, but people fail to realize that unless individuals share a common culture, it is thoughtless to assume they have the same understanding. Not all cultural groups share the same behavioral norms expected in traditional schooling environments, so it is imperative that educators teach the necessary social skills for students to successfully navigate the classroom setting. You may have noticed earlier that I used the phrase "mistaken behavior" instead of "misbehavior." That was very intentional on my part. "Mistaken" acknowledges that students are still learning proper social cues and expected behaviors, and sometimes they will make mistakes. Let me give you a practical example of how school culture and home culture can sometimes contradict each other, causing conflicts in behavior expectations.

Now, if any of you have ever taken the opportunity to attend a Black church service, you know it is quite an experience. If you haven't, no worries—I'll paint the picture for you. Imagine a preacher is standing at the front of the church teaching a message. Other than his voice, the room is completely quiet, and out of nowhere, you hear someone yell out, "Preach pastor!" No one turns to look to see who says it, and the pastor doesn't miss a beat. In fact, the encouragement pushes the pastor to preach with even more passion and fervor. Then, a few moments later, you hear another person yell, "Say that!" then another yells, "Hallelujah!" And this pattern continues until the pastor completes the sermon and takes a seat. What I just described illustrates the African American tradition of orality. It is very common for members of the Black community to engage in a call-and-response approach to communication that does not require one person to speak at a time. Accordingly, many Black students take this same tradition with them into the classroom, which is in direct conflict with the expectations of raising their hands and waiting their turn instead of just responding verbally. Correspondingly, students who display this type of behavior in classrooms are viewed as being disrespectful, quickly labeled as discipline problems, and consequently face disciplinary actions just for being themselves. However, this is just the tip of the iceberg; early problems adjusting to the classroom environment may also have long-term consequences and effects on every other aspect of the schooling process. Additionally, early childhood behavior problems have been linked to negative social and academic outcomes, such as insecure attachment to teachers, poor peer relationships, phonological problems, reading delays, and language deficits (Dominguez et al., 2011).

Perhaps one of the greatest contributions to these cultural disconnects is that most teaching models claim to be culturally neutral and based on the needs of all children, when in fact they are established by mainstream education principles rooted in whiteness. Accordingly, many teachers truly believe that these models serve all children and thus fail to realize just how important culture is in the learning and development process—both the culture of the students and their own. Consequently, they feel little need to alter their teaching styles or adjust their expectations according to each child's cultural and developmental needs. However, each educator and student represents their own set of cultural values and beliefs that provide the frame of reference for classroom interaction. For the educators, these values and beliefs dictate how they teach, what they teach, and how they assess student achievement. This is particularly detrimental when there is a cultural mismatch between students and teachers. When educators are not familiar with their students' cultural nuances and fail to establish authentic relationships with them, it is very easy to begin to characterize them according to popular stereotypes, whether good or bad. These stereotypes are very often indicative of our biases, both implicit and explicit. Now, I want to take a moment to encourage you all to pause and reflect, because this is typically the moment in this course where a hush falls over the room, and students begin to nervously fumble with their pens or readjust in their seats. It's okay! We all have them! We all have preferences for certain groups over others and believe certain stereotypes to be true, whether we choose to admit it or not. But we don't have to let them control our interactions or overshadow our teaching practices as long as we are first willing to confront them (see Pause & Reflect 3.3). Take a moment and refer back to Activity 2.3 (Struggle Groups), presented in Chapter 2.

Pause and Reflect 3.3

As you work through this reflection, I implore you to be transparent and vulnerable with yourself. It's the only way you can really begin to unpack your biases and position yourself to truly form authentic relationships with culturally diverse children and families.

List all the stereotypes you can think of about the following groups: whites, Blacks, Hispanics, Asians, Africans, and any other group that you are likely to encounter in the communities in which you aspire to teach.

Next, identify where you heard the stereotype. Family? Friends? Media?

How have these stereotypes impacted your interactions with those groups in the past, and how might that translate into your teaching practices?

To avoid misjudging and stereotyping the learning and development of culturally diverse children and families, educators must be culturally competent and confident in their abilities to effectively educate all students. Culturally relevant pedagogues prepare students to succeed in mainstream culture while affirming their home cultures. These teachers understand that each child enters their classroom with their own set of cultural values and beliefs that shape who they are and where they come from. Bourdieu (2018) used the concept of cultural capital to define the attitudes, values, and lifestyle of an individual. Cultural capital varies between race and class and is also influenced by factors such as family structure and religious beliefs; therefore, it determines how an individual speaks, behaves, and thinks. Effective teachers must be able to use these cultural differences to develop their teaching strategies. They must also be able to assess not only the cultural appropriateness of academic instruction but also the cultural fairness of assessments, ensuring that all biases are eliminated (see Activity 3.2). Here are some possible recommendations to consider:

- Take the time to understand your own cultural background and how it impacts your beliefs about education, your teaching practices, and the biases you hold toward various ethnic groups.
- Become knowledgeable about the cultural background of your students and how it influences their behaviors and beliefs by establishing authentic relationships with your students and families.

Activity 3.2 Culture and Development Video

This assignment is designed to help preservice teachers integrate ideas, theories, and other content from the course with their own personal experiences over the course of their life.

Video Content

Background Information—Begin the video with a brief introduction of yourself, including a discussion of your cultural background and the corresponding beliefs about learning and development.

Developmental Domains—Next, identify a critical milestone or event that has profoundly impacted your life during your early childhood years (birth to 8 years old). Discuss how it has affected each of the three domains (physical, cognitive, and psychosocial). Be sure to make a connection between your experience, your cultural upbringing, and theoretical perspectives related to each domain.

Example: Here's an example of how a psychosocial milestone might be discussed:

When I was in kindergarten (5 years old), I had a good friend named Kaitlyn, and we did everything together. We played in the centers together, sat beside each other at lunch, and were inseparable during recess. Kaitlyn's birthday was coming up, and she had been telling me about her birthday party every single day, and how much fun we were going to have, which was very exciting. I couldn't wait to go and even told my mom about it. Well, one day during dropoff, Kaitlyn's mom came into the classroom and gave some of the other students envelopes to put into their book bags. When I saw she didn't have any more, I went and told her I wanted one. She just looked at me and said, "I do not have any more" and left. I went to Kaitlyn and asked why I didn't get one, and she said, "'Cause my daddy said brown people cannot come to my house." I immediately started crying. I remember no longer wanting to be brown because I thought it was bad. This is not surprising; the textbook states that self-esteem at this age is primarily based on the feedback of others, particularly negative and positive feedback from others. When I got home and told my mom, she was very upset. She told me that my brown skin was beautiful and that some white people are mean to Black people because they don't understand how amazing we are. She told me I don't need to be anywhere I'm not wanted. She also told me that God made me exactly the way he wanted me to look, and he did not make mistakes.

The following example illustrates how to make connections to a theoretical approach in the cognitive domain:

My mom told a lot of my family about what happened, and everyone had a similar reaction to my mom's. I was told how beautiful I was and how mean some people can be for absolutely no reason at all—that some people won't like me just because of the color of my skin, but I shouldn't worry about it because their opinion doesn't change the fact that I'm an amazing person. Their not getting a chance to know me was their loss. This illustrates the <u>theory of mind</u> as described in our text. I became aware of my own thoughts and realized that just because Kaitlyn's daddy said brown people couldn't come to her party didn't mean that brown people were bad at all.

> **Conclusion**—In your conclusion, **summarize the influence of culture on your milestones.** For example, how did your cultural beliefs and values impact how you and your family responded to the event?

Incorporating Critical (Sociopolitical) Consciousness as a Strategy to Meet the Developmental Needs of Culturally Diverse Students

I hope that by now, you're beginning to see just how important it is to critically examine normative standards of child development as a measure of student success. Because white middle-class culture is valued as the norm, those students who reflect it tend to excel, while those who do not remain far behind. The familiarity with the school culture for these white middle-class students is demonstrative of the benefits associated with the power and privilege of being white within the field of education. This is also the very power and privilege that perpetuates systemic inequalities while minority students are continually blamed for their own academic failure. Take into consideration the achievement gap between white students and BIPOC students. It is often used to emphasize the underachievement of students of color. However, research has identified developmental gaps in measures of achievement as early as 18 months. Now, let's take a moment to unpack this a bit. These gaps are evident before students even enter the K–12 school setting, so what is it all about? What is it that white children have that their BIPOC peers do not? My response: experience and opportunity. For these students, their home and school cultures closely mirror one another; therefore, the transition into the school environment is natural. They already have a certain level of mastery of developmental skills to which some students of color have never been exposed.

Hence, developmental disparities and differential school readiness levels stemming from low socioeconomic status, race, and ethnicity emerge in the early stages of child development, with young Black children scoring lower on assessments of proficiency and cognitive development. Unfortunately, school readiness criteria often fail to address the inequities of life experience and opportunities. Accordingly, most economically disadvantaged students of color enter schools lacking the necessary skills and knowledge to succeed in the school environment, which has a significant impact on how they adjust to the classroom setting, master course content, and engage in prosocial behaviors with their peers and teachers. It is imperative that educators begin to critically examine educational inequities, such as the overrepresentation of students of color in special education, suspensions, and expulsion. Educators must become advocates for the children and families they serve.

As advocates of equity, educators must first be willing to accept that schools were never designed with children of color in mind and thus are not structured for them to thrive and develop with ease. Furthermore, we must realize that the notion that teaching models are neutral is a false narrative, problematically reflecting a single perspective focused on members of the most privileged group and thus marginalizing everyone else. You must understand that traditional teaching models use whiteness as the analytical lens through which all learning and development are assessed, ultimately positioning all other ethnic groups in a greater position to fail. Many of us have heard the quote commonly attributed to Albert Einstein, "Everyone is a genius. But if you judge a fish on its ability to climb a tree, it will live its whole life believing that it is stupid." Thus, it is imperative that educators be intentional about the messages they send to their students, especially as they relate to race and culture. It is also important to acknowledge that these messages are both verbal and nonverbal (see Activity 3.3). Children pay just as much attention to educators' actions as they do to their words, whether positive or negative. Here are some possible recommendations to consider:

- Position all children for success by taking an asset-based approach to learning and development. Focus on how the strengths of the child can be used to support further development.
- View development holistically, understanding that it is more than performance connected to reaching developmental milestones; it is also about a child's ability to navigate the world in which they live.

Activity 3.3 The R.I.P Discussion Assignment

The name of this activity is a strategic play on words: For this assignment, R.I.P. stands for Reflect and Respond, Investigate, and Present and Participate, but it also has the traditional meaning, Rest in Peace. Accordingly, this assignment has dual purposes:

1. To strengthen and reinforce preservice teachers' academic abilities by incorporating reading comprehension, reflective thinking, critical thinking, research skills, organization, and presentation skills.
2. To challenge preservice teachers to put to rest any deficit perspectives they hold about young children who do not meet normative standards of child development.

The assignment is directly tied to the designated readings in the course. I encourage you to engage in this activity with any readings that really challenge your perspectives the most. It has three primary components:

Component 1: Reflect and Respond

To get started with this assignment, ask yourself the following questions:

1. What content from the readings resonated with you the most, and why?
2. What content from the readings challenged you the most, and why?
3. What are some questions that come to mind regarding what challenges you the most about the readings? Questions must be open-ended.

Component 2: Investigate

Next, identify at least one of these questions that you want to research. You'll be looking for answers to these questions. Through your investigation, you'll identify a resource (an article, video, or infographic from a reputable source) that gives insight into the question.

Component 3: Present and Participate

Finally, share what you discovered with a peer, and explain how it has increased your understanding and challenged your perspective.

Conclusion

Considering the varied approaches to child development, it cannot be treated as one-size-fits-all. Culture is one of many factors that influence development across domains. Culture is the foundation of who we are and what we believe, and it ultimately frames how we navigate the world around us.

As educators, we must understand the value of child development theories as a guideline for understanding normative expectations, and as a road map to position culturally diverse children to achieve equitable outcomes with their white peers. These theories should not be used as summative evaluations of the learning and development of culturally diverse students because they were not designed for them.

References

Ayers, W. (2001). *To teach: The journey of a teacher*. Teachers College Press.

Banks, J. A. (1992). African American scholarship and the evolution of multicultural education. *The Journal of Negro Education, 61*(3), 273–286. https://doi.org/10.2307/2295248

Bourdieu, P. (2018). Cultural reproduction and social reproduction. In *Knowledge, education, and cultural change* (pp. 71–112). Routledge.

Dominguez, X., Vitiello, V. E., Fuccillo, J. M., Greenfield, D. B., & Bulotsky-Shearer, R. J. (2011). The role of context in preschool learning: A multilevel examination of context-specific problem behaviors and classroom process quality to low-income children's approaches to learning. *Journal of School Psychology, 49*(2), 175–195.

Fogel, H., & Ehri, L. C. (2006). Teaching African American English forms to standard American English-speaking teachers: Effects on acquisition, attitudes, and responses to student use. *Journal of Teacher Education, 57*(5), 464–480.

Hart, B., & Risley, T. R. (2004). The early catastrophe. *Education Review, 77*(1), 100–118.

Humphries, M. L., Keenan, K., & Wakschlag, L. S. (2012). Teacher and observer ratings of young African American children's social and emotional competence. *Psychology in the Schools, 49*(4), 311–327.

Masten, A. S. (2001). Ordinary magic: Resilience processes in development. *American Psychologist, 56*(3), 227–238.

McDevitt, T. M., & Ormrod, J. E. (2020). *Child development and education* (7th ed.). Pearson.

Papalia, D. E., & Martorell, G. (2021). *Experience human development* (14th ed.). McGraw Hill.

Pence, A. (2011). Early childhood care and development research in Africa: Historical, conceptual, and structural challenges. *Child Development Perspectives, 5*(2) 112–118.

Schafer, J. R., Ezirim, M., Gamurorwa, A., Ntšonyane, P., Phiri, M., Sagnia, J., Salakana, L., & Bairu, W. W. (2004). Exploring and promoting the value of Indigenous knowledge in early childhood development in Africa. *International Journal of Educational Policy, Research, and Practice: Reconceptualizing Childhood Studies, 5*(3), 61–80.

Whiting, G. W. (2006). Promoting a scholar identity among African-American males: Implications for gifted education. *Gifted Education Psychology Press, 20*(3), 2–6.

PART II

WHEN CHILDREN GO TO SCHOOL: HONORING DIVERSITY AND DIFFERENCE AS A MORAL IMPERATIVE

FOUR

Practicing Culturally Relevant Pedagogy with Special Education Students

LaPortia Mosley and Laura Vines

THE WORLD OF SPECIAL EDUCATION is like a beautifully handcrafted blanket. Every strand has a place that requires patience, determination, and love. Every time you work those strands through the lived experiences of your students and yourself, you make your blanket even more beneficial for all. However, let's not kid ourselves into thinking that making a blanket is easy. Special education is not a walk in the park. Making a blanket is difficult, and it is painstaking work. Honestly, it requires grit and tenacity. There are highs and lows. At times, you may have no idea what to do next, and you may even want to quit. But, as educators, we keep moving forward. We find the drive to meet the needs of every student who walks into our classroom. It is vital that, as educators—in general education or special education—we give all students learning opportunities that allow them to grow past classroom experiences. Not every blanket will be the same, but it can provide the same warmth at the end of the learning process if you're willing to put in the work.

Positionality Statements

LaPortia Mosley (she/her)

I identify as a middle-class, able-bodied, Black cisgender woman. I was raised in a small rural town in Georgia where everyone knows everyone. Between my childhood and my adolescent years, my family went from low income to middle class. My parents worked hard to provide for me and my siblings. They relentlessly pushed college for us. I can still hear my dad saying, "Go to college so you do not have to work as hard as I do." My parents were able to put us all through college. We have all have degrees, and my youngest brother is set to graduate soon. However, regarding race, sexual orientation, and religious affiliation, there was not much diversity in my small town. Anything out of the "norm" was highly frowned upon and led to my following what was expected of me and never challenging the norm. I did not experience much diversity until I started my first teaching job and moved hours away from my hometown. It was then that I realized my own biases and complicity in sustaining societal norms. As I worked through my years of teaching, I realized that my lived experiences and opportunities were not the same as everyone else's. I was naïve in thinking that everyone was afforded the same opportunities that I had. I have pushed myself over the years to challenge the norms and make it my goal for every student to see themselves recognized in the classroom and in society.

Laura Vines (she/her)

I too grew up in a small rural town in Georgia with incredibly hardworking parents who stressed independence and development of the individual. I don't know if my mindset is a product of my upbringing, my region, my generation (X), or just plain stubbornness, but I hate being "put in a box." I am complex, still evolving, still incomplete, but I often feel like an outsider or observer. I think this mindset is what originally drew me to science. In fact, prior to becoming an educator, I was a hardcore labcoat- and closed-toe-shoe-wearing, hair-pulled-back female research scientist. As such, I assumed that observation was one of my superpowers. I thought that being a culturally relevant pedagogue meant primarily focusing on racism within the classroom. I could not have been more wrong. Culture is really what makes us unique.

Key Terms:

- **504 Plan:** this term refers to Section 504 of the U.S. Rehabilitation Act of 1973, which ensures necessary accommodations and services for students in public and private programs that receive federal money. It is designed to match the needs of elementary through college-age students who have one or more impairments that limit major life activities but that do not qualify as formal disabilities under current legislation.

Discrimination based on disability in public and private programs that receive federal money is prohibited.

- **Co-teaching/team teaching:** in the context of special education, a general education teacher collaborates with a special education teacher in the development, implementation, and assessment of material within an inclusion classroom.
- **Culturally Relevant Pedagogy (CRP):** an instructional approach that facilitates academic rigor through accessibility, cultural competence, and critical consciousness to teaching and learning.
- **Differentiated Instruction (DI):** teaching and providing supports ahead of time to support how a child learns.
- **DisCrit:** the shortened name given to the study of the intersection of disability studies and critical race theory. DisCrit explores how bias and concepts of "normality" are influenced by racism (implicit and explicit).
- **General education classroom:** a classroom where at least 70% of students do not meet special education eligibility, and students receive instruction from a certified teacher using general curriculum.
- **Gifted:** students who are considered to have above-average general intelligence.
- **Inclusion classroom:** the practice whereby students with classified disabilities are educated within a general education classroom for most of the school day and receive individualized accommodations/supports or services.
- **Individualized Education Plan (IEP):** a plan developed by professionals, parents, and educators based on a child's needs and abilities. An IEP lists supports and accommodations to be provided, as well as goals.
- **Individuals With Disabilities Education Act (IDEA):** a law that provides federal aid toward free and public education for special education and related service programs for students aged 3–21 who have one or more specific disabilities as defined by law.
- **Least Restrictive Environment (LRE):** the principle that students with disabilities should be in a general education classroom as much as possible and should only be removed when the disability is so severe that accommodations/services within these settings cannot be provided to adequately support learning.

- **Mainstreaming:** the practice whereby students who receive special education services only participate in some general education activities (e.g., lunch, recess, specials).
- **Response to Intervention (RTI):** a multi-tiered data-driven interventionist approach that screens all students to seek and to identify academic weaknesses and/or behavior needs in students to provide additional support as directed by the Elementary and Secondary Education Act (ESEA).
- **Self-contained classroom:** all instruction is provided by a special education teacher within a small classroom setting.
- **Special Education (SpEd):** an instructional approach in which a student's individual differences, identified disability/ies, and needs are accommodated to provide specialized quality education.
- **Universal Design for Learning (UDL):** providing students choices in how learning is conducted and/or how understanding is expressed.

Key Ideas:

1. ***To promote academic rigor in special education, you must:*** foster relationships with your students, be a facilitator of learning, and guide your students through the learning process and offer students real-world opportunities so they can make real-world decisions.
2. ***To promote cultural competence in special education, you must:*** ensure students' identities are affirmed and are represented in the classroom environment, content, and instruction, while adapting and modifying modalities to address learning needs.
3. ***To promote critical consciousness in special education, you must:*** acknowledge and address systemic barriers for students with disabilities while empowering students.

Special Education and CRP

Culture is important to all of us—it is the lens through which we see and interact with our world. Culture is not just race; likewise, culturally relevant pedagogy, or CRP, is the instructional approach that brings accessibility, relevancy, and application to material (see Chapter 1 for more information).

To illustrate the power of CRP, we present the following for consideration. How often have we thought, or heard a student say, "Why should I care?" or "When am I ever going to use this?" Or look completely disengaged. In many ways, adults have forgotten a lot about how it feels to be a child. After all, how often do you walk on the right, single file down the hall or interrupt authority figures when they are talking. Typically, adults have freedom and control over their impulses and the materials they encounter, and many children do not.

I, Laura, want to share with you an instance when I personally experienced the power of CRP. I live in a region of Georgia completely different from the one where I grew up. Several years ago, I was a special education (SpEd) paraprofessional in an inclusion classroom where the thermostat was always set to "August in South Georgia" warm. This was problematic because at the end of the day, it was so hard to keep from falling asleep if I wasn't actively doing something. One day, I was doing something mundane, like filing papers, while the teacher was introducing the regions of Georgia. Suddenly, the teacher started a slide show about the Appalachian Plateau! My ears perked up, I turned my head, and I swear this feeling was so vivid, I still remember how it felt. It felt as though my brain was lighter and open. My brain devoured each slide. I recognized the places shown and immediately accessed memories and connections to the material. I was even able to share an experience from my childhood and show my scars during the typical-animals-found-in-this-region slide (lost "kittens" in a tree that were mean bobcat kittens). This was a life-changing and eye-opening experience that drives home the point: It's easy to forget facts, but it's hard to forget experiences. Therefore, CRP is probably the single most important thing we, as educators, will learn during our preparatory programs; it must be considered first and foremost in all we do if we want to bring accessibility, learning, and recall to our students, and cultivate belonging, pride, curiosity, wonder, and excitement.

Like in science, pedagogical knowledge and practice are cumulative. I've always believed that being an educator is akin to being an apprentice. Educators never stop learning from those who came before us, from those we work alongside, and from our students. As such, it is important to understand that the field of SpEd, in its purest form, especially inclusion, is the very cumulation and embodiment of critical pedagogy. This is illustrated by the overlap of theories of special education founders with the teachings of countless pedagogues pertinent to the development of classroom management and child development. These founders include Michael Apple, bell hooks, Lilia Bartolome, Deborah Britzman, Jerome Bruner, Michael Eric Dyson, Henry Louis Gates Jr., and Shirley Steinberg, all of whom propose(d) models of learning where all voices are valued and encouraged to bring relevancy, increase engagement, and reinforce the value of the individual (Kirylo, 2013). Another founder is Paulo Freire, who believed that education from one's peers is an important part of the learning process because students are "unfinished" and constantly absorbing, reflecting, trying, and evolving. After all, education is not just rote memorization of facts absorbed from one's teacher. The purpose of education is to prepare and equip individuals to lead independent, informed, satisfying, and productive lives. Therefore, by extension, our classrooms of today should reflect life, work, and citizenship of tomorrow by valuing diversity and cultivating relationships, critical thinking, creativity, collaboration, and a sense of social responsibility in our students. This concept is not new. In fact, this engagement model is heavily influenced by Maria Montessori, of the famed Montessori pedagogy, and Margaret Bancroft, who began their work with children with special needs (Kirylo, 2013). More recently, shapers of special education theory and best practices have included contemporary pedagogues exploring the intersection of disability studies and critical race theory, known as DisCrit (see Annamma et al., 2013, for more information), as well as many notable theorists contributing to the field of critical disability theory who posit that the field should move away from its historical emphasis on deficit, disorder, and dysfunction and toward empowerment and humanization, celebration of neurodiversity (e.g., Armstrong, 2017), and advocacy; others warn of the shortcomings of these societal models (Shakespeare & Watson, 2010) and posit a more complex view (see Eilers, 2020, and Shakespeare, 2013, for a review). For the latest research, I recommend the *Journal of Disability Studies in Education*.

Background of Special Education

Throughout history, those with disabilities have long been marginalized, especially in education. Before the enactment of the Education for All Handicapped Children Act (EHA) in 1975, children with special needs were often denied access to public education. In fact, in 1970, 5 short years before enactment, only one in five children with a disability received an education, and some states went so far as to ban children with special needs from the classroom (United States Department of Education [USDOE], 2022). Further progress was made with the passage of the Individuals with Disabilities Education Act (IDEA) in 1997 and its subsequent reauthorizations. Now, more than 65% of students with disabilities spend more than 80% of their day in general education classrooms. Others may spend most of their day in self-contained classrooms or be "mainstreamed" and participate in some general education activities (e.g., electives, lunch, science, and/or social studies). Other progress of note includes the more than 786,000 infants and toddlers who receive early intervention services (Office of Special Education Programs, 2022; USDOE, 2022). In fact, more than 14% of all students today receive some form of special education support (American University School of Education, 2021). These data do not include those students who receive support through 504 plans, or response to intervention (RTI) support. Although much progress has been made, significant inequalities that have life-altering ramifications remain, including inequalities in funding, training, and execution, and a disproportionality of minorities (eligibility, placement environment, and discipline) (see Annamma et al., 2013, and National Center for Learning Disabilities, 2020, for more information). In short, the field of SpEd acknowledges historic and ongoing shortcomings and continues to aim to empower and equip this marginalized group via individualized accommodations that address abilities and special needs while ensuring education for all.

While this may differ across states, students receiving SpEd services typically fall within one or more of the following categories: Autism Spectrum Disorders, Significant Development Delays, Intellectual Disabilities, Deafblind, Orthopedic Impairments, Other Health Impairments, Specific Learning Disabilities, Speech-Language Impairments, Traumatic Brain Injuries, Visual Impairments, Emotional and Behavioral Disorders, and Deaf/Hearing Impaired (Georgia Department of Education, n.d.). "Gifted" students—those who are considered to have above-average general intelligence—are also considered by some to fall within the field of SpEd. Once you delve into the various categories, an overarching theme begins to emerge: There is no typical disability, even within the same category. Two students may have the same condition, but the way the condition impacts academic achievement varies greatly. The question is, how can we best serve our students receiving services? Consider that educators have a toolbox of techniques at their disposal, rather than a rubber stamp. In most instances, the teaching techniques listed could be found in any effective classroom.

Additionally, overwhelming evidence has shown that a productive and enriching learning experience requires students to actively participate in learning (see Chapter 2 for more information). How is this accomplished? Yes, active learning and engagement uses a CRP approach! It is my belief that CRP is the foundation for all learning because at the heart of education are genuine, authentic relationships built and supported by the appreciation for and nurturing of the individual. According to Maslow's hierarchy of needs, before any learning occurs—not rote memorization, but actual learning/processing and application of knowledge—aside from physiological and safety needs, students must feel loved, recognized, and valued. All children want, and need, to be seen, heard, and valued. To meet these needs, we must acknowledge our students' culture. It is our duty to help students use their lens/culture to make sense of and actively engage in the world around them. This comes from an educator forming a genuine relationship with the student and bringing cultural reflectivity and interests into the classroom's instructional opportunities. This is valid whether the student has autism, has an emotional behavior disorder, or is gifted. It all boils down to relationships, consistency, and a classroom community of mutual respect, trust, and minimal distractions.

I return to our overarching question: If no two students possess an identical set of strengths and weaknesses, how can we best serve our students receiving services? It is essential that we, as educators, do not "give way to the narrative" that we are the sole provider and the end of all knowledge within the classroom. To be effective educators, we must become students of our students by discovering their Funds of Knowledge (see Chapter 2 and Index for more information). We must discover and cultivate our students' assets and strengths. Think of knowledge as putting together a puzzle; there are multiple ways to begin, but the result will be the same. To accomplish this, we must consider these questions: What does it look like to teach SpEd to promote academic rigor? What does it look like to teach SpEd to promote cultural competence? What does it look like to teach SpEd to promote critical/sociopolitical consciousness?

Promoting Academic Rigor in Special Education Classrooms

Academic rigor occurs when a high level of student learning is expected, supported, and demonstrated. The goal of education is not just rote memorization of facts, but equipping individuals to lead independent, informed, satisfying, and productive lives. In the real world, we are rarely drilled on math facts or asked to diagram a sentence, but we do use our foundational knowledge in higher order tasks—analyze, evaluate, and/or create—in making sense of and living in our world. While revised Bloom's taxonomy (Krathwohl, 2002) is often cited, it is important to examine what these higher order concepts mean. Analysis refers to taking an unknown set of data/information and looking for meaning; this requires separating the relevant bits from the irrelevant. Analysis is not a "plug-and-play" concept. Along the same lines, *evaluate* is taking information and judging it using known standards and criteria, and *create* involves taking what you have assessed and applying the pattern/message in a new and novel way. Create is not, and will never be, something you find on Pinterest. Therefore, to preserve knowledge and learning, you must adapt and differentiate while keeping content rigorous. You want to be your students' cheerleader and facilitate the learning process. You won't be by their side for the rest of their lives, but the skills you provide them with will. Challenge your students to ensure that self-efficacy is supported and nurtured, but also throw out any preconceptions of what assessments look like (repetition does not mean mastery; repetition is just busywork). As an educator, you must give students real-world opportunities so they can make real-world connections. In doing so, you'll be teaching in a way that promotes academic rigor (see Pause & Reflect 4.1).

Pause & Reflect 4.1

A Peek Inside the Classroom: K–12 Self-Contained Autism Classroom

Mosley—I can recall being tasked with teaching measurement to my students. Measurement can be a difficult concept to convey to students, especially when they have no prior knowledge of the subject. I made a conscious choice to build a relationship with each one of my students and figure out what excited them in and outside of the classroom. By building a relationship with my students, I was able to learn that my students loved hands-on activities and food. I knew I had to incorporate those passions into my lessons, so my students had buy-in and excitement about what was being taught. Therefore, I transformed one of my measurement lessons into a lesson that my students could make connections with and transfer the skill to use later in their life. I moved my measurement lesson from the classroom to the cafeteria. I dressed up as a waitress and brought in ingredients from home for making muffins. As I taught my lesson on measurement in the cafeteria, my students took turns using measuring cups to complete the recipe for making muffins. They were able to make real-world connections; they saw the importance of measurement and learned why it was important. I moved past a worksheet and guided my students while learning. Not only did I teach them a math concept, I also taught them a life skill.

Pause. Reflect. Think about a lesson that you're getting ready to teach. How can you teach that lesson in a way that allows a student with special needs to walk away with a transferrable skill?

Next, you'll find tips on promoting rigor while maintaining differentiation and rigor in a SpEd classroom:

- Minimize audible/visual distractions.
- Know your students and optimize engagement.
- Provide headphones and minimize clutter when possible.
- To enhance understanding and aid with recall, review key vocabulary along with any pertinent images before reading.
- Use differentiated-leveled passages (with highlighted keywords, large text, and increased spacing).
- Include QR code links to explanatory videos (with captions) or links to verbal instructions or narration of passages.
- Use LEGOs to create models of events, to demonstrate organs and cells, and for story retells (beginning, middle, end).
- When lessons are presented to whole group, provide differentiated handouts of notes (omit keywords for fill in the blanks and to promote active listening).
- Reduce the number of problems.
- Print out sheets of large-grid graph paper to assist with alignment of rows and spacing.

- Read and explain word problems using manipulatives, drawings, etc., highlight keywords, and identify steps using different colors.
- If math journals are used, preprint and paste problems in journals ahead of time to give the student more time.
- To minimize repetition on assessments while maintaining rigor, you can test students' ability to solve problems; to correct or evaluate the quality of a fictitious student's work; and, finally, to solve a problem an alternate way and show the steps along with a narrative of their thought process (written or recorded).

Promoting Cultural Competence in Special Education Classrooms

Happiness is such an individual and subjective state of being, but it really is our key motivator in everything regarding our students. Being that happiness is so subjective and personal, it is heavily impacted by one's culture. Remember, culture is what is important to each one of us, and it is the lens through which we see and interact with our world. So, what does it look like to teach SpEd to promote cultural competence? It boils down to whether students are being seen and whether their self-efficacy is being supported and nurtured. Your success in addressing this will be your students' motivator (see Pause & Reflect 4.2). First, become a "student" of your students (discover their likes and interests). Are their likes reflected in your room, discussions, read-alouds, content, and activities? Does your room physically reflect their needs?

Pause & Reflect 4.2

A Peek Inside the Classroom: Second-Grade Classroom and Fifth-Grade Inclusion Classroom

Pause. Think about your classroom. Does it reflect your students? Think about your décor. Think about your books. Think about the holidays you highlight. Think about what is deemed "respectful" mannerism in your classroom. Does it reflect cultural competence?

Mosley—After going to a teacher conference one summer, I realized that my cute, Instagram-worthy classroom lacked something for the upcoming year: my students and what made them. As I reviewed my PowerPoints, I realized the clip art was not representative of all my students. However, that was not hard to change. I fixed it and felt accomplished. I moved on to the next task. As I reviewed my classroom library, I quickly realized that my books did not reflect my students' lived experiences. Therefore, I knew it would be difficult for my students to make connections during class discussions. I went on a hunt to find books that mirrored my students. I recall going into my local bookstore and leaving absolutely upset and surprised. I could not find a single book with a person of color as the main character. I could not find one book with a person with a disability as the main character. I could not find one book highlighting different types of families. I ended up ordering several books online. My friends and family also donated books to my classroom. My classroom slowly started to transform—not because I bought some books and changed some slides, but because I invested time in getting to know my students, learning more about their cultures, and incorporating learned concepts into my lessons. I studied my students. I will never forget getting a new girl in the middle of the school year in second grade. She placed her bookbag on the hook and squealed. She pointed at a book I had in front of the classroom and exclaimed, "Look, she looks just like me! Please tell me you are going to read that book!" When she saw herself reflected in the classroom, she felt safe and ready to learn. She felt part of the community as soon as she walked in because she saw herself mirrored in the classroom.

Sometimes you don't realize that you need work in an area as an educator until it meets you at your front door. I recall teaching in a fifth-grade inclusion classroom and finding out that I was pregnant. During my pregnancy, I learned that my child would be born with a birth defect, and I had no clue how to explain disabilities and birth defects to my class. However, it knew it was important because it was not just my lived experience, but the lived experiences of countless others. So, I chose a read-aloud that would foster an experience through the eyes of students with disability. The book is called *There is No Such Thing as Normal.* It's a picture book that walks you through the lives of different individuals with a disability. One page highlights cleft lip and palate, and I was able explain my child's birth defect before she was born. Through class discussion, I learned that one of my student's family members was born with a cleft lip and palate, too. Through read-alouds and class discussions, I was able to break the mold of normalcy in the classroom. I opened a piece of my world to my students, and in turn, they were able to share their world with me.

Following are some tips on promoting cultural competence when setting up and maintaining your SpEd classroom:

- Ensure that you can provide personal space between students if space allows and reduce visual distractions (reassess anchor charts/posters/classroom theming).
- Keep personal workspaces clear of unrelated materials, especially when working one-on-one and assisting small groups.
- Assist and encourage students in ways to keep their desks, folders, supplies, and personal spaces organized.
- Be sure that students can physically navigate your room, especially during an emergency.
- Offer a refocus space in case you have a child who likes to retreat to decompress (be sure they can be always seen).
- Don't take things personally. Always remain calm.
- Avoid public reprimands.
- Redirect or pull students aside privately or use nonverbal cues to communicate inappropriate behavior.
- Celebrate and reward positive behavior.
- Provide advance alerts before transitions (e.g., "When I say 'go,'" "In 5 minutes").
- Provide silent visual timers for in-class assignments and assessments.
- Consider vision or hearing concerns when assigning student seating. Proximity is ideal.
- Keep directions simple.
- Make sure you have students' attention before giving directions.

Promoting Critical (Sociopolitical) Consciousness in Special Education Classrooms

As stated earlier, school is not a vacuum. This applies to what our children face and the messages (conscious and subconscious) they receive outside our four walls. This is especially true for students who receive special education services, as highlighted by the very existence of DisCrit. We cannot change the world our children face outside our classroom, but we can nurture relationships and ensure that all are seen, valued, and heard within. Despite our best intentions, we can never truly speak for or represent others. Culture is so multifaceted and individualized that the best way to promote critical and sociopolitical consciousness is to give our students opportunities to interact with one another and express themselves individually. Relationships are transformative! They contribute to our own sense of self, and they dispel existing subconscious bias and any future agents of bigotry or ignorance—for to criticize is to assess for bias. Incorporate small-group collaboration and keep groupings as random as possible (you can assign students numbers and use randomizers online or a program such as ClassDojo). Give students challenges that foster thinking outside the box (I like read-aloud STEM challenges). It is a gross overgeneralization, but students with special needs are already adept at navigating our world in unique ways. Another means to promote critical and sociopolitical consciousness is to incorporate into lessons age-appropriate current events, historical contributions, and roles, read-alouds authored by those who are marginalized or not represented in our communities, and assessments in which students create personal associations/connections. Whatever you choose, ensure that all voices are heard.

Conclusion

If SpEd is the culmination of CRP and best educational practices combined, and funding is available through federal (e.g., IDEA) and state (e.g., Section 504, ESSA) funds, are there any factors that serve as obstacles in applying theory into practice? Absolutely! Practice can often be more complicated than theory. Lack of time, lack of training (identifying early signs of specific learning disorders, supports, etc.), the heterogeneity of humans, comorbidities of disabilities, the lack of access to specialists (e.g., doctors, therapists, trainers, tutors), "hands on deck" (assigned paraprofessionals, support from home, support from school administration, etc.), and even the field of education marginalizing the subject area in educator programs all contribute to the complexity of practical application. For these reasons, SpEd teacher burnout is a clear and present danger, with an estimated 25% turnover rate each year: twice the rate of general education teachers (American University School of Education, 2021). If you peruse any school district's job board, you're likely to see numerous requests for SpEd teachers. Consider: Who suffers when these positions go unfilled? The students. Students will lack stability, structure, and an on-site advocate, and staff will go without a highly trained specialist and sounding board.

So, what's next? As I have frequently told my elementary students, if school was meant to be easy, we could all leave, lock the door, and start our careers right now. Mistakes are opportunities for learning and growth! Let this be your mantra. Allow yourself patience and grace. I've been there. Working consistent 60-plus hours a week in the classroom benefits no one, regardless of best intentions. You cannot be all things to all people. Your family will suffer, your health will suffer (i.e., via insomnia, poor dietary choices, stress, etc.), and, because you're stretched so thin, you may even manage to self-sabotage by undoing any extra benefit you'd hoped to gain from those extra hours. Accept that you may not be a "Ms. Frizzle" (Cole, 1986–2010) your first year (or even second), but know that with each successive year comes experience and a toolbox of successes and "never-agains." Again, prioritize what matters: relationships. Classrooms are microcosms of our idealized world. Remember, our students will one day grow into adults, and the lessons and skills they learn (e.g., academic skills, socio-emotional skills, having a sense of self, being aware of how they treat others) within these four walls will affect how they see and interact with the world. Change what you can. This begins with us modeling empathy and respect. Relationships are transformative. I cannot stress games, choices (universal design for learning framework), and small groups enough; consider independent and collaborative work among peers with teacher oversight, and at least a few times a week with a significant active teacher component—anything to break the monotony and remove yourself from the front of the classroom and into the "trenches." Above all, remember to maintain confidentiality, especially with students receiving services. An adult would shudder at the thought of having their personal business laid bare to the world. Imagine this from the viewpoint of a child (it's especially hard when children are so perceptive). Consider having individualized folders—hard copy or electronic—ready to go that contain modified assignments and accommodations to support differentiated instruction. When personally meeting with small groups, use inconspicuous group identifiers (e.g., geologists, botanists, zoologists, entomologists). Finally, only share a child's anecdotal observations, information, and progress with their case-assigned SpEd teacher, grade-level co-teachers (who also serve the child), assigned specialists (if applicable), parents/guardians, and admin (i.e., those who attend a student's IEP meeting). Each child is a precious gift. See the good and ignore any prior teacher "warnings." We all deserve a clean slate. After all, most of us personally know how damaging labels can be (i.e., conscious/unconscious bias), as well as how transformative that "one teacher" can be.

There's is no rubber-stamp solution for how to best serve students receiving SpEd services within the classroom, because there's no typical disability, even within the same category. Add this to the developmental heterogeneity of humans, perceived stigma, and overstretched teachers and caregivers, and it's very likely that the number of students with categorized disabilities within our classrooms is underreported. Instead, I encourage you all to become students of your students. Observe. Try to look at your classroom through the eyes of your students. Does it reflect them and their needs, or does it follow the current zeitgeist? Look at the faces of your students. In general, are they happy? Focus on their Funds of Knowledge. Learn what makes your students tick. What can they talk your ear off about? What do they enjoy? What is important to them? How do your students like to express themselves? Adapt and differentiate but keep content intact. Challenge your students to ensure that self-efficacy is supported and nurtured. Also, throw out any preconceptions of what assessments look like. Remember, you're assessing knowledge and understanding, not regurgitation. Most important, however, by becoming a student of your students, you demonstrate to each child that they are seen, heard, and valued.

References

American University School of Education. (2021). *Why is there a special education teacher shortage?* https://soeonline.american.edu/blog/special-education-teacher-shortage

Annamma, S. A., Connor, D., & Ferri, B. (2013). Dis/ability critical race studies (DisCrit): Theorizing at the intersections of race and dis/ability. *Race Ethnicity and Education, 16*(1), 1–31.

Armstrong, T. (2017, April 1). *Neurodiversity: The future of special education?* Association for Supervision and Curriculum Development. https://www.ascd.org/el/articles/neurodiversity-the-future-of-special-education

Cole, J. (1986–2010). *The Magic School Bus*. Scholastic.

Eilers, N. (2020). Critical disability studies and "inclusive" early childhood education: The ongoing divide. *Journal of Disability Studies in Education, 1*(1–2), 64–89. https://doi.org/10.1163/25888803-00101004

Georgia Department of Education. (n.d.) *Eligibility categories.* https://www.gadoe.org/Curriculum-Instruction-and-Assessment/Special-Education-Services/Pages/Eligibility-Categories.aspx

Kirylo, J. (2013). *A critical pedagogy of resistance.* Sense.

Krathwohl, D. R. (2002). A revision of Bloom's taxonomy: An overview. *Theory Into Practice, 41*(4), 212–218.

National Center for Learning Disabilities. (2020). *Significant disproportionality in special education: Current trends and actions for impact.* https://www.ncld.org/wp-content/uploads/2020/10/2020-NCLD-Disproportionality_Trends-and-Actions-for-Impact_FINAL-1.pdf

Office of Special Education Programs. (2022). *IDEA Section 618 State Part C Child Count and Settings.* https://data.ed.gov/dataset/idea-section-618-state-part-c-child-count-and- settings/resources#

Shakespeare, T. (2013). Critical realist approaches to disability. In *Disability rights and wrongs revisited* (2nd ed.). Routledge.

Shakespeare, T., & Watson, N. (2010). Beyond models: Understanding the complexity of disabled people's lives. In *New directions in the sociology of chronic and disabling conditions.* Palgrave Macmillan.

United States Department of Education. (2022). *A history of the Individuals with Disabilities Education Act.* https://sites.ed.gov/idea/IDEA-History

FIVE

Practicing Culturally Relevant Pedagogy with Multilingual Learners

Alexandra J. Reyes and Anne Valauri

YOU'VE PROBABLY HEARD A LOT of talk about how our schools are changing, and how teacher education is struggling to keep up. One of the foundational elements of critical pedagogy is knowing who your students are. To be responsive educators, we must understand and value the backgrounds of our students, including their home languages and cultures. Currently, approximately 10% of K–12 students in U.S. public schools are labeled as English learners (also referred to as ELs—more on that later). Effectively, this means that 1 in 10 students should legally be receiving targeted English language development (ELD) support above and beyond the typical English language arts classes. Even so, the type of support and structure of the program vary from school to school (see Table 5.1 for a breakdown of programs), and not all multilingual learners are designated "EL" or receive services. Many multilingual students do not qualify for services based on assessment scores, have "exited out" of ELD programs, or have waived out of services. This means that, we have many more multilingual learners in our classrooms than the official EL statistics suggest.

Who Are Multilingual Learners? A Note on Terminology

In a school setting, the terms for students you might hear or be familiar with are "English learner" (EL) or "English language learner" (ELL). For a long time, schools referred to students as "limited English proficient" (LEP). Although some schools, districts, and federal agencies still use this term, there has largely been a move away from LEP because of its deficit orientation. While EL or ELL are probably the most commonly used terms in schools, there is still an overemphasis on centering English in these labels. A more recent turn has been toward the use of the term "emergent bilingual" (EB), which aims to capture the development of both languages, and the fluidity of language learning. This term attempts to move away from the privileging of learning English over the home language. Some argue that the use of "emergent" in the term still retains connotations of limitation. Additionally, "emergent" has specific meaning in language development contexts, which can be confusing.

Other terms you may have heard include "English as a second language" (ESL), "English to speakers of other languages" (ESOL), "language minority," and "culturally and linguistically diverse students." Each of these terms serves a purpose, but none adequately captures the complexity of multilingualism. We use the term "multilingual learner" to highlight the hybridity and plurality of developing English as an additional language. The term also aims to capture the many different languages (and language varieties) children may speak or be exposed to at home, as often families speak more than two languages. Multilingual learners may be at any stage in the development of their languages and at different proficiencies in each.

Table 5.1 covers some of the more common types of English language development (ELD) and bilingual education (BE) programs in the United States.

Table 5.1. English Language Development (ELD) and Bilingual Education (BE)

Program Type	Language(s) of Instruction	Description
Full Immersion (aka Submersion)	English only	Mainstream monolingual education; no specialized ELD support; no ESOL specialized teachers; assimilation to English is the goal; often called "Sink or Swim."
Pullout	Majority English; home language may be used for support	Mainstream education; periodic (typically daily or weekly) ESOL instruction with specialized teacher outside the mainstream classroom; assimilation to English and/or remediation is the goal.
Push-in	Majority English; home language may be used for support	Mainstream education; specialized ESOL teachers or paraprofessionals enter the mainstream classroom to provide English language support; assimilation to English and/or remediation is the goal.
ESOL (aka ESL)	Majority English; home language may be used for support	Mainstream education; specialized ESOL teachers provide ELA instruction (in lieu of mainstream ELA class); assimilation to English and/or remediation is the goal.

Program Type	Language(s) of Instruction	Description
ESOL Cluster Sites/Schools	Majority English; home language may be used for support	Students receiving ELD services are clustered at certain sites where ESOL specialized teachers work; students may be bussed to cluster sites for weekly ESOL immersion days; assimilation to English (without regularly missing specific content instruction) is the goal.
Sheltered English Instruction	Majority English; home language may be used for support	ESOL specialized content area teachers provide content instruction with language supports; assimilation to English *and* grade-level content learning is the goal.
Transitional Bilingual Education	Up to 50% home language initially; English is prioritized	Home language instruction is included to develop initial literacy; home language is decreased as English instruction is increased; assimilation to English and grade-level academic learning is the goal; often referred to as "early exit" bilingual.
Developmental Bilingual Education	Up to 90% home language initially; often 50/50 (or less) by fourth grade	Home language instruction is used to develop initial literacy; content area instruction in home language and English; specialized bilingual teachers provide content instruction in both languages; bilingualism/biliteracy and grade-level academic learning is the goal; often referred to as "late exit" bilingual.
Dual Immersion (aka Two-Way Bilingual Education)	Up to 90% home/target language initially and gradual shift to 50/50; or 50/50 throughout (depending on model)	EL students and native English speakers receive content and literacy instruction in English and the (non-English) target language; specialized bilingual teachers provide content instruction in both languages, or specialized teachers teach specific content areas in each language; bilingualism/ biliteracy and grade-level academic learning is the goal; also referred to as "two-way immersion" (TWI).

Note. ESOL = English to speakers of other languages; ESL = English as a second language; ELA = English language arts. Adapted from Garcia et al., 2008.

Whether or not you are an ESOL teacher, have migrant or refugee students, have students labeled as ELs, or are teaching a class with no EL students, chances are, you'll have multilingual learners in your care. Multilingual learners benefit from additional support, regardless of their designation or language proficiencies. In this chapter, we'll explore some ways that we can employ a humanizing pedagogy to provide educational experiences that are culturally relevant, responsive, and sustaining. We will have opportunities to consider how we might provide accessible instruction that is academically rigorous, advances cultural competence, and fosters critical consciousness.

Positionality Statements

Anne Valauri (she/her)

I am a White cisgender heterosexual woman who grew up in a middle-class household in the Midwest. While my own grandparents' immigration from the Balkans after the fall of the Ottoman Empire influenced my work with immigrant and multilingual children and families, I recognize how access to whiteness in the United States led to a very different experience from those of many of the families I have worked with. I am from a large Midwestern city and went to relatively diverse public schools, though at the time, diversity mostly meant that it was about 50% White students and 45% Black students, with a very small 5% remaining; most people I went to school with had been born in the U.S. Midwest. I attended an Eastern Orthodox church, and my religious community comprised people who spoke a multitude of languages; they were from the Balkans, the Middle East, East Africa, and countries that had been a part of the Soviet Union. As an adult, I have lived and taught abroad in countries where multiple languages were spoken other than English. I taught in a bilingual Head Start program in Texas at a time when I was semifluent in Spanish, and I have worked in early childhood classrooms that serve families with diverse national and regional origins. I also have a multiracial family, and while that doesn't mean I deal with racial oppression personally, I know what it means to worry about a loved one in certain areas or getting pulled over. I consider myself able-bodied—though I have an autoimmune disorder—because much of the time, I don't have to think about it. I still have a lot of work to do in many areas, especially in unpacking my own relationship to ability.

Alex Reyes (she/her/ella)

I am a bilingual, bicultural cisgender Latina. I benefit from certain privileges: U.S. citizenship, good education (public schools all the way!), and able-bodiedness. My ethnically ambiguous appearance is as often an asset as it is a hindrance. My earliest years were spent in a very diverse low-income neighborhood in Miami, Florida. I was surrounded by teachers, neighbors, relatives, and friends of all different backgrounds. Although I grew up in a predominantly English-speaking house, my father was a Bolivian immigrant, and the Spanish language was always present. Many of my formative summers were spent in Bolivia, where my sister and I stayed with our monolingual (Spanish-speaking) Mama Lola. Multilingualism has always been natural to me; our identities are significantly tied to and informed by our language communities. I became a Spanish teacher and then pursued ESOL after working with emergent multilingual students who thrived when adequately supported. As an English-dominant university-educated professor, I am granted a degree of respect for my multilingualism. As a marginal member of the Latinx community, I am acutely self-aware of the shortcomings of my Spanish and am often self-conscious about my latinidad. My Otherness grants me advantages in some spaces and throws up barriers in others. In my practice, I strive to honor and encourage students' various cultures, languages, and identities, even as I struggle to find my own place within the community and learn to live in the third space.

Key Terms:

- **Dynamic bilingualism:** "the development of different language practices to varying degrees in order to interact with increasingly multilingual communities" (García & Kleifgen, 2010, p. 42).
- **English learner** (EL): an individual who is learning the English language as a second language.
- **Home language:** the language an individual uses at home and/or within their community, either with both family or friends.
- **Language ideologies:** our underlying beliefs or ideas about language that impact how we view and use language.

- **Multilingual learners:** individuals who speak a primary language or home language other than English, who are in the process of learning the English language.
- **Translanguaging:** is the practice of integrating features from multiple languages to accomplish communication tasks.

Key Ideas:

1. ***Multilingual learners engage in sophisticated and cognitively demanding processes in their daily lives.*** With the right support, multilingual learners can successfully engage in academically rigorous learning.
2. ***Each of us has valuable cultural and linguistic resources.*** Centering students' cultural and linguistic resources in the curriculum and classroom helps them learn about themselves and each other, advancing cultural competence.
3. ***Understanding how different languages and identities function in schools and society is key to critical consciousness.*** Recognizing and challenging our beliefs about language and culture can move us toward a more humanizing pedagogy.

Supporting Multilingual Students for Academically Rigorous Engagement

Researchers and practitioners have long known that high expectations are important for student success (e.g., see Ladson-Billings, 1995a, 2014). Even so, many (wrongly) believe that high expectations and academically rigorous content are reserved for "talented," "gifted," or "honors" students. Academic rigor benefits everyone and can be achieved in a variety of ways. As educators, we have the responsibility to learn about our students, understand their Funds of Knowledge, and help them develop their skills to better access content and learning. For example, many multilingual students act as language brokers for their families. They translate documents, interpret conversations, and often take on a host of adult responsibilities because of their positions as multilingual and multicultural beings. Language brokering is a sophisticated process; it's complex, nuanced, and cognitively demanding. Acknowledging and building on these skills is one approach to incorporating rigor in your teaching.

Providing appropriate supports is another way we can develop accessible and rigorous content instruction. What does it mean to support students' learning needs? Often, when teachers approach differentiation, they start by "teaching to the middle" and modifying their lessons from there. Rather than classifying students as low, middle, and high achievers (or whatever euphemisms your school uses to level students), let's reframe our thinking. What if we turned our efforts toward making learning accessible for all students, and set that as the norm? What if we built academic rigor into all our teaching and provided support so that all students—regardless of English proficiency—could successfully access content? Instead of lowering the bar, we could (1) give students credit for their cultural and linguistic knowledges, and (2) give them a boost.

One way to be mindful of how we plan for accessibility is to use the Sheltered Instruction Observation Protocol (SIOP) model (Echevarria et al., 2016) to evaluate your lessons and guide your planning. SIOP is a tool that forces us to think through every step of the lesson planning and delivery process to ensure we are providing adequate supports for multilingual learners—EL students in particular—so they can access content and achieve academic success. Whereas differentiation is often treated as either watering down the curriculum or giving extra assignments, SIOP is a framework for providing ground-floor entrance to content and building upward to ensure that all students have equitable access to rigorous content. The eight SIOP components are lesson planning, building background, comprehensible input, strategies, interaction, practice and application, lesson delivery, and review and assessment (Echevarria et al., 2016). The SIOP model emphasizes English language development support by including explicit language objectives that complement content objectives, varied language interactions, and purposeful opportunities to apply the language in the academic context (see Activity 5.1).

Activity 5.1 Language Supports

Step 1: Read the paragraph in the box that follows, and think about the following:

- What are you able to understand?
- What strategies did you use to help you interpret the paragraph?

<table>
<tr><td>

AN LÁRIONAD NÁISÚNTA RÉIBOL 1798

Ar do chuairt buailfidh tú le príomhdhaoine an Éiri Amach, glacfaidh tú páirt inár gcath úrscothach 4D ar Vinegar Hill Experience, gheobhaidh tú amach conas a d'oibrigh airm na tréimhse agus foghlaimeoidh aghaidh ar chumhacht 10,000 duine go maith oilte agus dea-armtha Fórsaí na Corónach.

</td></tr>
<tr><td>

Step 2: Now read the paragraph that follows, and think about the following:

- What are you able to understand?
- What strategies did you use to help you interpret the paragraph?

</td></tr>
<tr><td>

About the Rebellion Experience

One of the great visitor attractions in County Wexford

Fanned by flames of Revolution in America and France, the events of 1798 in Ireland are etched forever on Irish history. Vividly re-told in an exciting interpretation of events the "Rebellion Experience" at The National 1798 Rebellion Centre is not to be missed. On your visit you will meet the key figures of the Rebellion, participate in our state of the art 4D battle of Vinegar Hill Experience, discover how weapons from the period worked and learn in gruesome detail how some 20.000 insurgents faced the might of 10.000 well-trained and well-armed Crown Forces.

</td></tr>
<tr><td>

Example borrowed from the National 1798 Rebellion Center website (http://1798centre.ie/about)

</td></tr>
</table>

Note: Activity 5.1: Language Supports and image was adapted from the National 1789 Rebellion Center website (https://1798centre.ie/about). Reprinted with permission.

In Activity 5.1, you were probably not able to decipher much in the Step 1 paragraph, beyond the year 1798 and a 4D Vinegar Hill Experience. This simple expository paragraph would not be very challenging for a student who was literate in the Irish language, but for those of us who don't know (much) Irish, the paragraph can be difficult. Even when employing decoding strategies (sounding it out, using context clues, etc.), the text's meaning may remain inaccessible. In the second step, a person who is literate in English would be able to understand the words, although the significance may be unclear (see the next section for more on the importance of cultural context). Consider what supports were provided in the second step (e.g., translation, images) that would help a reader understand the meaning. What other SIOP supports could we include to make the reading even more accessible to non-Irish speakers? Highlighting and defining key vocabulary, identifying language objectives, and connecting the content to previous learning and students' backgrounds would remove some barriers and make the reading more approachable. How might we include more language supports throughout our teaching to give multilingual learners the opportunity to engage with rigorous academic content and build their biliteracy?

Centering Students' Languages and Cultures in the Classroom

Imagine your future classroom. What types of print are on the walls? What kinds of books and materials are on your shelves? As you consider this future classroom, take a moment, and think about the languages of the materials—are your materials, both in texts and on the wall, in languages other than English? Are resources readily available to support translation? Do the materials in your books and on your walls represent the students you would serve?

So much of how we think education ought to be comes from our own educational experiences and what we grew up with, particularly if our language or culture was privileged in society. If you grew up speaking mostly English in an English-dominant environment, and then your school reproduced and reified English dominance, the way you design your classroom, the materials you choose, and how you treat your students are likely to be influenced by your experiences.

To begin to disrupt this pattern and move toward cultural competence, the first thing you need to do is recognize yourself as a cultural being; you have parts of your identity, including the language(s) that you speak, that may be privileged or marginalized by schools and society. For those who benefit from it, language privilege, like all privileges, is often difficult to see. Consider these questions: How was your home language treated in the schools you attended?

Was everyone expected to understand English? Were you expected to learn English if you did not grow up speaking it? What languages did your parents or caregivers speak?

In addition to understanding how languages are positioned, it is also important to consider the plurality of students' home cultures and the many different language varieties there are. In Activity 5.2, you're asked to consider how cultural context can impact communication, building relationships, and learning.

Activity 5.2 Language and Cultural Context

1) Read the following recipe:

Recipe for Trifle

- 1 package of ladyfingers	- 5 mL vanilla
- 1,000 mL double cream	- 6 eggs, separated
- 350 mL whole milk	- 500 mL cream sherry
- 75 g castor sugar	- 40 g berries

1. Add the sherry and berries to a blender. Blend for 30 seconds. Strain the seeds.
2. Heat half of the double cream over a double boiler. Slowly add in egg yolks while stirring so the egg yolks temper. Add castor sugar and vanilla. Remove from heat and let cool.
3. Lay the bottom of a trifle dish with half of the ladyfingers. Pour berry mixture over lady fingers and let soak.
4. Whip remaining double cream.
5. Add a layer of custard mixture to the dish, then add a layer of whipped cream.
6. Add another layer of ladyfingers and add berry mixture, let soak, then add another layer of custard.
7. Top with whipped cream and berries.

2) Respond to the following questions:

1. Were any of the ingredients unfamiliar to you?
2. Did you have all the ingredients on hand?
    - If not, would you be able to buy all the ingredients at the local supermarket, grocery store, or supermarket?

3. If you were able to get all the ingredients, could you successfully follow every step of the recipe?
4. If not, what parts of the recipe would be challenging?
   - How could you address those challenges to complete the recipe?

Even if you speak English every day, understanding an unfamiliar context can be very challenging. Language variety (aka dialect) and culture need to be considered in communication and building relationships with multilingual learners and their families. In addition, while language and culture are deeply tied together, there is great variety even among speakers of the same language, given linguistic variation and differing cultural references between groups. Particularly if you are a monolingual English speaker, you need to think about the plurality of cultures that exist in the classroom. Just because two students speak the same home language does not mean they will speak the same variety or even have the same cultural references. No person is a singular representative of their racial, cultural, ethnic, or linguistic group; culture is not a monolith.

Part of developing cultural competence as an educator is building relationships that will help you understand and appreciate the nuances of different student home languages and cultures. Ask yourself: What are ways that you can respectfully learn about students' backgrounds? How can we embrace and promote cultural and linguistic diversity in the classroom? Building connections with students' families is a key part of learning about their cultural and linguistic assets. However, while developing relationships with families can be vital to learning about students' lives, it is important to understand the history and context of home–school relationships in the United States, particularly with multilingual immigrant families (see Pause & Reflect 5.1).

Pause & Reflect 5.1

Imagine you're a multilingual immigrant caregiver who has come from a country with an educational system completely different from that in the United States. Imagine trying to figure out that system in a language that you do not speak (or that at least is not your primary home language) so your child can receive the best education possible. Imagine that you're expected to chaperone a field trip, but you can't, and this expectation was never communicated clearly to you. For the rest of the year, the teacher believes you "don't care" about your child's education and treats you rudely.

How would this impact your relationship with your child's school?

___

How would a child feel if this happened to their parent or caregiver?

___

Learning From and Listening to Families

On top of the language discrimination, racism (if you are not White), and xenophobia that multilingual immigrant families might experience, the U.S. educational system is often needlessly complex. Many families have time demands (e.g., work and childcare) in addition to the language barriers and cultural expectations that don't always allow them to come into the classroom. Home–school practices in early childhood and elementary education often disregard and alienate many families, particularly immigrant families, through unfamiliar or incongruent practices, while labeling families as "not caring" for not participating in these practices. This often ties back to how educators connect "good" classroom engagement practices to the way things were for them growing up or how people who are like them would engage with the classroom. Most elementary teachers in the United States are English-dominant, White, middle-class women; this is not reflective of the children and families who are served by the education system, which furthers this deficit positioning (see Pause & Reflect 5.2).

Pause & Reflect 5.2

What do you think of when you hear the term "parent involvement"?

___

Do your ideas reflect what your own school looked like when you were growing up?

Scholars and advocates have pushed back against the term "parent involvement" and toward a more inclusive and interdirectional term, "family engagement." Family engagement means listening to families and learning about who they are and what they want for their children. This takes humility on the part of an educator, and a commitment to listening and being responsive, as well as respecting family boundaries. This also might mean being creative if you and the families speak a different language—such as engaging translators, older siblings, or sometimes students themselves to help you make connections, especially in informal interactions (picking up a student from class) versus formal interactions (conferences).

To be a culturally competent educator, you must not only recognize yourself as a person with a cultural and linguistic background that may be more privileged or marginalized in society, but also recognize your students as individuals with rich cultural and linguistic resources. Educators can learn about these resources through authentic, caring relationships with students and families, and by bringing these languages, cultures, and identities into the classroom in meaningful ways that do not just incorporate but push and extend. This goes beyond a shallow "celebration of differences" and asks us to center students' culture and language in the classroom. Centering languages other than English sends messages to students and families that their lives and resources are not just valued, but central to education. This can also send messages about listening and thus build trust with family members; Tobin et al. (2013) noted that many multilingual immigrant family members feel that home language is "something valuable, fragile, and at risk of disappearing" (p. 65), noting how the loss of home language can also feel like the loss of home culture.

When I (Anne) taught at a Head Start program in Texas, about 85% of the parents/caregivers in my classroom spoke Spanish as their primary language and the language of their home. While I was semifluent at the time, I also had a wonderful assistant teacher who was from Cuba, and though she spoke a different Spanish than the families who were primarily from Mexico and Central America, she helped us if we ever ran into language misunderstandings during home visits or meetings with parents or caregivers. A lot of parents really wanted their children to learn English because they wanted them to have what they saw as a leg up in kindergarten. At the same time, I remember meeting with one mother who asked that her son have an opportunity to maintain his Spanish in the classroom. His older siblings were in elementary and middle school and mostly spoke English at school. Because of this, they tended to speak only English at home, which she didn't understand. Her youngest son was the only one who still spoke mostly Spanish, and she wanted him to maintain that connection with her. I wanted to respect the wishes of parents to have their children learn English, and I equally wanted to make sure that this mother's desires were heard and honored, so I conducted the class in about 50% Spanish and 50% English. This situation will not be true for every class, given that each family and their desires for their children are different, but as an educator, you should get a sense of families' goals for their children, and consider these in how you engage with home languages in your classroom.

How can you center children's home languages and cultures in your classroom?

- Have texts in your students' home languages! Many popular children's books have been translated or have side-by-side bilingual English versions. Make sure to include literature that reflects not just your students' languages, but also their cultures. This should be based in your relationships with students and families, otherwise you risk relying on stereotypes instead of deep background knowledge
- Make sure your environmental print (or the print in centers and on the walls) is in students' home languages in addition to English. There are many ways to get help with translation if you don't speak or read the language—from accessing district and school resources, to asking family members for help, to looking online (though always be careful of online translations!).
- If you're in an early elementary classroom, have your centers reflect students' lives; again, this should be based in knowledge drawn from your relationships with families, not stereotypes or preconceptions.

Make sure all items at your centers—from dramatic play materials to math and science manipulatives—are labeled in the languages of your classroom community.

- If you don't speak your students' home language, it might not be realistic for you to become fluent in that language in a short amount of time. However, you can always learn words and phrases, particularly as you interact with family members.
- Make texts with your students and bring family stories into your classroom. This allows for opportunities to engage in oral storytelling, bilteracy or transliteracy, and centering student home lives. For example, Marshall and Toohey (2010) had students from a predominantly Punjabi Sikh community in Canada record their grandparents' stories of life in India and then translate their stories into a student-made picture book for the class (in your own classroom, you can decide whether to have students translate or compose in their home languages). Students can create a text that not only reflects the cultures of the classroom, but also, as in this case, pushes back against centering Western histories in the stories we tell.
- Invite family members in to share parts of their lives with the class, and make sure you plan ahead for translation assistance if needed. Be careful to make sure no one is singled out, particularly if they are the only member of a particular group in your classroom.
- Position yourself as a learner, and let students teach concepts or parts of their lives in their home language to the class. This will not only allow for student agency, but also position them as vital classroom resources whom other classmates can go to and learn from.

Language Ideologies and Making Space for Dynamic Language Practices

Ladson-Billings (1995b) noted that "not only must teachers encourage academic success and cultural competence, they must help students to recognize, understand, and critique current social inequities" (p. 476), or to develop critical consciousness. Critical consciousness requires not only considering your own identities and language practices, and how these are positioned in society, but also thinking about the roots of your ideas about languages and language practices. Activity 5.3 helps us identify our ideas about both language and speakers of certain languages or language varieties, why we might think or feel this way, and how we were socialized to develop these attitudes.

Activity 5.3 Language Ideologies Inventory

Take a moment and fill in the blank for each prompt. Do not censor yourself; just write down the first response that comes to mind. (Adapted from an activity by Jamie L. Schissel)

1. When someone says "ain't," I think ______________________________.
2. British accents sound ______________________________ to me.
3. Who do you picture when you hear that someone sounds "country" when they speak?

   ____.
4. When a friend knows how to use "whom," I think __________________ about them.
5. When I hear a teacher describe a student's language as "broken English," I think

   ______________________________________ about the student.
6. When I hear a teacher describe a student's language as "broken English," I think

   ______________________________________ about the teacher.

Note: Activity 5.3: Language Ideologies Inventory was adapted from the personal correspondence of Jamie Schissel. Reprinted with permission.

Think about your responses. Where did these ideas come from? From your own school experience? From your family? Friends? Our underlying beliefs or ideas about language, which impact how we view and use language, are referred to as *language ideologies*. Understanding language ideologies can allow for a more asset-based view of students and families because it can help us recognize and acknowledge our beliefs and assumptions about certain types of languages and people who use those languages. Exploring language ideologies helps us name the ideas we hold and understand the origins of our beliefs. These beliefs and assumptions emerge from our own experiences and communities, and they inform which language practices and speakers we value, and which we put down or dismiss. Think about how you responded to the questions in Activity 5.3. What shaped your ideologies about language? In the United States, differing attitudes toward multilingualism have shaped attitudes, policy, and research about multilingual students and their families. Earlier in the chapter, we describe taking an approach in the classroom that allows for home language to be maintained. This is known as additive bilingualism, as opposed to subtractive bilingualism. Subtractive bilingualism, in which home language is often not used, forbidden, or used sparingly, is the result of language ideologies that perpetuate the belief that one needs to take away a language to learn another (e.g., in the United States, this means subtracting home languages in favor of English).

Moving away from this narrow view, scholars have put forward the concept of dynamic bilingualism, or "the development of different language practices to varying degrees in order to interact with increasingly multilingual communities" (García & Kleifgen, 2010, p. 42). Dynamic bilingualism goes beyond additive bilingualism to embrace heteroglossic rather than monoglossic language ideologies. Monoglossic language ideologies are built on the belief that languages exist in isolation and should remain separate, and they position monolingualism as the norm. Monoglossic ideologies often promote prestige languages and language varieties over nonstandard or vernacular language features. By contrast, heteroglossic language ideologies honor more fluid, hybrid, multilingual language practices. These practices may incorporate features (e.g., grammatical structures and vocabulary) from multiple languages and language varieties, prioritizing communication over rigid form.

As critically conscious educators, we must interrogate where and how we develop our ideas about languages so we can better understand how deeply ingrained dominant language ideologies (i.e., monoglossic, English-only) are, and how they shape practices and expectations in schools. When we recognize and challenge how our own language ideologies may lead us to perpetuate harmful teaching practices, we're in a better position to value and lift up dynamic language practices in the classroom. This may include making space for translanguaging (García, 2009) in the classroom. Translanguaging is the practice of integrating features from multiple languages to accomplish communication tasks. As we noted earlier, language learning is not always linear or absolute; often, multilingual students are further marginalized because their language practices are neither mainstream "standard" English, nor strictly of the monolingual home language. Because language learning and practices are fluid, students often develop hybrid language practices, and these may include standard and nonstandard features. Culturally sustaining educators welcome translanguaging and other hybrid language practices as vital resources for developing communication and fostering critical consciousness.

What can valuing and embracing dynamic language practices look like in the classroom?

Multiple studies have demonstrated not only how multilingual students' hybrid language practices are highly thought out, but also how they can be transgressive (Martínez & Morales, 2014), pushing back against narrow and harmful language ideologies that view them from a deficit perspective. To an educator, this can look like learning about student hybrid word play and language practice and valuing them on both an intellectual and a transformational level. Examining our ideologies through a raciolinguistic lens (Rosa & Flores, 2017) allows us to push back against ideologies that students (particularly students from racialized backgrounds) need to fit their language practices toward "appropriateness"—especially given that notions of classroom appropriateness are mostly determined by the teacher, who, in the United States, is predominantly White, female, middle class, and English dominant (see a pattern here?). A speaker's identity often influences how their language is viewed; "bilingualism and multilingualism tend to be seen as assets for White English-speaking economically advantaged children, [but] are often positioned as liabilities for children of color from economically disadvantaged backgrounds" (Souto-Manning & Martell, 2016, p. 6).

In addition to recognizing how our own ideas of language are influenced by dominant language ideologies, another step in the classroom is to not only honor language practices that push back against these ideologies, but also to name the dominant ideology itself. There is power in naming how oppression functions in schools and society, and, thus, in facilitating students' own interrogation of dominant language ideology, perhaps through an activity like the one at the beginning of this section, Activity 5.3. Whereas in the past, many educators avoided "tough" conversations around racism or language discrimination with elementary school students, more and more research has come out in recent years suggesting that children as young as preschool age notice not only difference, but also inequality. When an understanding of how dominant language ideologies function is woven together with an interrogation of other forms of systemic oppression, students are able to not only better decode the messages they receive about themselves and their communities, but also fight back.

Challenges and Opportunities

As critical teachers of multilingual learners, we face many challenges. For example, many schools are not adequately resourced, harmful language ideologies are pervasive, and residency status impacts the daily lives of many students in the community. We view these challenges as opportunities to trouble the status quo and develop creative solutions. With input and support from students and families, we can address and overcome many barriers.

Many school districts are not yet equipped with all the resources needed for translation, interpretation, and support in languages other than English. Even if they are, it can be difficult to find translation assistance outside home–school conferences, such as for less formal interactions. If you're facing the challenge of a lack of school district–provided multilingual resources, as you get to know students' families, you may collaboratively identify or develop informal and local resources for translation with the families in your classroom.

Unfortunately, subtractive bilingualism is still a very prevalent attitude in many school districts around the country. This deficit attitude typically stems from a lack of knowledge about multilingualism or an unwillingness to change among those who benefit from monolingualism. Although research shows that multilingualism benefits all students, English-only language ideologies are deeply held and difficult to disrupt. As a critically engaged educator, you may have to be an advocate for students to speak and maintain their home languages at school.

And while this is not specific to multilingual students and families, you may have some students who are dealing with uncertainties around residency, whether fear of deportation or having their citizenship status up in the air. In addition, deportation, or immigration-based detention of a loved one can be deeply traumatic for students who experience this either firsthand or through family. We must be sensitive to these issues and work to connect families to resources and services. Gallo (2017) recommended that educators be aware of discriminatory practices and negative comments toward undocumented family members. We can actively signal accepting attitudes, and consider hosting Know Your Rights workshops or other advocacy and resource-based events.

Conclusion

Engaging in critical pedagogy with multilingual students promotes both student success and belonging in the classroom, and advocacy skills they can take into the community. Because of dominant monoglossic language ideologies that perpetuate deficit notions of languages other than standard academic English (and the speakers of those languages), education in the United States is often not set up for members of marginalized communities to thrive. However, educators can move to disrupt these trends in working toward an educational space that (1) provides rigorous instruction and adequate supports, (2) centers student home and hybrid language practices and cultures in meaningful and affirming ways, and (3) aims to disrupt English dominance and monoglossic ideologies in schools by naming those ideologies, interrogating them, and making space for hybrid language practices.

References

Echevarria, J., Vogt, M., & Short, D. (2016). *Making content comprehensible for English learners: The SIOP model* (5th ed.). Pearson.

Gallo, S. (2017). *Mi padre: Mexican immigrant fathers and their children's education*. Teachers College Press.

García, O. (2009). *Bilingual education in the 21st century: A global perspective*. Blackwell.

García, O., & Kleifgen, J. A. (2010). *Educating emergent bilinguals: Policies, programs, and practices for English language learners*. Teachers College Press.

García, O., Kleifgen, J. A., & Falchi, L. (2008). *From English language learners to emergent bilinguals. Equity Matters: Research Review No. 1.* Campaign for Educational Equity, Teachers College, Columbia University.

Ladson-Billings, G. (1995a). But that's just good teaching! The case for culturally relevant pedagogy. *Theory Into Practice, 34*(3), 159–165. http://www.jstor.org/stable/1476635

Ladson-Billings, G. (1995b). Toward a theory of culturally relevant pedagogy. *American Educational Research Journal, 32*(3), 465–491. doi:10.3102/00028312032003465

Ladson-Billings, G. (2014). Culturally relevant pedagogy 2.0: aka the remix. *Harvard Educational Review, 84*(1), 74–84.

Marshall, E., & Toohey, K. (2010). Representing family: Community funds of knowledge, bilingualism, and multimodality. *Harvard Educational Review, 80*(2), 221–242.

Martínez, R. A., & Morales, P. Z. (2014). ¿Puras groserías?: Rethinking the role of profanity and graphic humor in Latin@ students' bilingual wordplay. *Anthropology and Education Quarterly, 45*(4), 337–354.

Rosa, J., & Flores, N. (2017). Unsettling language and race: Toward a raciolinguistic perspective. *Language in Society, 46*, 621–647.

Souto-Manning, M., & Martell, J. (2016). *Reading, writing, and talk: Inclusive teaching strategies for diverse learners, K–2.* Teachers College Press.

Tobin, J., Adair, J. K., & Arzubiaga, A. (2013). *Children crossing borders: Immigrant parent and teacher perspectives on preschool for children of immigrants.* Russell Sage Foundation.

SIX

Classroom Management: History and Application

Chelda Smith Kondo and Montana Smithey

A UNIVERSAL EXPERIENCE IN THE UNITED States is exposure to the classroom setting—whether as a student, teacher, parent, observer, or media. Think for a few moments about what good classroom management looks like and sounds like based on your own experiences, and what you believe good classroom management to be. Before you continue reading this chapter, complete Activity 6.1, writing down at least three responses in each column.

Activity 6.1 Looks and Sounds of Classroom Management

Good Classroom Management Looks Like:	*Good Classroom Management Sounds Like:*
1.	1.
2.	2.
3.	3.

Healthy, sustainable, and effective classroom management must be humanizing—unequivocally. While the mechanics require academic engagement, thoughtfulness, preparedness, organizational skills, and flexibility, humanizing relationships are fundamental and primary. Historically, the cultural standards for idealized behavior are restrictive to Black, Indigenous, and People of Color (BIPOC) students—these standards minimize cultural identity and demand that those students stay in "their place." That "place" usually implies not challenging, questioning, or changing the established cultural standards. A critical pedagogue learns and practices expanding their standards of "good behavior" beyond respectability to facilitate a classroom community that is authentically inclusive of diversity—diversity of thought, culture, and behaviors.

Positionality Statements

Chelda Smith (she/her)

One of the hallmarks of being a "Black girl" is creative self-expression. It brings me absolute joy to manipulate my physical representation using wardrobe, hair, nails, and accessories to express a particular aesthetic. I went to a historically Black college and university (HBCU) for my undergraduate degree. There, from the maintenance personnel to the university president, self-expression using hair, accessories, and wardrobes was the cultural norm. Truly, every day could look and feel like a fashion show, and at no point did one's effort and energy toward self-expression undermine their intellectual capacity, talents, knowledge, and skills. I got my doctorate at the University of Minnesota, a predominately White institution (PWI), where I was rarely in the presence of other Black people. There, I felt pressured to aggressively alter my self-expression to (hopefully) be taken more seriously for my intellectual capacity. To assimilate, I went as far as erasing and hiding my personal life. Ultimately, I stopped wearing earrings and changing my hairstyles, and I wore mostly neutral and solid colors. My goal was to be associated only with the intellectual contributions I made, or not noticed at all. Thus, I managed myself by minimizing my cultural identity in hopes of achieving upward mobility and approval from my mostly White and middle-class peers and professors. This had harmful effects on my mental health, resulting in severe anxiety and depression, and it has taken years to heal from the trauma of an internalized inferiority complex. When I consider how to approach healthy classroom management, my university experiences inform my practice.

Montana Smithey (she/her)

Being a White, cisgender, able-bodied woman has been advantageous in countless ways—but especially in schools, because they are gendered, classed, and racialized. Schools have been built with people like me in mind—at least on the surface. When I experienced domestic violence in my childhood and young adult life, my privileged identities helped me to mask that trauma. Being a White girl is the typical identity of who is "good," "smart," and "normal" in schools. While I leveraged those privileges toward academic achievement, the burden of masking deteriorated my mental health. Even now, I try to hide my anxiety the best I can—mainly to appear independent and strong, and avoid biases associated with mental health and "not having it together." Empathizing with those having less privilege and for whom schools are designed to dehumanize, I approach classroom management as essential to inclusion, community, and humanization.

Key Terms:

- **Authority Figure:** an individual who has or represents power.
- **Traumatic Event:** an event that causes immense stress.
- **Traumatic Responses:** the short-term and long-term effects resulting from a traumatic event.

Key Ideas:

1. ***Our cultural lenses and biases influence how we create healthy, sustainable, and effective classroom management.***
2. ***Having an informed and appreciative knowledge of a student's cultural background can positively influence our capacity to build intercultural rapport and engage in effective and culturally responsive classroom management.***

Brief History of Classroom Management

We empathize with classroom teachers who feel underprepared to effectively manage their classrooms. Broad educational research and teacher preparation have failed to critically research classroom management. What remains are unresearched tips, tricks, and formulas purchased or downloaded for free online. It is no wonder that teachers, overwhelmed by the behavioral challenges they face in the classroom, resort to prepackaged "solutions," discussed later, that inevitably fail. Any exploration of classroom management that is not rooted in the humanity of students (cultural competence), that does not acknowledge and work to dismantle systemic inequity (critical consciousness), and that does not include engaging and challenging instruction (academic rigor) will be ineffective.

In the 1930s, B.F. Skinner began applying learning theories to disciplinary approaches. He concluded that rewarding teacher-desired behavior and ignoring or punishing the teacher's undesired behavior was an effective behavioral modification technique. While this approach may seem logical and effective to some, it mirrors that of animal training, and it does not facilitate self-regulation. Notions of cultural competence and critical consciousness were not only irrelevant but also antithetical to the goal of controlling pupil behavior. Humanistic psychology, which gained popularity in the 1950s, informed classroom management by emphasizing self-actualization and relationship building. Still, as psychologists navigated embracing the uniqueness and individuality of young people, the United States was actively segregated, and the humanity of BIPOC was debatable to authorities and to the nation's leaders. Heck, Rosa Parks didn't refuse to give up her seat on the bus until 1955!

One of the fundamental issues with humanistic psychology was its roots in morality and goodness. Defining "goodness" using White, heterosexual, patriarchal, Christian, middle-class cultural standards for idealized behavior is dehumanizing. Moreover, this definition blames, criminalizes, shames, oppress, and excludes those on the sociocultural margins of society. We see the enduring effects today in the ways Black people are criminalized in the legal system and in classroom settings and presumed guilty unless proven innocent—even posthumously (Trayvon Martin, Breonna Taylor, George Floyd, unfortunately . . . et cetera). It is also evident in the ways in which Black girls are adultified; the presumption is that their undesired behaviors are always intentional, without consideration of what is developmentally appropriate. Still, classroom management strategies developed from a humanistic psychological approach aim to help students understand themselves, better work with adults, and develop more productive behaviors. The humanistic approach also gives students choice in their learning, promotes creativity, and emphasizes individual expression while allowing them to understand their own thoughts and feelings. Sound familiar? It is very much like social-emotional learning, which aims to have students practice and refine their self-regulation.

Dreikurs et al. (1974) expanded Alfred Adler's work on individual psychology to a classroom management model in 1971 called *discipline without tears*. This model emphasizes the importance of students feeling a sense of belonging in the classroom, receiving status, and experiencing recognition. Moreover, this approach rejects punishment and reward. Theoretically, students behave or misbehave to communicate how they are feeling about their sense of belonging, status, and recognition in each environment. Ideally, teachers should be in tune with students and their perspectives to recognize their needs as they relate to their desire for a sense of belonging, status, and recognition—and respond accordingly. Using this model, teachers would also empower students to be their own decision makers, allowing them to be reflective of the ways in which they think about themselves and their own emotions. However, there exists a disjuncture between BIPOC youth experiences of community and belonging, and the way most teachers expect them to behave while restricting their experience of community and belonging in the classroom. But a classroom without a healthy community is a classroom that is not well managed. It might be controlled, or it may be out of control, but, as we will explore in this chapter, controlled and managed are not the same.

Since Dreikurs's model was introduced, an array of approaches to classroom management have surfaced, from Tom Gordon's 1974 teacher effectiveness training to the University of Oregon's Positive Behavioral Interventions and Supports (PBIS) experimentation in the 1980s. Jacob Kounin's (1970) large-scale systematic study of classroom management found that "withitness" was central to effective classroom management. In 2006 and 2007, as preservice teachers, we learned about withitness as a skill to hone and perfect. Withitness is the art of awareness, or what some consider as teachers' "having eyes in the back of their heads." It is more complicated than this, however, because it involves sensitivity to mood changes, tone, relational dynamics, engagement levels, and many subtle factors in sustaining a healthy and humanizing classroom.

Kounin (1970) also explored other practices central to effective management, including seamless transitions, preparedness, clear communication of expectations, and maintaining variety and challenges in students' academic work. Tulley and Chiu (1998) found six discipline strategies that teachers most often use to respond to undesired behaviors (see Figure 6.1). Except for the third discipline, explanation, these practices are ineffective and disengaging, in direct opposition to community-building and engagement. Still, many of us know someone who responds to fear of punishment as a guide and motivation for ideal behavior. Worse yet, school-based management systems like ClassDojo are rooted in these dehumanizing practices.

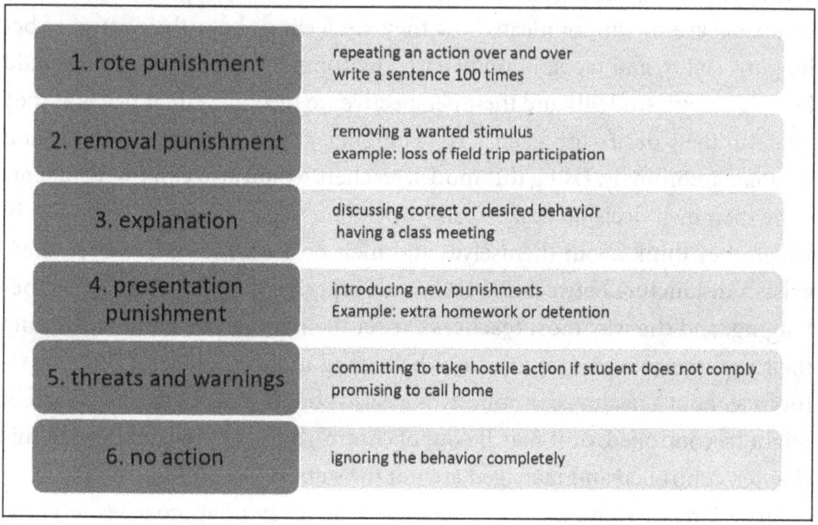

Figure 6.1. Six discipline strategies.

Problematic Systems

Let's discuss two prominent classroom management practices that are popular in classrooms today. They stem from what we have learned about behavior from psychologists and theorists over the past century and are promoted as best practice; however, they are problematic.

I, Dr. Smithey, taught elementary school for 6 years, and I regret to inform you that I was an avid user of the clip chart method because it was the only way I had seen others around me manage a classroom. Although I learned alternative approaches in my teacher preparation program, it was easier *for me* to maintain the status quo and do what had always been done to fit in. There I was, with a perfectly laminated chart of purple (outstanding), blue (great job), green (ready to learn), yellow (think about it), orange (consequence), and red (call home/office). Wooden clothespins, each with student's name written on it, were all crowded around green at the start of each day. Depending on the situation, I or the students would move those clips up or down as a way of rewarding and punishing behavior throughout the day. That's research-based, right? A student breaks the rule, and they clip down and receive their consequence. If I happened to remember, I would "catch them being good" and allow students to clip up, rewarding that behavior. And before students entered the classroom again, I would reset all clips back to green each morning—another best practice—starting each day new. It was challenging to be consistent in using the chart because I was relying solely on my memory and ability to be attentive. Back then, I didn't understand how this system could be problematic, and I hadn't unpacked and resolved my own traumas, biases, and triggers, which surely informed my judgment around whose clips went up and whose went down. I just knew it helped "control" my classroom, justified giving out consequences, and was an easy way to communicate with families. My students had a daily folder or planner that went home, and I would simply include the color that reflected how their day went. Although convenient, the clip chart approach is problematic because it is a form of public shaming, and every misbehavior, regardless of the offense, is treated the same via a tiered system of consequences (see Figure 6.2). It also establishes and reinforces student reputations, disproportionately affecting Black and Brown youth, under-resourced students, boys, and special education students.

Another trendy classroom management system is ClassDojo (www.classdojo.com). Although we have not implemented it ourselves, we have observed its use in the classroom for many years, including the classrooms of our children. ClassDojo became popular in response to the movement toward positive reinforcement. Imagine walking into the classroom and sprawled across the screen is a set of 20 avatars that have student names underneath. Some kids have 6 points, while others have 45 points. Up in the corner of the screen is the number of points the entire class has earned. A teacher scans the room and sees students on task and awards points. Hey, that is researched-based too—giving points to positively reinforce a desired behavior. In walking around within the classroom, you might even hear a sound effect as points are given to students: "Ding, ding." A teacher may also choose to take away points from students who are not on task: "Whump, whump." Those sounds fill the air as students look up at the screen, wondering who earned or lost points, because most of the time, the sounds replace verbal exchanges

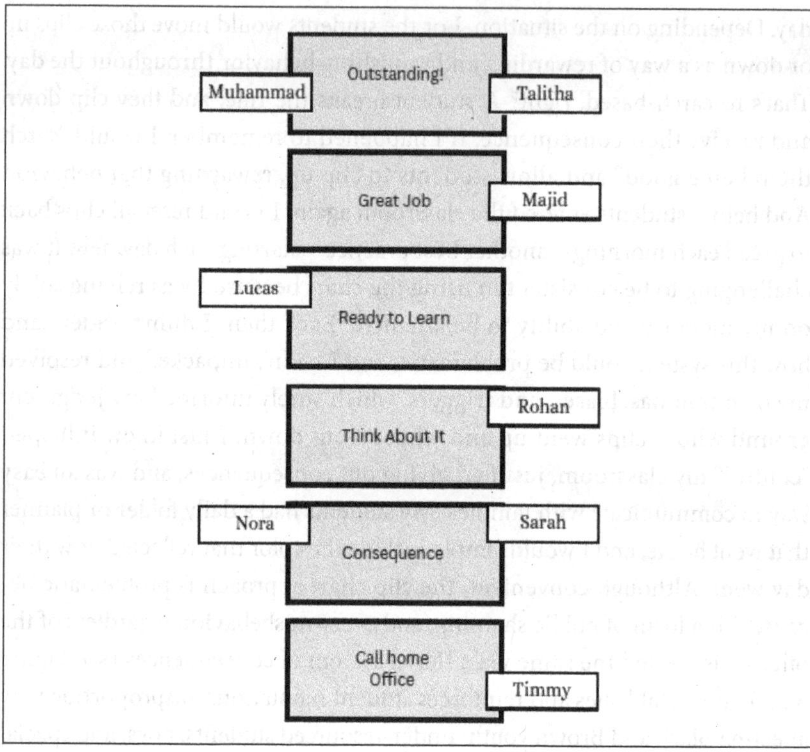

Figure 6.2. Problematic systems.

between teachers and students. In this platform, teachers can also set point goals for individuals or the whole class. Communication with families using ClassDojo is easy, too. Parents download the app on their phone and can see what their children have been praised for (or why they have lost points). This classroom management strategy is problematic because it dehumanizes students. Students are being conditioned on what is acceptable behavior and unacceptable behavior with sound effects that mirror Pavlov's experiments from the 1890s that involved dogs salivating from the sound of a bell. Although platforms like ClassDojo are designed as a positive reinforcement tool that focuses on removing subjectivity and centers observable behaviors (e.g., staying on task, following directions), more often, we have witnessed the opposite effect from its use.

Although both tools are convenient and systematized, and they streamline the communication to families, neither accounts for teacher biases or for the emotional wellness of children. Both systems rely on the disempowerment of students. Research shows that both tools exploit student motivations to please the teacher or earn points (dojos) rather than foster the intrinsic motivation to be cooperative for the sake of one's learning and that of their community (Manolev et al., 2019). Students learn to perform "good behavior" according to the whims, biases, and cultural standards of the teacher, which is a form of control. Moreover, public shared management systems such as these intensify "and normalize the surveillance of students" (Manolev et al., 2019, p. 36).

Culturally Responsive Classroom Management (CRCM)

Just like multicultural education, the evolution of classroom management has involved a wide range of approaches. In this chapter, we'll highlight the most transformative approaches that take up critical pedagogy. "CRCM is a pedagogical approach that guides the management decisions that teachers make" (West, 2022). Taking on a humanistic (as opposed to authoritarian) approach to classroom management, CRCM embraces the notion that people can control only themselves, not others. Therefore, teachers should not attempt to control students, but be in cooperative relationship with them. CRCM also embraces cultural differences as assets to be centered and appreciated in classrooms, rather than silenced and marginalized. In so doing, CRCM inclusively honors the ideals of humanistic and individual psychology. Moreover, the conditions of oppressed people are contextualized in systemic ways that do not victim blame. For example, poverty, disability, nationality, and/or ethnicity are not debatable identity markers on a moral hierarchy. Rather than blame the stereotyped, this approach centers on addressing, challenging, and dismantling stereotypes and the practice of stereotyping.

Through CRCM, teachers can "recognize that the goal of classroom management is not to achieve compliance or control but to provide all students with equitable opportunities for learning and they understand that CRCM is 'classroom management in the service of social justice'" (Weinstein et al., 2004, p. 27). Thus, CRCM is critical pedagogy that humanizes everyone—student, teacher, and society. Like culturally relevant pedagogy, the goal of CRCM is to:

- Advance academic achievement through rigorous and engaging instruction.

- Develop and sustain cultural competence with and among students and communities through mutual respect, inclusion, and authentic rapport.
- Advance critical consciousness through the challenging and dismantling of systems and structures that marginalize specific students and communities.

CRCM directly aligns with critical pedagogy, culturally relevant pedagogy, and culturally sustaining pedagogy because it requires the teacher to work and understand themselves first and continuously before they engage in the liberatory work of teaching and guiding others.

In October 2008, the Metropolitan Center for Urban Education produced a brief titled *Culturally Responsive Classroom Management Strategies*, which outlines five tenets for practicing CRCM. The remainder of this chapter and Chapter 7 will itemize how you can begin actualizing these principles using common aspects of teacher development toward effective classroom management.

1. Recognition of one's own cultural lens and biases
2. Knowledge of students' cultural backgrounds (see Chapter 2)
3. Awareness of the broader social, economic, and political context
4. Ability and willingness to use culturally appropriate management strategies
5. Commitment to building caring classroom communities

Recognition of One's Own Cultural Lens and Biases

Teacher's Role

In case you missed it when it was stated previously: The only person you can ever control is yourself. Central to self-control is self-awareness. In Chapter 2, we did some work to help you better understand your identities and biases. Here, we're going to process your triggers and comforts. Triggers are events or situations that ignite an intense response. Trigger sources can range from memories and smells to behaviors, places, or even people. When an individual is triggered, they may behave "out of character" or beyond self-control. Response to triggers can be emotional (crying, or showing panic, anxiety, or anger) or physical (becoming violent, aggressive, or self-isolating). Typically, being triggered alters behavior. Classroom teachers are not immune to triggers and often find themselves caught off guard. For example, if symptoms of a common cold (i.e., sneezing, coughing, runny nose) cause you to physically distance from people, clean excessively, or compulsively wash your hands out of fear of germ exposure, a lower elementary classroom would not be a comfortable or compatible place for you to work. It also would not be positive for the children.

As a teacher, you are responsible for managing the tone in your classroom. If you are yelling or out of control, it would not be surprising if your students learn from your behavior that yelling is an appropriate way to communicate. When we're triggered, we're typically rattled or taken out of our preferred way of existing. We can't stress enough how important it is that you are aware of how your tone comes across to others. One of the best ways to figure out whether something is a trigger for you is to see how you react to it. But before you can appropriately respond, you must be able to name it.

The next exercise is designed to help you be proactive about recognizing some of your triggers in the classroom and consider some possible coping skills to better manage yourself. Activity 6.2 features common classroom experiences that one might expect when they teach elementary school. If any of these are a personal trigger of yours, consider healing them before you go into a classroom.

Activity 6.2 Teacher's Trigger Inventory

	Potential Trigger	Your Potential Response
	Yelling	
	Disorganization	
	Throwing objects	
	Touching/being touched	
	Being interrupted	

	Potential Trigger	Your Potential Response
	Crying	
	Repeating instructions	
	Mistakes	
	Eye-rolling	
	Profanity	
	Insubordination/defiance	
	Being challenged	
	Tardiness	
	Talking back	
	Talkativeness/excessive talking	
	Excessive questioning	
	Cheating	
	Hitting	
	Name-calling	
	Daydreaming	
	Talking out of turn	
	Tantrums	
	Nail-biting	
	Nose-picking	
	Impoliteness (not saying "please" and "thank you")	
	Finger-sucking	
	Off-task disruptions (doodling, tapping, giggling, etc.)	
	Joking	

On a more important, and potentially egregious, note, you may be triggered by demographic differences. When triggered by these groups, you may:

- Dismiss student potential for academic achievement
- Not respect students, their family members, or community
- Avoid certain students altogether
- Create some physical, emotional, or mental barriers that prevent relationship building

- Be verbally aggressive or abusive toward specific students
- Fear those students, their family members, or community
- Overly punish certain students
- Discredit certain students' academic achievements

It is incredibly unjust for students who belong to specific demographic groups to have a teacher who is triggered by their identity—their mere existence. Thus, this portion of the inventory serves as an opportunity for you to evaluate whether any members of the groups listed in Table 6.1 represent a struggle group for you; if they do, consider how you can minimize harm in the classroom (if you decide to become or remain a teacher) as you do the healing work required to become someone who is not triggered by these communities.

Table 6.1 lists a few demographic groups that we are socialized to demonize, criminalize, mistrust, and/or avoid. Indicate whether you struggle with these groups (see Chapter 2) and begin doing the work to address your biases.

Table 6.1. Demographic Groups (Part I)

Mark (X) as applicable	**Demographic Group**
	Houseless (high mobility, temporary housing, tent, shelter, etc.)
	Visible disability (blind, deaf/hard of hearing, in wheelchair, etc.)
	Neurodiverse (ADHD, autism spectrum, etc.)
	Fat bodied
	Lower socioeconomic status (working class, below poverty line, under-resourced)
	Black (African American, African diaspora, Caribbean, etc.)
	Latinx (Central and South American)
	LGBTTTQQIAA+ spectrum (lesbian; gay; bisexual; transgender; transsexual; 2/two-spirit; queer; questioning; intersex; asexual; ally+
	English learner
	Undocumented immigrant

We're not solely focusing on deficits; we can also talk about what your comforts in a classroom are and whether an elementary environment is best for you (see Table 6.2).

Table 6.2. Comforting Groups & Experiences

Mark (X) as applicable	Comforting Groups & Experiences
	Comforting others through physical touch
	Helping others regulate their emotions
	Modeling healthy self-regulation
	Ethnic, racial, linguistic, ability, and socioeconomic differences
	Being corrected
	Being around BIPOC people
	Accommodating others
	Humanizing others
	Vulnerability
	Imaginative play and learning

If all the commonly seen or experienced concepts or groups listed in Tables 6.1 and 6.2 make you feel purposeful, then perhaps being an elementary school teacher is a good fit.

Authority Figure

Surely, you've heard the saying that a good teacher doesn't smile before Christmas. The idea is that teachers should be very strict to gain control of their students (through distance and fear) before showing a gentler and kinder side of themselves. This is central to authoritative teaching, which emphasizes gaining student respect by being uncompromising. The definition of respect we use in both personal and professional life is the ability to be self-actualized within a community. A teacher who does not compromise—truly, a person who does not compromise—is a lonely teacher who isolates and marginalizes others. We promise that there are ways to accomplish your shared goals in the classroom without having everything go your way. It will require more understanding on the students' part, more flexibility on your part, some creativity, and trust.

If there's one area where you should be authoritative, it's not your classroom management, but your content knowledge. You want to have mastered the content within the standards across the subject areas for your current grade band, and one grade level above and below. You also want to be able to teach the content and skills in a variety of ways. Take, for example, the skill of teaching a child to tie their shoelaces. The most common way this skill is taught is through the bunny-ear method. You may have learned to tie your own shoelaces that way, but it doesn't mean it's the only way, or the most effective way, for the type of learner you are teaching. As an effective teacher, you'll want to master a variety of ways to teach the same concept or skill (in this case, tying shoelaces)—the bunny-ear method, the squirrel-and-the-tree method, loop-it-and-swoop-it—and you'll also want to have a variety of resources to help (i.e., actual shoes with laces, a cardboard cut-out shoe, books, or bicolored laces). What I just described is differentiation in the method of tying the shoelace and in the resources and content for tying shoelaces (see Figure 6.3). That is the space where you want to become an authority (see Disclaimer 6.1).

Figure 6.3. Shoe-tying skill. Wikicommons.

Disclaimer 6.1

This doesn't mean that you'll master all content—that's nearly impossible. It just means you'll have studied the content and skills enough to meet students where they are and bring them up to standard. If you run into a situation where you don't have adequate resources or knowledge to address their content or skill deficiency, you'll want to have mastered being autodidactic and resourceful enough to teach yourself or to find others who can help you master it. That way, you can return to the student, perhaps the next day or the next week, and meet their learning needs.

Awareness of the Broader Social, Economic, and Political Context

A culturally responsive teacher works to develop skills of observation and relationship building—but at a deeper level than we may be thinking. These skills are important because often, when you are observant and truly know your students—their full selves (e.g., race, ethnicity, class, gender, sexual orientation, ability)—you can be proactive rather than reactive. When I, Dr. Smithey, think back to my time as a teacher, I thought I was observant as situations came up in my classroom, and I reacted appropriately. On the surface, I knew my students and a bit about their families. All the typical "things to do" we learn about in teacher preparation: I asked students what they did after school, went to family events held at the school, and even attended some football games. In some ways, I attempted to know their Funds of Knowledge. I knew what my students were interested in, and I participated right along with them. I am laughing to myself as I write, remembering the students trying to teach me Double Dutch at recess, and all the times I fell on my face. I smile as I recall wearing my collection of Silly Bandz with pride (throwback to teaching in 2010). I thought it was enough, but it was not. Honestly, some years, I wondered what I was doing wrong, because it seemed like I was always "putting out fires," and it was exhausting—meaning that sometimes I was constantly being reactive to disruptions and, unfortunately, escalating situations because of the way that I responded as the teacher. It only took me 15 years to realize I had not done the work to confront my own biases and triggers that had been driving the way I was trying to "control" my classroom—no wonder it wasn't working. Knowing *them* was not enough; I also needed to know *me* (see Chapter 2) so that we could become a healthy *us*. I had not developed skills of careful observation and relationship building in the ways that I needed to. I was aware of basic behaviors that showed me they were not engaged in learning—I could tell when they were bored, or I would notice patterns of students' "needing" to use the bathroom every time we started writing or math. However, I was not completely familiar with my triggers (see Activity 6.2) or their triggers, either inside or outside school. It may be easier to recognize school-based triggers, especially over a period as you can start to see patterns, if you're observant and document what you see. For instance, school-based triggers could be:

- Negative interaction with a teacher or peer
- Arguments or bullying
- Hearing certain words, like "no"
- Removing or touching something that belongs to the student
- Public shaming (remember those trendy management tools)
- Change in routine, schedule, or a person
- Particular feelings (e.g., bored, overwhelmed, confused, embarrassed, ashamed)
- Failure, correction, or critique
- Testing or certain assignments
- Loud or bright classroom
- Physical touch
- Transitions

However, non-school-based triggers are harder to see, and they can easily be based on assumptions and stereotypes—especially if you exclude families from the conversation and only get to know students and their families on the surface. Non-school-based triggers could be:

- Housing insecurity
- Inadequate sleep
- Hunger or food insecurity
- Incorrect (dosage or type) or insufficient medication
- Financial/employment security of caregivers
- Immigration status of self, caregivers, or loved ones
- Sickness or unmet need for medical treatment
- Conflicts at home or in the community
- Peer groups outside school
- Poor digital well-being

To be proactive in the classroom, as opposed to reactive, it is important to be observant of triggers that students may have, as well as signs that they are becoming agitated or bothered by those triggers.

Recognizing student triggers is part of a 7-phase acting-out cycle (Colvin & Scott, 2014) (see Table 6.3).

Table 6.3. Phases of the Acting-Out Cycle

Phase	Description
Calm	A student is participating and engaged in the classroom environment, generally following rules and expectations.
Trigger	A student begins to respond to, or is reminded of, a previous situation, often unconsciously.
Agitation	A student cannot manage their own response to one or more triggers independently and becomes visibly bothered by showing emotion or physically fidgeting with hands or moving from place to place.
Acceleration	A student begins to show a misbehavior and often directs their response toward an individual, such as a peer or a teacher.
Peak	A student disrupts the classroom environment, and typically the learning cannot continue.
De-escalation	A student lessens the behavior.
Recovery	A student is no longer agitated, often re-engages in the classroom environment, and returns to the calm phase.

The purpose of this next activity is to become familiar with the phases of the acting-out cycle in the classroom—specifically, the phases that lead up to the peak phase. We want you to become so observant that you recognize what keeps your students most engaged in learning during the calm phase while you're also in tune with, and aware of, individual triggers in students. First, choose a student with whom you want to behaviorally be more proactive and less reactive. Then, use the chart in Activity 6.3 to make observations over a series of days. You'll notice that the chart shows the acting-out cycle in reverse order. As you practice observing, the goal is to notice the triggers and signs of agitation before acceleration. Finally, consider your next steps as the teacher, and complete the prompts under the chart.

Activity 6.3 Phase of Acting-Out Cycle Activity

Phase of Acting-Out Cyle	Day of the week:
Acceleration What happened? Specifically, what was the misbehavior? Who was the misbehavior directed toward?	
Agitation How was this student showing me they were bothered by a trigger before the misbehavior happened?	
Trigger What school-based triggers were noticed before the student became agitated? What do I think I know about non-school-based triggers the student has?	
Calm What was happening in the classroom before and while the trigger occurred? How do you know the student was engaged and was responsive to the teacher before the trigger occurred?	

Look at your notes from several days for patterns across stages. What do you notice? What do you wonder?

In looking at the triggers, identify school-based versus non-school-based. If you identified one or more non-school-based triggers, are they based on facts or assumptions you made? Why should you think about facts versus assumptions?

Trauma-Informed Pedagogy

According to the National Child Traumatic Stress Network, "A traumatic event is a frightening, dangerous, or violent event that poses a threat to a child's life or bodily integrity." Traumatic experiences range from natural disasters and substance use disorder to physical, sexual, or psychological abuse. Traumatic experiences also include police killings of members of a child's racial demographic group. Having witnessed or experienced trauma at least once, especially repeatedly, children can sense danger even when there is no danger.

> Traumatic reactions can include a variety of responses, such as intense and ongoing emotional upset, depressive symptoms or anxiety, behavioral changes, difficulties with self-regulation, problems relating to others or forming attachments, regression or loss of previously acquired skills, attention and academic difficulties, nightmares, difficulty sleeping and eating, and physical symptoms, such as aches and pains. (National Child Trauma Stress Network, nd)

These trauma responses are behaviors we deem inappropriate in the classroom, yet, if you reflect on the last 5 years alone, children have been exposed to:

- The Covid-19 global pandemic that has killed more than 1 million Americans
- Exponential increase in hate crimes targeting Asian Americans, including a mass shooting on March 16, 2021
- More than 120 school shootings since 2017
- The U.S. border crisis that has involved detaining, separating, and caging asylum-seeking children at the Mexico–U.S. border.
- Enduring distress and dislocation of Native Americans, who face severe climate challenges and exploitive policies of the U.S. government
- More than 1,000 people shot and killed by police in 2021, with the rate of fatal police shootings of Black people being much higher than that for any other race or ethnicity
- Russia's invasion of Ukraine

Compounding trauma is real, and children are not healing at the rate of exposure. Children (aka students) are affected by these traumatic events, especially those who experience trusted adults as perpetuators of harm. Furthermore, experiencing racial discrimination and oppression increases the risk of trauma symptoms. Keep this in mind the next time you want to decide that a child's trauma response is not appropriate and therefore deserves punishment. Acting out, aggression, hyperactivity, poor social relationships, defiance, immaturity, poor academic achievement, poor attention span, and inadequate self-concept are among the most common behavioral challenges that teachers struggle to manage in classrooms. Sound familiar?

Trauma or Misbehavior?

Activity 6.4 is an inventory to help contextualize student behavior—we can't seriously engage in CRCM without deep considerations of the impact of trauma.

Activity 6.4 Trauma or Misbehavior

Directions: Indicate T for trauma response and M for misbehavior

T	M	Behavior
		1. Perfectionism
		2. Clinginess
		3. Excessive shyness
		4. Apathy or working far below potential
		5. Physically violent
		6. Loss of emotional regulation
		7. Difficulty transitioning
		8. Verbally abusive
		9. Extreme fatigue
		10. Loss of appetite
		11. Irregular attendance
		12. Social isolation
		13. Profane language
		14. Stealing
		15. Fear or distrust of others

In the next Activity (6.5), you'll reflect and list on how you might de-escalate the 15 behaviors listed in Activity 6.4, especially as you consider your triggers and your comforts. Furthermore, consider how your response to any of the behaviors—whether it's misbehavior, trauma related, or indicative of some neurodivergence—might help the student feel empowered while remaining an active and valued member of the classroom community. If you already guessed that you need to learn your students' triggers and comforts to best respond to their needs, especially during a trauma response, you are absolutely right!

Activity 6.5 Plan to De-escalate

Example: Facilitate deep breathing exercises
1.
2.
3.
4.

Remember, when a child exhibits undesired behaviors, your role as the classroom teacher is to do no harm, and help them feel validated, seen, and able to re-engage. By all means, do not agitate the child further; this isn't the time for sarcasm, joking, teasing, aggression, power struggles, ultimatums, or doing anything that would amplify the child's emotional disturbance. Your goal is to remind them that they have an ally in a safe place to regulate their emotions and get back to the task at hand. Moreover, you want to allow the child to continue to function within the community, so the goal is to de-escalate and help them to recover as quickly, quietly, and seamlessly as possible; this way, their peers are not disturbed, and learning can continue to thrive.

De-escalation

Figure 6.4 shows five de-escalation phrases that you might adopt to meet your needs when a disturbance occurs in the classroom. In Activity 6.6, you'll revise the phrases to reflect your tone and language preferences so that you're authentic when you use them.

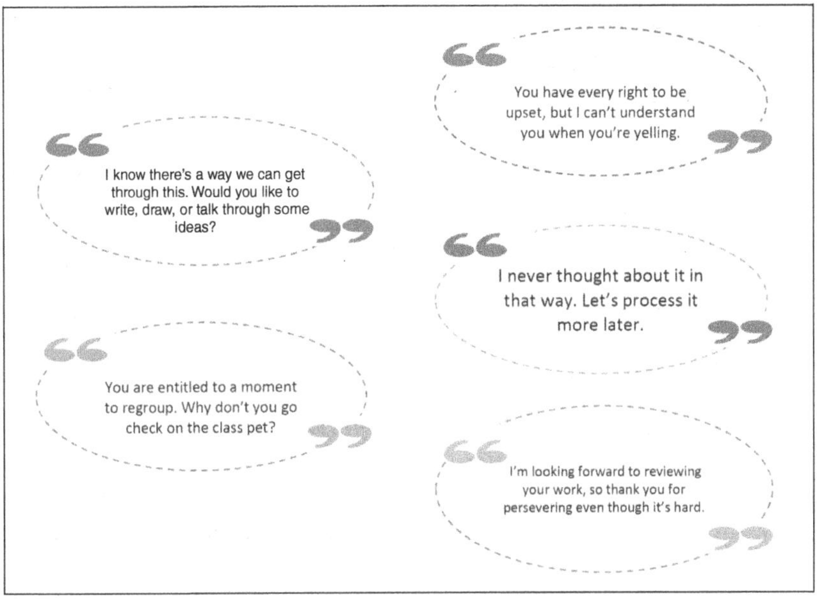

Figure 6.4. Five de-escalation phrases.

Revised de-escalation statements

Activity 6.6 Revised De-escalation Statements

Directions: Read through the bubbles in Figure 6.4. Write a revised statement for each, based on how you would say it.

1.	
2.	
3.	
4.	
5.	

Conclusion

This chapter has explored the roots of classroom management, its various iterations, and why traditional classroom management has failed to live up to its potential. In Chapter 7, we'll discuss more explicitly how you can practice

CRCM, using and modifying what you already know and understand about classroom management. At all times, it is important to remember that notions of appropriate and proper behavior are culturally influenced, and a teacher's perceptions of student's worth, identity, and behaviors have lasting consequence. You, as the classroom teacher, are powerful. Thus, what you validate or invalidate can alter a child's sense of self and relationship to school. Be aware of inconsistencies in how consequences are administered (e.g., teacher favoritism or targeting) and what is praised.

Moreover, as you consider how to practice CRCM, the disproportionality in suspensions, special education referrals, gifted or accelerated recommendations, expulsions, and even arrests become salient. Teachers who are change agents are keen to enter classrooms as disruptors of disproportionality that further marginalizes. However, if you're unaware of your power, your positionality, and your biases and triggers, you'll likely reinforce the dehumanizing classroom management practices that dominate schools across the United States.

References

Colvin, G., & Scott, T. M. (2014). *Managing the cycle of acting-out behavior in the classroom.* Corwin Press.

Dreikurs, R., Cassel, P., & Kehoe, D. (1974). *Discipline without tears.* Dutton Adult.

Kounin, J. S. (1970). *Discipline and group management in classrooms.* Holt, Rinehart and Winston.

Manolev, J., Sullivan, A., & Slee, R. (2019). The datafication of discipline: ClassDojo, surveillance and a performative classroom culture. *Learning, Media and Technology, 44*(1), 36–51.

Metropolitan Center for Urban Education. (2008, October). *Culturally responsive classroom management strategies.* https://www.asdn.org/wp-content/uploads/Culturally-Responsive-Classroom-Mgmt-Strat2.pdf

National Child Trauma Stress Network. (n.d.). *About child trauma.* Retrieved August 2, 2022, from https://www.nctsn.org/what-is-child-trauma/about-child-trauma

Positive Behavioral Interventions and Supports. (2012, June 19). *Positive behavioral interventions and supports: History, defining features, and misconceptions.* https://www.pbis.org/resource/positive-behavioral-interventions-and-supports-history-defining-features-and-misconceptions

Tulley, M., & Chiu, L. H. (1998). Children's perceptions of the effectiveness of classroom discipline techniques. *Journal of Instructional Psychology, 25,* 189–197.

Weinstein C., Tomlinson-Clarke S., & Curran, M. (2004). Toward a conception of culturally responsive classroom management. *Journal of Teacher Education, 55*(1), 25–38.

West, E. (2022). *Culturally responsive classroom management for Native learners.* Indigenous Education Tools. https://indigenouseducationtools.org/bf/11

SEVEN

Culturally Responsive Classroom Management

Chelda Smith Kondo and Montana Smithey

IN CHAPTER 6, WE EXPLORED the first three tenets of culturally responsive classroom management (CRCM), as articulated by the Metropolitan Center for Urban Education (2008). This chapter will address the final two tenets: ability and willingness to use culturally appropriate management strategies, and commitment to building caring classroom communities.

Self-Analysis

Now that you've read Chapter 6, we'll begin here with a self-analysis exercise pertaining to your beliefs toward classroom management. Read each idea in Activity 7.1 and decide if you agree (A) or disagree (D).

Activity 7.1 Self-Analysis

Directions: Indicate A for agree or D for disagree for each statement or belief.

Statement/Belief ***Based on a culturally responsive classroom***	**A**	**D**
1. Every single person in each classroom is worthy.		
2. School policies and practices can limit students.		
3. Basic needs of students in the classroom are their physiological needs, such as water, warmth, sleep, clothing, shelter, food, and air.		
4. Rules are the heart of culturally responsive classroom management.		
5. Rules and procedures are set at the beginning of the school year and should not change.		
6. Procedures require a good amount of preplanning on the part of the teacher.		
7. Students rarely have triggers connected to their behavior.		

Statement/Belief ***Based on a culturally responsive classroom***	**A**	**D**
8. School rules and policies are biased toward certain demographic groups.		
9. Having a student take a time-out in another room is an appropriate consequence for misbehavior.		
10. A tiered system of consequence (e.g., warning, time-out, call home) is better than logical consequences to misbehavior.		
11. Teachers should have favorite students.		
12. The greatest classroom management tool is engagement.		
13. Chronic disruptions are best managed through consistent consequences.		
14. The only person a teacher can control is themselves.		
15. Misbehaviors are universally known and understood.		

As you read this chapter, pay close attention when these ideas pop up; we'll revisit them at the end. In Chapter 2, you took a deep dive into your identity as a teacher and learned how to better understand the context in which you teach—all of which is central to establishing CRCM. In this chapter, we incorporate those ideas while considering the practical application: what CRCM looks like and sounds like in the classroom (see Activity 6.1). We will explore ways to build and maintain a caring classroom community and examine the importance of being willing to use culturally appropriate management strategies. Traditional classroom management texts begin with how to establish rules and procedures in the classroom, as well as strategies to enforce them, and this text is no different. However, you'll notice that in this chapter, we emphasize classrooms as spaces where students feel safe, have a sense of belonging, and are given a chance to grow in their self-actualization—the idea that students are working toward realizing their talents, their potential, and who they are as people. We consider rules and procedures that support these ideas, as well as enforcement of such rules and procedures that humanizes students and provides a path toward restoration. You may come across nontraditional ideas, such as having favorite students, and practical strategies that teachers can use when chronic disruptions to the learning environment occur.

Positionality Statement

Montana Smithey (she/her) and Chelda Smith (she/her)

A White and Black teacher educator walk into a bar (LOL, just kidding!). Although we, Dr. Smithey and Dr. Smith, have both become teacher educators, our journeys have been starkly different. Our positionality statements in Chapter 6 explain some aspects of our identities, but they're not the only factors that inform our approach to classroom management. As mothers of school-age children who have varying needs academically, socially, and emotionally, we are biased in our defense and promotion of classroom management that is culturally responsive. Despite our demographic differences, we are both advocates for our children—and children similar to them—to be seen for their assets, not only their challenges.

Key Terms:

- **Chronic Disruptions:** behaviors that occur throughout the day that are seen to interfere with the function of the classroom.
- **Physiological needs:** the needs of students to do well within the classroom. These include a sense of safety, a feeling of belonging, a sense of self, and self-actualization.
- **Procedures:** an established way or series of actions that are planned within a classroom.
- **Proximity:** to be near one another in a given space.
- **Rules:** a set of specific regulations within a classroom.

Key Ideas:

1. ***To build a caring classroom community, teachers must humanize students, allow them to have a sense of belonging in the classroom, and establish norms, rules, and procedures that are enforceable and culturally relevant.***
2. ***To use culturally appropriate management strategies, teachers embrace disruptive students, become observant, and use engagement in learning as a tool.***

Commitment to Building Caring Classroom Communities

A caring classroom community is vital to the academic and social success of your students, and you. To be clear, if there is active tension in your classroom, neither you nor your students will enjoy entering or being in that space. Classrooms need joy, and students need to belong. Next, I, Dr. Smith, share some of my favorite ways to establish a classroom community, as part of Activity 7.2.

Activity 7.2 Establishing a Classroom Community

1. I assume that every single person in my classroom is more than capable of achieving grade-level proficiency and beyond.
2. I assume that every single person in my classroom is inherently worthy of a healthy learning experience.
3. If I have a student (or several) who has a deficit-based reputation within the school or with a specific teacher, I assume that their previous teachers, along with the school policies and practices, have limited that student. I then make it my personal responsibility and mission to alter the relationship that the child and their family have with schooling.
4. I see students beyond academics. Student success is not limited to grades.

From this list, which is most important to you and why? What would you add to the list?

____

____

____

Even if you have in mind how you want to establish a caring classroom community, it is important to recognize students' basic needs, including their physiological needs. These include a sense of safety, a feeling of belonging, a sense of self, and self-actualization. Their sense of safety is not limited to physical harm, though that is incredibly important; it also includes their ability to try new things, to make mistakes, and to be received with grace. Their sense of self is deeply tied to their cultural identities being valued and incorporated into the classroom environment and curriculum. Their self-actualization is rooted in their ability to name themselves and evolve from that naming as they gain greater understanding. Physiological needs refer to biological basics such as water, warmth, sleep, clothing, shelter, food, and air. These needs are basic requirements for human survival. In the case of classroom management, they are also basic needs for student engagement. If these needs are not met, no number of rewards or consequences will allow that child to thrive.

Classroom Rules

Many people think that rules are the heart of classroom management. They are not. More often, rules are the boundaries that teachers don't want students to cross so that teachers can accomplish their goals. There is no shortage of rules to be found on the Internet, and it's laughable how many of them are unenforceable or completely irrational for an elementary school student. We outline a few in Table 7.1.

Table 7.1. Classroom Rules

Not Enforceable	Irrational
Ask questions	Always be on time
Share new ideas	Come to class prepared to learn
Have a respectful tone	No talking at lunch
Always try your best	No using the bathroom or drinking water outside designated times

Both sets of examples are well-intentioned, as you likely noted, but they are not rooted in the reality of what the teacher can control, nor are they rooted, in some instances, in what the student can control, such as always being on time. Most elementary students do not bring themselves to school, so their arrival time is usually not within their control. And if their basic needs are not met, as we have already established, it is not likely they will come to class prepared to learn. It is also punitive to say that children can't socialize during lunch when surely, they're not allowed to socialize and talk during class.

This is not to say that rules are not important. It is only through maturity that we've learned that we can only rule ourselves. New, overwhelmed, or intimidated teachers often fail to understand that the term "rule" has two definitions: One is the expectation for how people conduct themselves and how procedures are executed, and the other is control or dominion over others. Please don't conflate the two or lean toward the latter. You know you'll have rules, so let's work on how to craft them. We recommend having the number of rules correspond to the grade level. If you happen to be teaching pre-K or kindergarten, no rules. Just kidding—kinda sorta. Pre-K, kindergarten, and first grade can all have one rule—respect—and it is more of an expectation than a rule. Inherent in that rule/expectation is respect for self, others, supplies, and learning. Through procedures, you can establish ways to help students honor that one rule/expectation (see Figure 7.1).

Figure 7.1. Respect.

I, Dr. Smith, personally subscribe to this rule being the only one, but if you insist on having more, don't exceed five. Here are a few norms that help establish a caring classroom environment and are enforceable and culturally relevant.

1. Use inclusive language
2. Keep our hands and feet to ourselves
3. Honor confidentiality
4. Be responsible for initiating healing and repair when we cause harm

Ideally, additional rules beyond respect would be established with your students over time, as you learn what the classroom community needs to be healthy and thrive. Although it is common to set rules and expectations on the first day of school, it is impossible to know the needs of each specific class before you get to know students. You might have noticed that all the suggested rules are written as positive statements. It's not necessary to offer rules in a negative tone. For instance, Rule 2 could have been, "Do not hit others," and Rule 3 could have been written, "Do not tell other people's secrets." Technically, that approach would communicate the same message; however, telling students not to do something often yields the opposite result, and positive phrasing is more inviting and empowering.

Classroom Procedures

Procedures, unlike rules, are the preplanned ways to maximize the learning day. The minimum number of procedures is five, and they are often dependent on the teacher, the students, and the teaching context. Some common procedures you'll want to preplan for and make sense of include:

- Taking attendance
- Facilitating assessments
- Distributing materials
- Collecting materials
- Transitioning between activities
- Accessing the bathroom or water
- Participating in group activities
- Submitting homework
- Requesting support
- Entering the classroom
- Acting in an emergency
- Lining up

The list of potential activities that need procedures is endless. Procedures help us do things effectively and efficiently, and they require a good amount of preplanning on the teacher's part. They require anticipating what might go awry and how the teacher might best respond. Procedures, like rules, must be practiced. Through practice, you learn when your procedures are too elaborate and how to simplify them for students. Remember: The goal is efficiency and effectiveness (see Pro-Tip 7.1).

Pro-Tip 7.1

Pro-Tip: Invite your most disruptive students to help you iron out the kinks in your procedures.

The best times to focus on establishing procedures and practicing them are the first week of school in both the fall and spring semesters, and after every school break. Mastery of procedures is key for an efficient classroom. Now, this doesn't mean that people will always follow those established procedures; sometimes people stray from them. Part of a teacher's plan involves how to welcome students back in or make modifications so that students can fully engage in learning. Procedures are important for our socialization in a community, for our cooperation, and for conflict reduction. Procedures are in place at home, places of worship, and restaurants—nearly everywhere. Like you, your students come from a world that also has procedures, so it's important for you to realize that those procedures may be different from your own. Your classroom needs to be a place that can sustain their home and community practices. Instead of thinking of a procedure as right or wrong, consider that your classroom procedures might work for that environment but not be effective elsewhere. This approach supports students in becoming bicultural by learning the most effective and efficient procedures for full participation in different environments.

Figure 7.2. Nonverbal Communication.

Some of the most effective procedures include communicating without speaking (see Figure 7.2). For instance, to get students' attention, you might clap a rhythm rather than trying to speak over them. Students echo this clapped-out rhythm, and with each iteration, the rhythm becomes more complicated. The first rhythm might just be three single claps, and some students will immediately tune in and repeat the rhythm. Subsequent rhythms might have a different tune to them, with five or six different claps, some fast, some slow. By the third iteration, nearly every student is paying attention and participating. A fun twist is switching to a finger-snapping rhythm that not only surprises students, but also brings them joy. Maybe you're not into clapping patterns, or you noticed that your students love musical instruments. You might use a tambourine or drum, and as musical patterns fill the air, students use their hands to indicate they are engaged. Another procedure that does not involve speaking involves the use of codes to signal the need to use the bathroom, get a tissue, or access water. In this instance, students raise their hand and show the code for water, which might be a thumbs up, or for bathroom, which might be crossed fingers (the index [first] finger crossed over the middle [second] finger). These silent procedures are useful for allowing students to express basic human needs without disrupting the flow of instruction.

One more example of a silent procedure we'd like to share is a way for students to engage in self-assessment of their learning. For us classroom teachers, one of the greatest threats to engagement and a cooperative learning environment is students not understanding the skills or content being taught. It is imperative that you have a way for students to communicate this to you without feeling shame. A silent declaration of either their mastery or the need for additional support—such as putting their palms together or placing their hand on their shoulder—is an excellent way to allow students to self-assess their progress toward mastery and request support.

Collectively, these nonintrusive, mostly silent procedures are also ways of reengaging students in ways that allow them to maintain their dignity, which is critical to establishing a caring and healthy classroom community and giving students a sense of belonging (see Activity 7.3).

Activity 7.3 Silent Gestures

Directions: List five silent gestures you might use to support nondisruptive student procedures.

1.
2.
3.
4.
5.

Enforcement of Rules and Procedures

Enforcing rules and procedures is not the best use of your limited instructional time. When a student breaks a rule or doesn't follow an established procedure, avoid responding emotionally. Teachers may send the child out of the classroom or stop teaching to call a parent or guardian. When we outsource behavioral management—by involving others—we are also outsourcing our relationship with the children. This is antithetical to the goal of having a classroom community where everyone in the classroom can thrive. Your goal is to keep everyone in the classroom, allow the tensions to settle, and model self-composure and grace while supporting students to reconcile and figure out how they can continue to actively participate in the community. Later, perhaps during a transition period or more discrete time, address the harm done. This allows you, as a teacher, to regulate your emotions so you're less triggered by, and less emotionally involved in, the offense. It also allows the student or students who crossed the boundary to see that they are still part of the community, and they have time to regroup and, later, adjust their behavior. In all, everyone should have had some time to cool down without compromising learning or the overall group dynamic.

Remember those silent procedures we talked about earlier? There are also some silent ways to enforce rules and procedures that can re-engage students when minor disruptions happen. One highly effective approach is proximity. While teaching or doing something else, you can physically go stand closer to a student who is off task. Do not touch the student—if you must touch something, lightly touch the desk. Often, just your physical presence close to the student will be enough to get their attention and bring them back to task. If you do speak to the student, affirm something they're doing correctly, or ask them a question related to the task in a curious (not disapproving) tone. Other silent ways to re-engage students or get their attention include writing short notes, making eye contact, or just becoming quiet. The goal is to continue the lesson and de-escalate any undesired behavior, which also means limiting the number of students involved (see Disclaimer 7.1).

Disclaimer 7.1

> Unless someone's safety is at risk—including the student themselves or you as the teacher—there's no need to immediately respond to undesired behavior. Take a moment to calm yourself.

When we have rules and procedures in place, typically we also impose consequences on those who do not cooperate. A punitive classroom environment requires consequences, and authoritative teachers often improvise those consequences, which inadvertently escalates disruptions. Avoid power struggles at all costs. You may win the argument, but you also lose a relationship. If you insist on having consequences, establish them in collaboration with your students, and ahead of any crisis. That way, when a child decides to depart from classroom expectations, they understand what they're getting into. This approach is also useful for you, as the teacher, because it limits improvising. Improvising in response to behavior could lead to irreparable harm, shaming, and conflict escalation. Develop logical consequences together as a classroom community and modify for students as needed.

Common consequences include silent lunch, walking laps at recess, or losing time from recess. These are harsh and rarely teach students the intended lesson. Logical consequences correspond to the misbehavior of the student. Examples are dedicating time for students to finish work; withholding classroom materials when used inappropriately; rehearsing a procedure; giving students a break because they need one (just like we all do); or engaging in a reflective conversation with students so you can understand their perspective—this is sometimes called a "time-in," as opposed to a time-out. Remember, a phone call home is extreme and should only come after several positive calls and an established positive rapport. Moreover, a call should involve seeking collaboration for improved outcomes, not further punishing the child.

Consequences should also have a path to restoration, so that students are not made to feel expelled from their classroom community because they made a mistake and triggered you. Restoration-based classroom consequences include having students write or have an action plan to prevent the infraction from occurring again; conducting practice sessions in which students master the desired behavior; and figuring out a way to restore the relationship that has been harmed or to fix the item that has been damaged.

Ability and Willingness to Use Culturally Appropriate Management Strategies

Favoring the Disruptive Student

I, Dr. Smith, once taught a fifth-grade child who greeted me each day with the phrase, "Good morning, bitch!" He was my favorite student, intentionally. This student, Jung, was so used to being removed from classrooms for being disruptive that he figured he'd be proactive by disrespecting me on the first day. Jung probably expected me to be triggered and kick him out. I was taking personal responsibility for creating a safe and loving schooling experience for this student and his family and being called the "b" word could not be what displaced me from my state of self-control. So, every time Jung greeted me this way, I pleasantly replied, "Good morning, Jung." I was consistently perky and kind about it because I couldn't control him—but I could control my response to his behavior. The school year has 10 months, and it was not until the last two that Jung finally stopped calling me the "b" word. And I was okay with that because Jung had his most successful academic year in my classroom. He was my favorite student because he became my teaching assistant. He tested all my procedures and was responsible for helping me keep time. Because Jung had a notorious reputation outside the classroom, I didn't send him out much, but I made sure he was comfortable inside. He even sat at my desk for most of his work time! Most teachers I have encountered would have kicked him out before he'd even made it across the door threshold. Instead of working on their triggers from that word, they would seek to control the student through consequences.

Now, having a favorite student is antithetical to practically any classroom management or any sort of community-building advice you might have heard—and I think it's fair for you to be skeptical. But hear me out: Given that children are kicked out or expelled from daycare programs when they are as young as 6 months, we can assume that elementary-age children are aware of who is valued and who is disposable in schools and communities. My intentional favoritism of a child who has been treated as disposable is an equity-based classroom management approach that compensates for years of marginalization—and by the time they have reached my classroom, this marginalization may very well be the sole reason they are still not well-adjusted at school. I'm always reminded that school is compulsory; the child has no option but to attend school. Many do not have the privilege of being homeschooled or attending private schools. Thus, I accept that if a child who is marginalized continues to show up in my classroom every day, they do not have a choice in the matter. But I have so much choice in, and power over, how I can help them to survive the day and the academic year and gain tools that will allow them to thrive in the long run. So, I make them my favorite!

I document everything amazing about my favorite student(s) in my notebook, in my phone, or some other place. This is incredibly important because "infamous" students are people accustomed to repeated invalidation. Therefore, they often conceal, minimize, and protect amazing aspects about themselves. It may take time for me to see they have specialized knowledge in a particular area or excel at certain skills. I make that list, so I don't forget how amazing these students are. Also, I know that my memory is not sufficient to compete with their deficit-based, often schoolwide reputation.

Preemptively, as soon as I discover the names of those students who will become my intentional favorites, I call their parents to express my enthusiasm and ask them to be partners with me so this school year can be the best their child has ever had. During that conversation, it's important for me to keep it short, express my commitment, and, if the energy feels right, ask the parents to share with me some amazing things about their child so I can be prepared to receive them. Once I start to record some good things on my list, no matter how small, I call home to share what I have observed. I make sure to call at least 3 times with only positive news so that we establish an understanding that, unlike other teachers, administrators, or other adults in this child's life, I see their inherent value and some of their Funds of Knowledge. I am excited about who they are, and I am not outsourcing my relationship with them. I am invested. Parents and I usually establish a positive rapport after several of these phone calls.

Making a student my favorite means that I also prepare myself to increase my tolerance for disruption. A child with a deficit-based reputation has learned that disruption is an effective way to gain attention. For all children—people, really—attention is important. If the child does not have a history of experiencing approval-based attention, the negative base will have to do. I personally find that the disruptive child is usually humorous. Rather than admonish that, I try to figure out ways to banter with them to de-escalate a situation when tensions rise.

Acknowledging Students' Inherent Value

Favoring the historically disruptive child also involves giving them roles and responsibilities in the classroom that help establish belonging. This could be as simple as having them be the person who collects homework or pass out papers, or as elaborate as co-teaching a concept or skill with you or assigning them a peer mentee. Perhaps the ultimate way to acknowledge a child's inherent value is to put them in a position of leadership or responsibility. My disruptive child will be the one who takes the necessary permission slips down the hall to the office. I trust them, and I let them know that I am trusting them to do a good job representing me and our established rapport. When they have done a good job and return looking for affirmation, I am casual. I let them know that, because I trust them, there's no need to make a big deal out of them rising to the occasion. They are fantastic, and fantastic people can accomplish responsible tasks, like delivering the permission slips. If they're distracted, or they don't complete the task as assigned, I'll understand that they tried. Later, we'll strategize about how to try it again and how to be better prepared for the obstacles they may encounter, so they might be successful in the future. Fantastic people learn from their experiences and try again. Because I understand that this favorite student of mine has a negative reputation in the school, I am sure to send them with a written note stating that

I have given them special permission to do this, and I am trusting them to accomplish this task. I only ask the adults they encounter to trust me to support this child in establishing a more positive relationship with schooling and learning environments.

At this point, you may be wondering, "Well, what about all the other students?" What about them? If we're going to be equity-minded in our classroom management and pedagogy, then we must recognize that the traditional teacher's pet has had plenty of opportunities to be responsible and to be a leader. We can also assume they will have continued opportunities, within and outside schools, to be affirmed. Perhaps what they are lacking are opportunities to take risks. These are the students to whom I do not give a rubric or an assignment exemplar. I don't want to further their people-pleasing tendencies of showing up in the classroom. They too need to feel safe making mistakes. A perfect example of a teacher's pet archetype is Isabela in the family Madrigal from the Disney film *Encanto*. Isabela didn't know that she could produce not only beautiful flowers, but also interesting, fun, creative plants like cacti. It is only when the pressure to be perfect is lifted that she can have a better sense of who she is, outside her family's expectations. This transformation also allows Isabela to be more inclusive of others, and less judgmental. These are dispositions we want to cultivate in every single student, and that's how we form healthy classroom communities.

I'd be remiss not to mention that controlling students and leaning on teacher's pets are teacher-centered ways of being in the classroom. Essentially, teacher's pets become teacher's assistants who help the teacher do less work. Controlled students allow the teacher to maintain the semblance of good classroom management, but also distance. A classroom management approach that has the teacher's needs or preferences at the center of its mission is inappropriate, unprofessional, and not culturally responsive.

Engaging Students in Learning

Again, engaging lessons is the most effective way to have cooperation and effective classroom management. Aside from knowing the content you are teaching, one of the most effective ways to be engaging is to be culturally relevant. That means that you're including your students' differences, communities, and home cultures in your lessons—not in an additive way but embedded and infused throughout. It will show up in the examples you highlight, in the resources you use, in the connections you make to real life, and even in assignments you assign. Project-based, or inquiry-based, learning is highly effective for students who are traditionally marginalized from schools. It can be incredibly empowering to figure out how your subject—be it science, social studies, math, literacy, physical education, or art—can speak directly to issues that children are making sense of in their everyday lives. This requires exceptional planning on your part, as well as creativity and mastery of your pedagogical content knowledge.

Chronic Disruptions

When a student is consistently engaging in the same misbehavior and causing chronic disruptions, there's an unmet need. Remember that your greatest classroom management tool is engagement. When students are engaged, they're cooperative. If you're facing chronic disruptions, it means that you have students who are not engaged, and maybe they're unable to be cooperative. Perhaps this is because what is being taught is not differentiated, is disenfranchising, or is simply disengaging. Maybe it's the result of something much greater than, and beyond, the classroom—consider Maslow's hierarchy of needs. Whatever the reason, leverage your positive rapport to help support your students. You may have to enlist the support of counselors or guardians but remain engaged. It's important that you all take some time, perhaps several moments, to figure out what's going on and how you can best help your student to re-engage. If parents or family members are contacted in the process of this conversation, make it clear that the goal is to help the student thrive in the classroom by being engaged. Allow the parent/guardian to function as the primary expert and the most invested person in the child's life. Ask them for advice and take that advice seriously. If the child is old or mature enough, ask them for advice, and take that advice seriously. Incorporate the suggestions into your practice so that the child can be engaged throughout your lessons, be an active member of the community, and work to cease the disruptions.

If you notice chronic disruptions, it is imperative that you, as a classroom teacher, take reflective notes to document what you're noticing and look for patterns. Remember those triggers and trauma responses from Chapter 6? Your documentation should be asset based, so you want to document details like:

- When the instances are not happening
- The possible triggers for when they do happen
- Some effective ways that the disruption has been mitigated, or stopped altogether
- What has not worked, on your part, so you don't take that approach again

It's also useful to record dates and times, along with detailed notes about what you're observing and what the student is exhibiting and experiencing (see Disclaimer 7.2).

Disclaimer 7.2

> Unless you are a child psychologist, you are not qualified to diagnose students with any disabilities or mental health conditions.

Avoid using stereotypes to pathologize students. Too often, teachers with poor classroom management determine that students have attention-deficit/hyperactivity disorder (ADHD) or another neurodivergence. Check your biases and go back to the drawing board. A child exhibiting chronic disruptions in the classroom is a child first—a whole human being who doesn't need another human being to decide that they are unworthy and a problem.

Major disruptions are usually onetime instances that might include fighting, injury to someone, a fire or chemical accident, or destruction of property. It is important you know who the point of contact is in your school, should you experience a major disruption. As a teacher, you have the discretion to determine how major it is. This is not the time to be petty. If a student whom you do not have a positive relationship with breaks a pencil that belongs to the class, it's not a major disruption, and it does not require external communication even though it involved destruction of school or classroom property. While responding in a petty manner might feel good in the moment, it will only harm your goals of having a positive classroom community. And, whether you realize it, other students are watching how you dehumanize others. Some are learning to mimic it, and others are just learning not to trust you.

Professionalism in CRCM means having studied student individualized education plan (IEPs) and 504 Plans ahead of crisis, ideally before the start of school year. It is vital that you know your school's emergency policies and exits, and effective ways to contact administrators in the case of an emergency. In all cases, remain levelheaded, and don't forget to attend to students who are not involved in the crisis. Keeping them engaged or giving them a sense of direction regarding how to function is as important as de-escalating the crisis, lest you leave room for another to spring up.

Reflection

Read through the scenarios in Activity 7.4 as a classroom teacher. Based on what you know and understand about CRCM, reflect on how you might have responded in each scenario. Would you have responded differently? What might you consider?

Activity 7.4 Reflection Scenarios

Belén is from Ecuador, bilingual, and from a low-income family. Belén is a student with ADHD who knows how to build intricate LEGO sets and draw pictures. She makes other people laugh with her jokes. Belén is talkative, so she struggles with social isolation. Belén lives with her aunt, uncle, and four cousins.
It is a Thursday morning, and I have just asked my 24 kindergarteners to clean up their centers and go back to their seats. I notice that quite a few have finished early, including Belén. She usually does. A few of them start returning to their tables, and I say, "I like how the green table is showing me they are ready." Some students who had not started cleaning up begin to put away their materials, and I continue with my positive reinforcement. "I like how the blue table is showing me they are ready. . . oh, thank you, yellow table, for following directions." I move toward Belén and say, "Belén, I already asked everyone to clean up and go back to their seat." She rolls her eyes, and I say a little louder, "Do not roll your eyes at me, that is disrespectful. I told you to clean up and go back to your seat." I take the game pieces from her hands, and she is quick to turn around. She grunts in frustration and stomps her feet all the way to her individual desk. Her desk is slightly away from the other tables because she is always telling other kids to shut up or poking them. I continue with the last of my positive reinforcement—"Thank you, pink table, for cleaning up like I asked"—and I look over at Belén,

who has her head down on the desk, her arms covering her head. I decide to let Belén calm down, and I move closer to the other tables so I can get them started on the next activity. I ask my students to take out a pencil and their writing journal. In hearing the word "writing," Belén starts complaining: "UGH, I hate writing. I am not doing it." I ignore Belén's outburst, especially because she is one of the smartest kids in the class, and I know it is not hard at all for her. I tell the students, "I want you to try your best to ignore Belén, I know she is distracting right now, but go ahead and turn and talk to a partner about what you are going to do this weekend." Belén says loudly, "I am not doing this work," and she runs out of the classroom. I go to my phone like I normally do, to let the front office know I need assistance because Belén has run away again.

Michael is a White student from a low-income household. Although presenting male, Michael prefers to use the pronouns they/them. Michael receives speech services twice a week during the school year. Michael knows about dirt bikes, ATVs, and video games, and tends to enjoy active learning. Michael lives with their mom and younger sister but stays with their grandma after school to help in the family store.

"Good morning Michael," I say. I see them look up at me, smiling as they put away their bookbag in the closet. My third graders file in for the day and finish up their morning work—even Michael, which surprises me. I give Michael a big hug and say, "I am proud of you, coming in and doing your work. I know you can have a great day." I share with a classmate, "Isn't he doing a great job, Destiny?," and she gives him a high five. You see, all year Michael has been a great student, making As and Bs, really enjoying school overall. Since coming back from winter break, Michael has not been doing their work, their grades falling to Ds. I start the math lesson for the day, and I notice Michael not doing any of the worksheets I handed out—again. "Michael, I need you to get your pencil and follow along with us." Michael stares at me and leans back, slumped in their chair. I finish up the math example and ask the rest of my class to try the next three with a partner. "Make sure you are sharing with your partner how you are solving the problem." I pair up Michael with Destiny because she is patient and encouraging, and those two have always gotten along. "Destiny, why don't you ask him the first question." Michael refuses to talk to her. "Michael, just go to the back table, you are going to have to work by yourself." Michael takes their work, throws it across the back table, and puts their head down on the desk. As the other students are working, I head to the back table and try to have a talk with Michael. "Michael, what is wrong? You had a great morning so far, don't ruin it." Michael moves away from me and pushes their papers to the floor. "Fine," I say. "I don't know what else to do with you. If you don't do your work, you'll have silent lunch and do it then."

Zakiyah is a Black student from a middle-income family. Zakiyah has an IEP for reading, primarily for comprehension. Zakiyah knows about local artists who often paint murals on bricks throughout the town, and she follows them on Instagram. She makes videos on TikTok, mainly dances and drawings. She lived in New York with her family but moved when her dad got a new job. They are currently living with a family friend.

"I made you a card, are you going to hang it up?" Zakiyah hands me a drawing. "Of course, you know I will—you are so good at drawing, thank you." I give her a big smile and go to my desk to hang up her picture next to all the artwork my fourth graders have been making me lately. My kids said their goal is to cover the entire wall with their artwork by the end of the year. Zakiyah joined our class in February, about 2 months ago, and gladly joined in this challenge. "Your picture is ugly," Mariah whispers as Zakiyah walks back to her seat. "What did you say? Do something. Do something," Zakiyah says, stepping closer to Mariah. Mariah mumbles under her breath, shaking her head and not looking up from her desk. I step between them and say quietly, "Zakiyah, go back to your seat and we'll talk about it in a minute." She says, "No" and flips her desk over. The contents of her desk spill all over the floor, and the class is silent, looking at me. "Zakiyah, I need you to pick up what is in your desk and have a seat. We can talk about it in a minute." She goes over to her cubby and starts packing up her bookbag. "I'm leaving this stupid school." I turn to give the class some directions: "Why don't you take out your classwork folder, and work on anything you need to finish up this week while I talk to Zakiyah and then Mariah, we need to talk too." The students pull out their folders and I say, "Zakiyah, you do not have to leave, we would miss you if you did." She slings her bookbag over her shoulder, goes to the door, and announces to the class, "Later losers," and walks out.

Conclusion

At the beginning of the chapter, you read a series of ideas and decided if you agreed or disagreed with them. It is our hope that we've given you a better vision of what a CRCM looks like and sounds like so that you might be empowered to try it. Take a few minutes to reread the series of ideas in Activity 7.1 and decide if you still agree or disagree. This activity, called an anticipation guide, is a strategy for engaging learners. You may not have realized it at the time, but at the beginning of the chapter, you recalled your own prior knowledge and then perhaps were curious as to which statements aligned with CRCM; this drew your attention to those aspects of the chapter. In making corrections to those you agreed and disagreed with, you have strengthened your knowledge through a stronger connection to your prior knowledge and long-term memory.

Remember, to build a caring classroom community, teachers must humanize students and allow them to have a sense of belonging in the classroom. In addition, procedures and clear expectations are more effective than rules and consequences. Finally, to use CRCM strategies, teachers must embrace disruptive students, become observant, and use engagement as a primary tool for learning.

Reference

Metropolitan Center for Urban Education. (2008, October). *Culturally responsive classroom management strategies*. https://www.asdn.org/wp-content/uploads/Culturally-Responsive-Classroom-Mgmt-Strat2.pdf

PART III

CONTENT AREAS

EIGHT

Math with Academic Rigor & Cultural Competency

Montana Smithey, Sam Rhodes and Alesia Mickle Moldavan

TAKE A MOMENT AND THINK back to when you were a student in a mathematics classroom. What do you hear and see? What are you and others doing? As you revisit the small details, what emotions do you feel? As you're thinking, circle the feeling, and fill in the blank (Activity 8.1).

Activity 8.1 Reflection

- Empowered
- Bored
- Humiliated
- Helpless
- Excited
- Anxious
- Other feelings:______________________________

What makes me feel these emotions and/or ideas about myself?__________

____

How do I think those around me feel?______________________

____

As you reflect on your past experiences, you might imagine a mathematics classroom with students quietly copying down formulas and procedures as the teacher furiously writes on the board. Even now, you may recall the anxiety of trying to keep up or waiting for the teacher to tell you whether you got the right answer. These experiences may have left you wondering if you belonged in the mathematics classroom at all—feelings that cause some people to wish to remain as invisible as possible in mathematics classes. On the other hand, maybe you thrived in that environment. You were good at taking notes and conforming to the cultural norms of school, so you felt successful as a mathematics student. It could very well be that you never experienced this kind of mathematics classroom. Maybe you recall a space that valued your unique ways of solving problems and a classroom that gave you the chance to share your thinking with others. In this classroom, you learned as much from your peers as you did from the teacher, and your personal identity, background, and experiences were tools that you could use to better understand the mathematics you were learning. Or perhaps you recall a mix of these classrooms over time, with experiences varying depending on where you lived, what grade you were in, or the kind of mathematics you were learning.

We ask these questions because taking the time to reflect on your feelings and experiences around learning mathematics is important, especially for those who teach mathematics. It is through reflection that you can begin to take ownership of how you view yourself and others as problem solvers and people who can do mathematics. It is through reflection that you can think about your role in teaching mathematics and what kinds of experiences you'll create for your students—including communicating what mathematics is, who it is for, and how we can use it to better understand culture and community. As we reflect on our mathematical stories, challenges, and privilege, we can start to explore what it means to reimagine mathematics instruction through the context of culturally relevant pedagogy (CRP).

In this chapter and the next, we will unpack what it looks like to teach and learn mathematics in ways that promote CRP and allow students to develop positive mathematical identities. A mathematical identity has to do with the way we see ourselves doing mathematics. It includes the beliefs, values, and attitudes we have as we learn mathematics, as well as the role that such identities play in empowering individuals to use mathematics to understand and challenge the world around them. We also want to highlight the dominant views that continue to perpetuate false narratives about what mathematics is and who it is for. The primary goal of this chapter is to have you reflect on your own experiences learning mathematics, consider the experiences of others, and think about what all this has to do with teaching mathematics as it relates to CRP. The journey is not an easy one; more than likely, you have had both positive and negative experiences. However, when we understand our personal experiences and identities with mathematics, we can become the transformative teachers that we want to be.

Another goal of this chapter is to acknowledge the pitfalls and traumas often associated with learning in settings in which little consideration is given to what students bring to the classroom. Our aim is to give you the tools necessary to get to know your students in ways you might not have considered before, while creating mathematics classrooms that allow students to bring their full selves (e.g., race, ethnicity, class, gender, sexual orientation, ability, immigration status) into the learning space. Knowing your students' full selves and mathematical identities will allow you to use what students already know and understand to disrupt a prepackaged curriculum that caters to the dominant group. By the end of this chapter, you'll have a solid foundation from which to continue your journey through Chapter 9, which focuses on developing critical consciousness through critical mathematical literacy and CRP. Our overarching goal across both chapters is to highlight how we can leverage CRP to invite new possibilities for mathematics teaching and learning.

Before we begin, it's important to address the purpose of including two chapters focused on mathematics in this book. More than likely, you're taking one or more classes where you feel like a math student again. These classes will build your understanding of mathematics across grade levels and your understanding of major concepts—*what* you'll be teaching students in your classroom. You're also likely to take a class on methods for teaching, or *how* to teach mathematics to students. Many classes may touch on both content and methods for teaching mathematics because they are equally important to know as a teacher. Regardless of the specific focus of your course, these chapters will guide you in making connections to teaching mathematics in culturally responsive ways.

Positionality Statements

Throughout this chapter, we, the authors, will give personal accounts of our experiences in mathematics. These are intended to highlight our positionality in relation to our experiences in mathematical education.

Montana Smithey (she/her)

I am a blonde-haired, blue-eyed White American woman and use the pronouns she/her/hers. I was born and raised middle to lower class in Connecticut, and throughout school, most of my peers and teachers looked like me. I glean a lot of privileges from what people can see, and I have used these privileges to further improve my life, reaping the benefits of being in and a part of the dominant White culture. I am a first-generation college student who used my social capital assigned at birth and education received during childhood to move to North Carolina for college, despite becoming financially independent. This independence translated into experiencing marginalization from my peers based on class during college. Ever since, I have become skilled in masking financial insecurity from others and minimizing class differences to reduce accompanying biases. To expand on my identity, a woman in academia, a mathematics educator, and a caregiver, I find myself balancing gender role expectations inside and outside the workplace while concealing instances of uncertainty with the content in order to be seen as independent and competent.

Sam Rhodes (he/him)

I am a White heterosexual male and use the pronouns he/him/his. I was raised in an affluent suburb in the United States, and I have spent most of my life in the upper middle class. After graduate school, I moved to Vietnam, where I became conscious of both my privilege and the power of leveraging identities. Identifying myself as an American in one setting and masking that identity to identify as a teacher in another setting allowed me to wield social power in ways that privileged me. After I returned to the United States, I realized that I was not afforded the same privileges from those identities. I quickly began to identify myself as a "math teacher" and, later, as a "professor" instead of a "teacher," given the respect that mathematics and academia have in our society. However, I have often struggled with mathematics being used as a proxy for intelligence and have felt trapped in situations where I felt unable to bring my full self to the room. Consequently, I find myself keenly aware of the identities that students develop when engaging with mathematics and how these identities can serve to privilege or hinder their learning of mathematics.

Alesia Mickle Moldavan (she/her)

I present as a White and able-bodied cisgender woman. Although I derive privilege from these identities, I would be remiss to say these identities tell my whole story. I am a quarter Japanese, and I use the privilege of presenting and identifying as White to benefit from the White-dominant culture I was immersed in for most of my schooling experiences. While I found my family's blended cultural and racial identities to be interesting to explore and compare, challenges in navigating the blended barriers of racial identity and suppressing one race over another often made me wonder why I should distance myself from one culture. To add to my identity complexities, I present as able-bodied despite having been born with a chronic health condition. While I make every effort to assure others that my health challenges do not define my ability—if anything, they empower me with heightened determination and resilience to reach my goals—I know that presenting as able-bodied allows me to hide my "invisible disability" and dismiss associated biases.

We share these identities with you because recognizing the privileges we have influences how each of us functions in the world and approaches teaching mathematics—not only in the ways we connect and communicate with people, but also in how we process and respond to the world around us. What drives our work in equity, identity, and CRP is the need to contextualize who we are and what we bring to the classroom, both as teachers and as students. As teachers, we must be aware of our own biases and how such biases impact our decision-making in the classroom. For students to let down their guard so their minds can explore and learn, they must feel liberated from the biases and stereotypes that often mask their potential. To be transparent, as collective authors, we each come to this work with implicit and explicit biases. As you read this chapter and the one that follows, you might see some of these biases reflected in our writing as our own lenses contribute to our evolving understanding of CRP as it relates to mathematics instruction.

Key Terms:

- **Adaptive reasoning:** being able to logically explain, justify, and reflect on the process.

- **Conceptual understanding:** knowing the why behind what you're doing and how numbers relate to each other.
- **Mathematical identity:** the beliefs, values, and attitudes formed while learning and teaching mathematics.
- **Procedural fluency:** knowledge of when and how to use methods flexibly, accurately, and efficiently.
- **Productive disposition:** seeing mathematics as a sensemaking activity, as relevant, and as a tool to use in life.
- **Strategic competence:** knowing and being able to call on multiple strategies to solve a variety of problems.

Key Ideas:

1. ***To maintain academic rigor, teachers must understand their mathematical identities and how identity relates to understanding what it means to be proficient in mathematics.***
2. ***To promote cultural competence, teachers use students' funds of knowledge in making instructional decisions and to maintain a focus on students' mathematical thinking.***
3. ***To develop critical consciousness, teachers critique the curriculum provided in ways that uncover what and who is privileged, and what and who is suppressed in those materials.***

The Impact of Mathematical Identities

Before we dive into what it means to be proficient in mathematics and what academic rigor in the mathematics classroom looks like, it's important for you to unpack your mathematical identity. Why, you ask? Well, because you're coming to this book with experiences that have shaped how you view yourself in the mathematics classroom. You already have an idea of what mathematics is and what it looks like to be good at mathematics. We want to support you in reflecting on how those ideas were formed and what experiences have shaped how you view yourself in the mathematics classroom, or your mathematical identity. To start this journey, graph your experiences over time using the reflective activity that follows (Activity 8.2). You'll see that the x-axis (horizontal) represents your learning experiences from kindergarten to the present.

Montana: "I know what you might be thinking. If you are like me, it is hard to remember what happened two weeks ago, let alone in kindergarten." Not to worry, just estimate. If it's helpful, you can think in larger chunks of time, like K–2 and 3–5. Now look at the y-axis (vertical); it represents the degree to which your experiences with mathematics were positive or negative. The line you draw on the graph will represent at what time points you had positive or negative experiences. As an example, Figure 8.1 shows our experience with mathematics over time. We included lightning bolts and a sun signifying low or high points that we describe in this chapter.

Montana: "As an example, my graph, I generally recall happy times in the mathematics classroom until about third grade, when I remember specific negative experiences, so my graph would show a steady line from K–2 toward the top of the graph (positive) and then a sharp decline (negative) around 3rd grade." Now, start at the beginning of what you can recall, and draw a line to represent your experiences over time, both positive and negative.

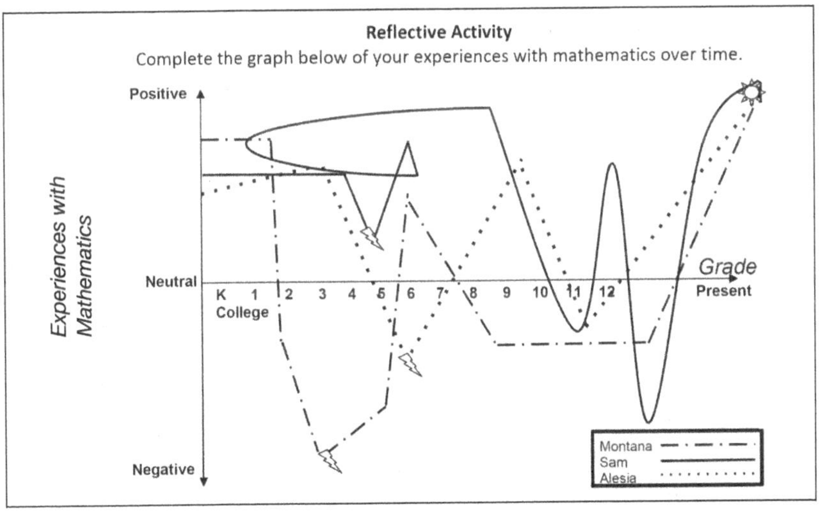

Figure 8.1. Reflective activity example.

Reflection on Mathematical Experiences

Take a few minutes to complete the graph based on your mathematical experiences (Activity 8.2). Then, reflect on your graph by considering the questions that follow.

Activity 8.2 Reflection on Mathematical Experiences Activity

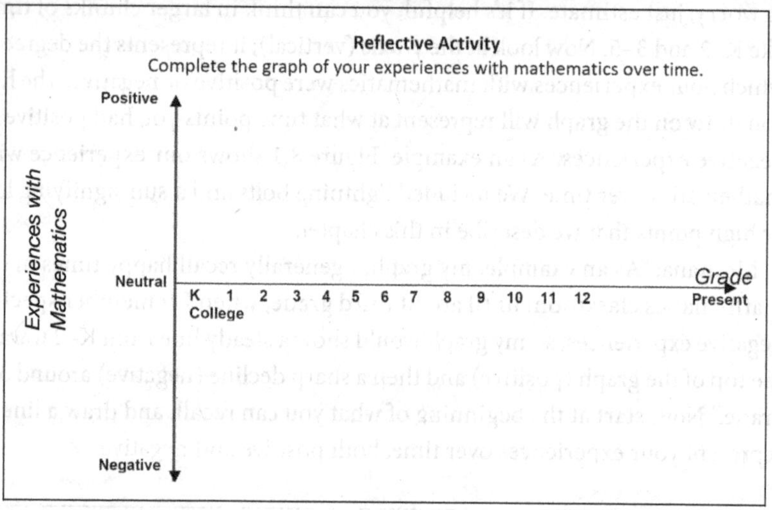

- Where are the high points on your graph?
- Where are the low points on your graph?
- What specific memories do you have of the teachers in mathematics classrooms who contributed to these high and low points?

More than likely, your low points align with times you felt helpless or dehumanized by teachers or peers when learning mathematics. Perhaps you found a "new" way to solve a problem and were told you couldn't use it. Maybe a teacher told you that you were "not a math person," or you attempted to share your mathematical understanding but were brushed off and dismissed.

Montana: "In third grade, I was made fun of by my peers for not knowing my mathematics facts, and my knowledge (or lack thereof) was on full public display. I remember my name was listed on the multiplication chart with a few of those silver foil stars under the 0s, 1s, and 2s facts. You know the kind—I used to love those stickers! The other kids did so well in mastering their facts and had many stars besides their names—and my peers would not let me forget it."

Alesia: "I recall how much fun I had in third grade learning multiplication and performing well on the problems of the day. But I also remember all the hours spent with a tutor during sixth grade while trying to learn how to perform measurement conversions when hospitalized for a pulmonary exacerbation that needed IV medications. Being ill and out of school made me feel like my mathematics abilities were being stifled and affected my confidence."

Sam: "In fifth grade, I recall lining up to go to specials while the 'good math students' got to stay behind to do mathematics enrichment. I longed to stay with them and do the fun math, but week after week, I lined up feeling frustrated, envious, and hurt."

Maybe you can relate to our stories, or perhaps you have a story of your own in which you were left feeling frustrated or dehumanized.

Let's look at the high points of your graph. It's likely that your high points reflect times when you experienced the true beauty and wonder of mathematics. Maybe you realized a connection between different concepts you learned, or you felt pride in having solved a challenging problem. You smile to yourself, recalling a time when you finally saw how mathematics related to your life, and how your lived experiences could be used to make sense of mathematical concepts and ideas.

Montana, Alesia, and Sam: "For instance, on our graphs, some of the highest points would be near the present day, when someone actually taught us why certain procedures actually worked, especially for fractions."

As we look over our collective experiences, we start to see that the thoughts and experiences we have had throughout our lives reinforce beliefs we have about ourselves; they also influence what we think mathematics is, who we think can do mathematics, and what it means to be proficient. For instance, you might be thinking, "I am definitely not a math person"—an identity that has become so rooted inside you that you make this statement as if it's a fact. To you, mathematics may be about being quick to find the right answers when you're given the formula. Or maybe you're thinking the opposite: "I love math because I've always been good at it. You give me a formula; I can follow it and understand it the first time. Plus, people usually come to me for help. I am definitely a math person!" We express this identity with pride and use it to show that we are smart—especially since our society, for some unknown reason, uses mathematics as the basis of assessing intelligence. This next activity encourages you to explore why others see themselves as "not a math person" or as "a math person" (see Activity 8.3). Take a few minutes to read through the instructions, conduct the interview, and reflect.

Activity 8.3 An Interview

> Find at least one person to interview who claims that they are "not a math person" or who has had notably negative experiences with mathematics. In addition, find at least one person to interview who claims to be "a math person" or has had notably positive experiences with mathematics. Take some time to develop a few interview questions for each person to better understand their experiences. What patterns do you notice? What do you wonder?

Regardless of which identity you have, we want to make sure we're clear that everyone can learn mathematics, and there's no such thing as a math person. Everyone can, and should, experience the beauty and wonder of mathematics. These statements might come as a shock to you, and you might not be on board with them yet (or, maybe you are, but you think they apply to everyone except yourself).

Montana & Alesia: "Trust us, some of us are still working on it too because for most of our lives, we struggled with mathematics, avoided it, and thought we weren't smart enough to be good at mathematics. Not to mention our family members constantly telling us how terrible they were at mathematics and that is where we got it from."

Guess what? Myth . . . busted! The temptation to believe these things is not surprising, given how our society perpetuates the myth that not everyone is capable of learning mathematics. However, research has continually shown that everyone can learn mathematics and achieve at high levels.

The fact of the matter is, CRP requires that we start with the belief that every student has brilliant thoughts and ideas. Every student has lived experiences that they can use to help them learn mathematics, and every student can thrive in mathematics classes. If we don't believe that about ourselves and those around us, we can't possibly believe it about our students. These facts about who can do mathematics don't invalidate the very real feelings and emotions that we may have around our own experiences with mathematics learning. Instead, they indicate that both positive and negative experiences shape our mathematical identities.

To help unpack how our experiences and identities are linked, let's use a metaphor as we analyze traditional mathematics instruction. Let's imagine that your goal throughout the school year is to design and create a piece of clothing. One day, the teacher says, "Today we will learn how to sew a zipper." The teacher models the technique, and then you practice on your own. You sew hundreds of zippers into fabric as the teacher circulates, pointing out mistakes. A few weeks later, after mastering zippers, you're told that the next goal is to learn how to sew on buttons. You've helped a family member sew buttons in the past, so you're excited that the class will be learning something that you already know how to do.

Unfortunately, your initial excitement is quickly replaced by dismay as your teacher tells you that the technique you learned at home is "wrong," and you must do it the way they are showing the class. Now reluctant, you watch passively as the teacher models the technique. When it's time to practice, you struggle to replicate the process. And to make things worse, you're working with different kinds of buttons that have varying numbers of holes, and it's difficult to adapt this technique to buttons with slightly different designs. After a while, you find yourself mindlessly repeating procedures without ever pausing to consider how the buttons or zippers look as part of the final product. You're not sure how these new techniques relate to experiences you have had outside of school, what their function is, or even what the larger piece of clothing is that you plan to make. Regardless, you're convinced that the style of the article of clothing that you are supposedly creating is not one that you'll ever want to wear, especially given the negative emotions and experiences you've had on the journey thus far.

This metaphor describes the experiences that many people have in traditional mathematics classes. So why does that matter? To truly understand and use mathematics in their lives, students need a purpose when learning it. Let's go back to the idea of buttons. Consider a single button. Without a purpose, a button is (mostly) useless. Maybe you have a drawer of forgotten buttons that you occasionally come across and consider throwing out, but you never know—you might eventually need it. Mathematics is the same. Not only is learning a formula without a purpose boring, but when the time comes to sew a button back on to an article of clothing, it's unlikely that the sewing technique you learned in school will perfectly align with the one needed to match the other buttons. In this way, teaching mathematics in ways that prioritize rote procedures over making connections to the lives and experiences of students results in static knowledge that students are often unable to use—even when it is needed in the future.

Imagine this scenario instead. Your teacher starts by asking what you want to create. Some students want to make jeans or dresses, others excitedly suggest coats or bags, and still others want to make an áo dài (a traditional Vietnamese garment worn for formal occasions)—all with very important reasons for their choices. The air is filled with students swapping stories about these items, and some have even modified pieces of clothing at home that they outgrew when they had a growth spurt. In this scenario, students can bring their interests, personal styles, and outside experiences to the sewing table. Learning how to sew zippers and buttons suddenly transforms from a rote activity to a magical part of the larger creation. Most important, as students look around at the beautiful items their peers create, they broaden their own understanding of the diverse uses of buttons and zippers. Learning mathematics can do the same: When we allow students to use their identities both to be creative and as tools to understand mathematics, classrooms transform into vibrant communities of student empowerment.

This brings us back to thinking more about what it means to be proficient in mathematics. We have spent some time unpacking our experiences in the mathematics classroom, learning about the experiences of others, and exploring our mathematical identities and how experiences and identities are connected. We want to highlight that often, what it means to be proficient in mathematics and what academic rigor looks like in the mathematics classroom are heavily influenced by those experiences and identities.

Montana: "Remember when I previously mentioned that I never really felt like a math person? I really thought being proficient in mathematics meant I had to be able to know my math facts quickly, know the formula, and correctly solve the problem each time—something we call procedural fluency. Unfortunately, that is how I defined proficiency in my classroom and how I measured academic rigor. Makes me cringe to this day—those sweet kids in my classes working in their workbooks filled with lists of equations to solve, gah! Little did I know, that was one part of being proficient in mathematics."

According to the National Research Council (2001), mathematical proficiency also includes conceptual understanding (knowing the why behind what you're doing and how numbers relate to each other); adaptive reasoning (being able to logically explain, justify, and reflect on the process); strategic competence (knowing and being able to call on multiple strategies to solve a variety of problems); and productive disposition (seeing mathematics as a sensemaking activity, as relevant, and as a tool to use in life). We know that's a lot to take in—basically, mathematics is so much more than just the right answers. It isn't "new math," contrary to messages from social media and in movies or television shows we watch. You may have seen the Disney movies *The Incredibles*. In the second movie is a scene where Mr. Incredible has to help Dash with his mathematics homework. Mr. Incredible shouts, "I don't know that way. Why would they change math? Math is math!" Well, this math has always been here, but many aspects of mathematics—like strategies that emphasize conceptual understanding before the formula—have been minimized. So, if you ever felt like mathematics was hard or somewhat disconnected, you were right! You were likely being shown just a handful of pieces of a much larger, finished puzzle, without any understanding of how those pieces got there in the first place. Our goal now is helping all students see the bigger picture. However, we can't work to re-elevate the four missing strands of mathematics proficiency without first understanding that we all come to the table with different experiences that have shaped our mathematical identities. Our identities influence what we think being proficient in mathematics means, how we view ourselves, and how we view our students. So, as we continue to work through our identities together, we hope you'll keep an open mind and take time to reflect along the way.

Incorporating a Student's Funds of Knowledge to Promote Mathematical Thinking

Students learn best when they connect new information to what they already know and understand. Students can commit that formal knowledge to long-term memory when they integrate the concepts into already established knowledge.

Montana: "I am terrible at keeping plants alive, and for a while, I gave it up completely. Recently, I thought you know, plants make me happy, so this time, I will try learning more along the way. I started with what I already knew about plants: They need water. I get it—that's pretty basic. Nonetheless, my plants suffer because I forget to water them. So, this time, I started with plants I could see out my window as a reminder—water me. But some plants still had trouble. I paid attention to the smaller details, like what the leaves looked like and what the soil felt like between watering. I read about the different plants via Google and watched YouTube videos. Slowly I've been building this knowledge base on how to keep my plants alive. Each time I get a new plant,

I can use what I already know to help it thrive while I continue to learn about the plant." Isn't connecting new information to what we already know so we remember it something we all need to do? Students are no different.

When it comes to the mathematics classroom, there is a history of separating context (the world around us) and mathematics. Students generally learn skills in isolation or privilege particular methods over others because those methods are used by the dominant group (Civil, 2016). For example, let's say a fourth-grade teacher is teaching adding and subtracting fractions with like denominators ($\frac{5}{5} - \frac{3}{5} =$ ___) and unlike denominators ($\frac{4}{10} + \frac{1}{5} =$ ___). Traditionally, the lesson would include the teacher modeling how to solve the equation step-by-step. Then, the teacher would give students a long list of practice problems meant to increase proficiency in solving those equations through repetition. The following week, a mixture of fraction equations would be given, and students would begin confusing formulas.

What if this teacher had taught the same skills but used contexts that were familiar to students? Students could then draw on their Funds of Knowledge (FOK) as they made sense of the problem. The result could be that students would understand when and why to use certain formulas, apply them to other situations, and remember these ideas long-term. It's important to note that the context chosen does matter. Let's say that this fourth-grade teacher considered students' FOK: Many students had mentioned participating in family meals, and the teacher had overheard them talking about some of their favorite traditional dishes—the majority of which were popular Mexican dishes.

Table 8.1. Problem Sets

Examples of a Problem Set without Context	Example of a Problem Set with Context
1 $\frac{1}{2} + \frac{2}{3} =$ 2. $\frac{9}{12} + \frac{2}{12} =$ 3. $\frac{5}{6} - \frac{3}{4} =$ 4. $\frac{3}{5} + \frac{3}{8} =$ 5. $\frac{7}{8} - \frac{1}{3} =$ 6. $\frac{12}{12} - \frac{11}{12} =$ 7. $\frac{4}{10} + \frac{1}{5} =$ 8. $\frac{1}{3} + \frac{1}{2} =$	1. On Saturday, Sandra went to Abuela's house for breakfast to eat one of her favorite meals, chilaquiles. Abuela is making chilaquiles, and the recipe requires ½ cup salsa. After adding salsa to the saucepan, she realizes that she accidentally used the ⅓ measuring cup. How much more salsa does Abuela need to add? 2. On the Día de la Candelaria, Diego went to their cousin's house to eat tamales for lunch. Diego was asked to put more filling onto the corn husks because there was so much filling left over. If there was already ⅓ of a tablespoon on each corn husk and Diego adds ½ of a tablespoon to each one, how many tablespoons are on each husk now? 3. After eating the tamales, Diego's Tía said they were the best tamales she had ever eaten and wanted to know how the recipes were different. Typically, Tía uses ¾ tablespoon of filling on each corn husk. How much more filling did Diego use than Tía?

In Table 8.1, you can see that students are working on the same skill of adding and subtracting fractions with like and unlike denominators. The first problem set focuses on students recalling the steps in solving the equations, whereas the second problem set allows students to use what they know about family meals and the dishes they love to understand the skill.

Montana: "I wanted to share that it was not easy for me to come up with the examples [in Table 8.1]. I had to research a culture different from my own, write a problem, make sure the problem was authentic to the recipe (i.e., uses salsa as opposed to flour), all while keeping in mind the fractions I wanted to use to meet a content goal."

We're not here to say that doing this work is easy—what we are saying is that it matters. Do you have to do these kinds of problems all the time? No, but there should be a balance, and students should readily see themselves and have the chance to use what they know to solve problems. Ultimately, when we detach contexts from mathematics, we're not only preventing students from using what they already know to make sense of new ideas, but also asking students to set aside their experiences and park their identities at the door. As a result, a teacher might emphasize just how useful mathematics is, but the message that students hear is that mathematics is not something they use in everyday life to explore the world around them—much less enact change in their communities (Matthews et al., 2022). In the next chapter, these ideas will be further explained.

We challenge you to ask a few students around you, "How do you use math in your life?" Often when we ask students this question, they answer, "When I do my homework," or "I do not know, at school?" Occasionally, students share times when they bought items at the grocery store. However, many students may not be able to clearly see the connections between their everyday lives and the mathematics they learn. For them, mathematics is confined to the classroom. To teach mathematics in ways that promote cultural competence, it is important to help students recognize the knowledge they already possess and how it can be used to *do* mathematics—and that mathematics and their lives are intertwined and inseparable. One simply does not make sense without the other. So how do we keep mathematics intertwined with contexts in relevant ways for the benefit of student learning? Well, we as teachers might select contexts that we believe are relevant to students, but sometimes what we think is a meaningful context to students is narrowed by our own lived experiences and identities. Thus, teachers should draw on students' FOK to influence their selection of meaningful contexts. Sounds like a tall order—so what does this look like in practice?

First, teachers need to find a way to collect students' FOK, such as by talking to students or completing a chart like described in other chapters (see Appendix). When thinking about what you want to ask students and while listening to them, consider what assumptions and biases you have about the student or their community that are affirmed or disrupted through this experience.

Activity 8.4 Funds of Knowledge: Interviewing a Student

Select a student who is different from you in at least one sociocultural way (e.g., race, gender, religion, socio-economic status, home language). Interview that student to collect their funds of knowledge and better understand their dispositions toward mathematics, places in their community, and the mathematical knowledge they already have (Foote et al., 2015).

Before the interview write at least three questions to ask the student in each of the following categories:

Prior experiences (in mathematics class, feelings about mathematics)

1)

2)

3)

Interests and places (at-home activities, places in their community)

1)

2)

3)

Strengths/curiosity (mathematics they know or want to know)

1)

2)

3)

Talk with the student for approximately 15–20 minutes using the written questions and ask follow-up questions based on the student's responses. Tip: If your student provides general or brief responses, try using the following prompts to show that you value their responses, and encourage elaboration: *Interesting, can you tell me more about that? Sounds fun, can you tell me about a time you went there? What does that look like?* Finally, reflect on your answers to these questions:

What assumptions and/or biases did I have about the student or their community that were disrupted through this experience?

____

____

____

How could I use this information from the student in an upcoming or future mathematics lesson? (If possible, connect to a specific standard or unit.)

____

____

____

Imagine the power in getting to know each of the students you teach in this way—what a vast amount of knowledge you could build on! You would learn about not only what they *do* know, but also the ways in which they exist in their communities. More than likely, you're thinking, how would I have time to engage with my students one-on-one for 20–30 minutes for these interviews? We understand—we've been there. The fast-paced nature of the day is intense. However, don't throw in the towel just yet—here are a few ideas. (1) Eat lunch with two to four students at a time and have the questions nearby to draw on to have conversations, especially during the first few weeks of school. (2) Create a chart of the questions on a clipboard and choose one question a week to be intentional about asking every student in the class at some point that week. (3) Use a platform or tool, like Flip or Google Forms, to collect information from students throughout the year. You can also send home a paper survey asking families about things they like to do or places they like to go in the surrounding community.

Okay, so you've gathered students' FOK in your class. Now what? How do you teach mathematics in a way that reflects what you've learned? In Activity 8.5, you'll collect images that you can use to teach mathematics and those students can use to make connections to mathematics content.

Activity 8.5 Interview Reflection

Collect images of places, activities, and strengths that students mention in their interviews to create a slideshow that you can use during mathematics lessons.

In Activity 8.6, you'll create a list based on your interaction with a student or group of students.

Activity 8.6 Interactions

What do I know about my students and their community? *(e.g., landmarks, locations, events, home activities, objects, things to do)*	**How might my students use what they know and are familiar with to learn mathematics?**

1) Use images collected in Activity 8.5 (Collect images of landmarks, places, events, home activities, objects, and things to do). Be sure to include images that are recognizable to students.
2) Create a slideshow that includes (a) the photo with a caption of its location, (b) the name of the skill or specific mathematics concept and its related standard, and (c) a question that could be posed to students to begin a conversation about the image. We used a place in our town that many people are familiar with.
3) Reflect: How might you include student voices in storytelling as part of the lesson?

____

____

____

Select a student who is different from you in at least one sociocultural way (e.g., race, gender, religion, socio-economic status, home language). Interview that student to collect their funds of knowledge and better understand their dispositions toward mathematics, places in their community, and the mathematical knowledge they already have (Foote et al., 2015).

Figure 8.2. Interview a Student's Funds of Knowledge.

So far, you've had a chance not only to gather students' FOK but also to collect images that are relevant and exciting to students (and ready for you to use in your lessons for the entire school year). Another part of promoting cultural competence is the ability to highlight student ideas and use their ideas to teach. In mathematics education, we call this *responsive teaching*. This approach to teaching centers student thinking in ways that consider the academic content within their ideas, and how those ideas are connected; the teacher then determines what ideas to pursue (Robertson et al., 2016). Teaching in this way certainly isn't easy. Teachers hold mathematics content in their minds, actively listen to what students are saying and doing, think through what students might understand (or not), and then decide what strategies or ideas to take up. We often see teachers responding to students' questions or comments, but a lot of that in-the-moment decision-making is hidden, inside teachers' minds (Jacobs et al., 2010). It's like putting on a pair of glasses. While we're circulating the room, looking at student work and making observations, we're wearing our own unique pair of glasses. These glasses serve as a filter through which we notice student thinking and decide how to respond. These ideas belong to children of all backgrounds, and it is important to recognize that the filter matters in how students are seen in our classrooms (Louie et al., 2021).

To develop critical consciousness, teachers critique the curriculum provided in ways that uncover what and who is privileged, and what and who is suppressed in those materials.

As teachers, we're often handed a mathematics curriculum the moment we walk into a classroom. Sometimes this curriculum is a set of standards or a pacing guide. Other times, we're given a textbook, workbooks, online resources, or even a script of what to say and when to say it. In any of these cases, we're being given a set of materials that guide what we're supposed to teach to students. This is known as the written curriculum, but a variety of other curricula also exist in the classroom, such as the taught curriculum (what a teacher actually teaches), the assessed curriculum (the part of a curriculum that is actually assessed), and the hidden curriculum (the norms, expectations, and values that are conveyed within the written curriculum), to name just a few.

However, just as we started this chapter with positionality statements to acknowledge that our perspectives and what we write are shaped by our own biases and identities, it is also important to understand that all curricula are shaped by the biases, perspectives, and identities of the authors and the teachers who enact them—not to mention, some publishers of written curricula gear their content toward states because the profits are higher. We want to emphasize that it is imperative that teachers remain cognizant of who is privileged and suppressed by each system and its curricula—both visible and hidden.

For instance, a curriculum that emphasizes fact drills privileges students who can quickly memorize and recall facts, even if they don't understand them, and it suppresses students who want to think deeply about mathematics.

Sam: "When I asked my son Brayden, who loves money, what 3 x 23 was, he responded by saying, 'Well, I know that 3 quarters would make 75 cents and I need to then subtract 2, three times, so that is 73 . . . 71 . . . 69. The answer is 69.' You might be thinking, 'That is really neat thinking!' But it's important to realize that by drawing on his personal experiences with money to solve the problem and think deeply about mathematics, Brayden solved the problem much more slowly than someone who simply memorized that math fact. Consequently, a system that emphasizes math facts likely never would have given Brayden the opportunity to share his thinking and may have even caused him to feel dehumanized by calling him 'slow.'"

Here's another example. Lessons that include statistics are often left for the end of the year—you know, if there's time—not to mention that the pinnacle of high school mathematics is calculus, not statistics. Yet, as will be discussed in Chapter 9, understanding data and statistics is essential in developing and leveraging critical consciousness to advocate for oneself and the community. So why isn't statistics given a more central role in the curriculum, and which groups of people are given access to learning and making sense of statistics? It brings us back to that question of who is privileged and who is suppressed in these situations.

Finally, consider that, despite the enormous contributions that many cultures have made to our understanding of mathematics—for example, Chinese, Greeks, Indians, Indigenous groups—they are rarely mentioned in our books or classes. While studying the history of mathematics and acknowledging current and past mathematicians from myriad cultures is certainly a start, the larger picture involves understanding that diversity of thought has given us many ways to make sense of and solve even seemingly basic problems. Did you know, for instance, that more than a dozen unique subtraction formulas can be found throughout history? So why is it that some curricula only allow students to solve subtraction problems using the method we all know (stacking the numbers and subtracting them using the formula)?

Regardless of which type you're talking about—visible or hidden—curriculum is value-laden, and it privileges some students or knowledge by suppressing others. The curriculum is an essential part of our working toward teaching in culturally responsive ways to critically analyze our teaching and curriculum. As teachers, we need to ask ourselves these questions: Who or what is being privileged by this curriculum? Who is being suppressed, ignored, or dehumanized by this curriculum? What are the ways I can work toward modifying or supplementing this curriculum to ensure that I meet the needs of every student in equitable ways?

Conclusion

The journey toward teaching mathematics in culturally responsive ways is far from over. However, we have found that teachers can make meaningful progress toward CRP by attending to three key ideas: academic rigor, cultural competence, and critical consciousness. In mathematics, these key ideas work together to help students develop subject competencies and productive identities. To maintain academic rigor, teachers must understand their mathematical identities and how identity relates to understanding what it means to be proficient in mathematics. To promote cultural competence, teachers use students' FOK in making instructional decisions and to maintain a focus on students' mathematical thinking. Finally, to develop critical consciousness, teachers must critique the curriculum provided in ways that uncover what and who is privileged, and what and who is suppressed in those materials.

References

Civil, M. (2016). STEM learning research through a Funds of Knowledge lens. *Cultural Studies of Science Education, 11*(1), 41–59.

Foote, M. Q., Roth McDuffie, A., Aguirre, J., Turner, E. E., Drake, C., & Bartell, T. G. (2015). Mathematics learning case study module. In C. Drake, J. Aguirre, T. G. Bartell, M. Q. Foote, A. Roth McDuffie, & E. E. Turner (Eds.), *TEACH Math learning modules for K-8 mathematics methods courses*. Teachers Empowered to Advance Change in Mathematics Project.

Jacobs, V. R., Lamb, L. L., & Philipp, R. A. (2010). Professional noticing of children's mathematical thinking. *Journal for Research in Mathematics Education, 41*(2), 169–202.

Louie, N., Adiredja, A. P., & Jessup, N. (2021). Teacher noticing from a sociopolitical perspective: The FAIR framework for anti-deficit noticing. *ZDM – Mathematics Education, 53*(1), 95–107.

Matthews, L. E., Jones, S. M., & Parker, Y. A. (2022). *Engaging in culturally relevant math tasks: Fostering hope in the elementary classroom*. Corwin.

National Research Council & Mathematics Learning Study Committee. (2001). *Adding it up: Helping children learn mathematics*. National Academies Press.

Robertson, A. D., Atkins, L. J., Levin, D. M., & Richards J. (2016). What is responsive teaching? In A. D. Robertson, R. Scherr, & D. Hammer (Eds.), *Responsive teaching in science and mathematics* (pp. 1–35). Routledge.

NINE

Math with Critical Consciousness

Sam Rhodes, Alesia Mickle Moldavan and Montana Smithey

Activity 9.1: Reflection

Take a moment to think of a time when you used mathematics to understand the world around you. What type of mathematics was used? How did your use of mathematics inform the way you or others around you made sense of a situation? Record your thoughts.

____

____

____

In considering this prompt, you may have thought about shopping at the grocery store, taking out a loan, or tackling a home project. All these scenarios are real world and certainly involve using mathematics. Or perhaps you recalled the countless times when students have interrupted lessons to ask, "When am I ever going to use this in life?" It's also important to consider why students often come to see mathematics as foreign and disconnected from their lives despite its real-world applications (such as grocery stores, loans, and home projects). When mathematics is only presented in ways that are disconnected from students' daily lives and lived experiences, it's no wonder students fail to see how and why mathematics matters.

In Chapter 8, you were asked to consider your own mathematics experiences and identity. You learned about the importance of working to cultivate positive mathematical identities within yourself and your students. You also considered ways to recognize the gifts and assets that each student brings to the mathematics classroom.

This chapter builds from these ideas to explore how student thinking and Funds of Knowledge can build connections for moving beyond the individual and toward a bigger picture—one in which the cultural nature of knowing and doing mathematics can be explored. We will examine instructional practices that foreground student thinking and prioritize the development of deeper conceptual understandings of mathematics. Finally, we will consider how we use mathematics, and for what purpose—an interrogation known as *critical mathematical literacy* (Frankenstein, 1990). Taken together, these practices can support students in using mathematics as a tool to develop critical consciousness, with the aim of better understanding issues of social justice and critiquing the world around them.

Positionality Statements

As with Chapter 8, we know that our positionality impacts the lens we bring to the mathematics classroom and how we address critical issues in mathematics education. Thus, we would be remiss if we did not expand our positionality statements from the last chapter to explicitly address how our positionalities impact this chapter. All three of us can specifically recall events in our lives that have shaped the way we view inquiry-based learning, social justice, and critical consciousness.

Sam Rhodes (he/him)

After spending a summer living and volunteering in Camden, New Jersey, I saw the lasting impact of those in power taking advantage of the city by using it to house a water treatment facility. This experience caused me to be sensitive to how power structures are used to advantage or disadvantage communities.

Alesia Mickle Moldavan (she/her)

My experiences tutoring students in Boys and Girls Clubs across Atlanta and Athens, Georgia, as well as working with students in inner-city schools in New York City, made me reflect on the various ways that cultural, social, and political influences have impacted student access to high-quality mathematics instruction and the resources needed for students to build their critical mathematical literacy skills. Countless times, I witnessed discriminatory social conditions and practices in school and community settings that privileged some students over others, leaving teachers to navigate the political powers that controlled mathematics learning during experiences both in and out of school. I continue to leverage these experiences to refine my own critical consciousness to make sense of mathematics, including how mathematics can be used to empower agency and advocacy.

Montana Smithey (she/her)

As a mother of four children, I have become increasingly conscious of who has access to childcare, sports, camps, and other experiences—particularly STEM activities—that enrich students' education. In many cases, the costs associated with these activities, particularly STEM camps, limit the feasibility of children participating, particularly those from families with more than one child. My personal experiences with these challenges have made me reflect on, and be sensitive to, how our society creates inequitable learning opportunities for our children based on class. These experiences emphasize our independent yet collective shifts toward developing critical consciousness to not only use mathematics to understand the world, but also inspire individuals to challenge injustices that inherently influence mathematics education.

Key Terms:

- **Critical consciousness:** in-depth understanding of the world due to exposure of social, political, and economic definitions.
- **Critical mathematical literacy:** understanding when to apply mathematical skills.
- **Inquiry-based learning:** a method that engages the students into making real-world connections through high-level questions.
- **Launch-explore-discuss model:** a learning cycle in which students are given opportunities to use current knowledge, to make sense of mathematical ideas and concepts, before being explicitly taught related formulas and procedures.

Key Ideas:

1. ***To maintain academic rigor, teachers must develop students' conceptual understanding of mathematics and use inquiry-based learning to inform tasks that are accessible to every student.***
2. ***To promote cultural competence, teachers must use students' Funds of Knowledge to guide instructional decisions and maintain a focus on students' mathematical thinking.***
3. ***To develop critical consciousness, teachers and students must not only engage in tasks that use mathematics as a tool to better understand issues of social justice, but also view the subject to enact change in their communities.***

Academic Rigor with Conceptual Understanding and Inquiry-Based Learning

Have you ever asked yourself, or heard another teacher say, "I spent a lot of time on this math concept, but now, it is like my students have never heard of it!" Well, you're not alone. We've been there ourselves, wondering where we went wrong and why our instruction seemed to work for some students but not others. We all strive to help *every* student, and it can be very frustrating when we don't meet that standard.

In those moments, it's easy to blame anything and everything but our instruction. Over time, we may become so accustomed to students' forgetting things that we automatically build review days (or even review months) into our curriculum. Conversely, you may have heard the saying, "It's like learning to ride a bike—you never forget!" We wonder, then, why is learning mathematics assumed to be different from learning other skills in life, like riding a bike? While we don't want to discount the value of review, we do think it's important to consider how mathematics teaching and learning can be more like learning to ride a bike. In doing so, we ensure that we're teaching our students in ways that allow them to remember the mathematics concepts and apply their knowledge in the future.

Empathetic Considerations for Teaching Mathematics

To answer this question, let's start by thinking back on our own experiences with mathematics; doing so may provide us with clues as to how this disconnect happens. Many of us can likely recall times when our teachers filled boards with endless work examples. Those examples consisted of various procedures that we were expected to memorize and then reproduce without explaining how we solved them. In these instances, our problem-solving thought process was likely confined to recalling facts and procedures that we had learned. Such examples are known as *low cognitive demand* tasks (Smith & Stein, 2018).

Usually, low cognitive demand tasks follow low cognitive demand instruction, such as gradual release (i.e., "I do, we do, you do"). By its very nature, gradual release is set up with the assumption that students are not creators of mathematics but need the teacher to show them what to do. In other words, the student's job is not to think, analyze, or make connections between ideas. Rather, the model confines student thinking to replicating teacher thinking through rote processes. Within this model, students are generally discouraged from asking why formulas work, or from finding their own ways to solve problems. Instead, the focus is on memorization and how steps should be followed. We ourselves recall "learning" with this model and asking teachers "why" something worked, only to have our questions ignored or deflected, or, even worse, to be discouraged from asking questions in the future. We remember the frustration of taking a test and trying desperately to recall a procedure that we never fully understood, and we remember the anxiety of taking timed drill tests that focused exclusively on *procedural fluency*: the ability to recall a series of steps and mathematical rules quickly.

Procedural Fluency in the Classroom

In classrooms where procedural fluency is prioritized, students who can quickly memorize and reproduce solutions are often labeled as "math people," while those who want to think deeply about what they're doing and why may be labeled as "struggling learners" and relegated to lower-level tasks and classes. Such labels contribute to tracking and to the disproportionate number of students of color in remedial mathematics classes in comparison with

White students. Such education discourages students from thinking deeply about mathematics and privileges students based on their ability to retain information—and it is extremely difficult to memorize things that we don't understand and have no association with! Here's a quick exercise to demonstrate this point: Spend 1 minute memorizing the following sequence. Then, close the book and write down, in order, as many of the letters as you can remember.

JFMAMJJASONDSMTWTFS

How did you do? Chances are, unless you related the letters back to something you already knew or experienced, you struggled to write down more than 5 or 10 letters in the correct order. If I drew on your Funds of Knowledge (FOK), however, and told you that the first 12 letters could stand for the first letter of each month of the year, and the last seven letters could represent the first letter of the days of the week, you would likely be able to replicate the sequence perfectly.

Prioritizing procedural fluency is like being asked to memorize the sequence by repeating it over and over (and over). However, prioritizing conceptual understanding—knowing "the why" behind each of the recalled steps and the flexibility to use reasoning in mathematical problem solving (Rittle-Johnson et al., 2001)—is akin to drawing on your existing knowledge of months and days of the week. You understand why the letters appear in a particular order because you can relate to the information behind it.

To further illustrate the differences between procedural fluency and conceptual understanding, let's return to the bike analogy. It's certainly helpful to be told where the brakes are and how to use them, or how the pedals work. However, it would be incorrect to assume that most people can learn to ride a bike simply by being told what to do. Rather, you learn by drawing from your past experiences—like riding tricycles—and then combining that knowledge with both what you were told about brakes and pedals, and what you experienced trying for yourself. In other words, you were given some foundational information and then tasked with drawing from your FOK to give it a try.

When you were learning to ride a bike, you likely got on the bike and fell over at some point. However, rather than being ridiculed (or ridiculing yourself) for falling, you were likely told, "It's okay, just keep trying!" Each time you fell, you learned. Maybe you learned what happens when you lean too far to one side, or when you stop pedaling fast enough. From this, you developed an understanding of why it is important to maintain balance and speed. In other words, you learned from falling.

When you learn in this way, you develop understandings that don't just vanish if you spend a few weeks roller skating instead of riding your bike. Moreover, you're likely able to quickly transfer your understanding to riding another bike, even if that bike has different gears, is a different size, or has a different purpose (e.g., road bike vs. mountain bike) than the one you learned on. Thus, despite differences between the bikes, you can transfer what you learned from one bike to another.

The same principles apply to mathematics teaching and learning. When students conceptually understand mathematics, they not only retain knowledge over time, but also are able to transfer their knowledge to solve new problems and make connections between ideas. Throughout these last two chapters, we have been asking ourselves, how we can make sure we are teaching our students in ways that allow them to *remember* the mathematics concepts and apply their knowledge in the future. There's not a simple answer, but we can start with teaching in ways that prioritize conceptual understandings and that engage students in mathematics learning that is relevant, meaningful, and rigorous.

For example, consider a time when you explored mathematics and the reasoning for its use rather than focusing on how you engaged with each step. Do you recall the joy you might have felt when you made connections between mathematical ideas on your own or "discovered" a new way to solve a problem? When we see ourselves as creators of mathematics and develop an understanding of why we're engaged in certain procedures, we can create conceptual understanding. In other words, our diverse and creative thinking can be celebrated and used as a springboard to deeper understandings of mathematics.

To build conceptual understanding, it is imperative that teachers provide opportunities for students to engage in high-cognitive-demand tasks. Such tasks can be described as nonroutine and open, eliciting multiple entry points for students to engage with the content and make connections to other relevant knowledge. These tasks also require deep, multifaceted thinking that involves more cognitive effort. As a result, students are required to monitor their own thinking and draw conceptual connections, and this encourages rigorous explorations with mathematics content.

It can be challenging to find ways to teach through students' ideas and cultural assets to support their making sense of the mathematics to develop conceptual understanding. One way teachers can do this is by encouraging students to explore and exchange their own ideas while simultaneously asking students questions about their strategies before explaining key vocabulary and procedures. This type of student-led instruction is known as *inquiry-based learning.*

Launch-Explore-Discuss

As we aim to prepare teachers to create inquiry-based learning opportunities that are more closely aligned to promoting academic rigor, we have found the launch-explore-discuss (LED) model of instruction to be extremely useful (Lappan & Phillips, 2009). The goal of the LED model is to present a learning cycle where students are given opportunities to use what they already know and understand to make sense of mathematical ideas and concepts before being explicitly taught related formulas and procedures. The LED model, which has similarities to the 5E model explained in Chapter 10, suggests a three-phrase approach for instruction related to problem-solving.

Launch

Before the lesson, teachers select a problem, like the one shown in Table 9.1, that aligns with the mathematical goals of the lesson. The problem chosen should meet a few criteria: (1) It should be relatable to students or draw on students' FOK; (2) it should be rigorous to allow for students to think deeply about the mathematics; and (3) it should allow students to develop conceptual understanding of mathematics to ensure student participation. High-quality problems can also involve societal issues to help students develop their critical mathematical literacy. One point we want to stress is that the purpose of the launch phase is *not* to teach students how to solve the problem. Once you show students how to solve a problem, you have taken away their opportunity to problem solve for themselves. Instead, the goal is to ensure that every student understands the problem and the context.

Within this stage, students don't yet need to know how to solve the problem, but they should have a firm understanding of what the problem says. For example, within the context of the problem in Table 9.1, teachers might invite students to share stories about where they have compared or rounded numbers in the world around them. As students share their stories, teachers can ask other students if they can relate to their peers' experiences. This way, the entire class develops a better understanding of what the problem is asking. Moreover, such conversations create opportunities for the teacher to press for reasoning, using questions like, "How do you know that answer is too low/too high/just right?" By engaging in conversation about how students are thinking, the teacher can support them in making connections between their lived experiences and the problem, turning these experiences into powerful problem-solving tools.

Explore

Once students have a strong understanding of what the task involves, they need the opportunity to think critically as they solve the problem any way they choose. Within this exploration phase, students can work independently, in pairs, or in small groups. Regardless of the context, students take on the mathematical work for themselves and are provided with access to various resources, such as manipulatives (e.g., blocks, number lines), to aid them in their exploration and allow them to touch and visualize the mathematics. Given that this work occurs before any formal instruction on the topic, it is unlikely that all students will solve the problem in the same way, creating a rich diversity of thought.

As students work, teachers circulate around the room to ask questions. The goal of this questioning is to elicit, build, and extend student thinking without funneling students to one method or answer (Carpenter et al., 1989). In other words, because students are capable and competent, we want to understand their thinking, not overwrite it with our own. At this point, you might be thinking, "But my students will make mistakes!"—and you'd be right. However, just like riding a bike, falling is part of the learning process. We don't learn by avoiding mistakes; we learn by making them and analyzing them. Moreover, within almost every wrong answer is correct thinking. Finding and building off what is correct is always more empowering than starting over.

By the end of the exploration time, students will have solved the problem in diverse ways, allowing the teacher to select strategies that highlight important mathematical ideas. For example, to show the connections between the operations, a teacher might select a student who used subtraction and a student who used addition to solve the same problem. Or a student may be asked to show their picture while another student shows an equation to make connections between the representational and abstract ways of solving the problem. In any case, the teacher is thinking ahead regarding how to generate productive discussion around student strategies in ways that highlight the students as competent and build on what they do know (even if they have mistakes in their work).

Discuss

The final step in the LED instructional model is facilitating a discussion around the student strategies and solutions selected during the exploration phase. While the discussion can be facilitated in a myriad of ways depending on the criteria to select strategies, students must be given various opportunities to present their thinking to their peers (Bill & Sherin, 2019). To construct their own understanding, students can collaborate with one another to unpack the similarities and differences between their work samples and reflect on the big mathematical ideas embedded in the problems.

To highlight the differences between gradual release ("I do, we do, you do") and LED, a sample mathematics concept that targets rounding via two lesson plans is presented in Table 9.1. These lessons are presented side by side to allow for comparison at each phase in the model.

Table 9.1. Comparing Instructional Model Approaches for Teaching Rounding to the Nearest 10

<table>
<tr><th>Gradual Release</th><th>LED</th></tr>
<tr><td>I do: Teacher models rounding to the nearest 10 with a set of 4 examples (42, 67, 35, 29) using the rhyme: "Find your place, look next door, 5 or greater . . . add one more. All digits in front stay the same. All digits behind . . . zero's your name." The teacher demonstrates how to underline the tens place and circle the ones place when saying the rhyme aloud, often referring to the anchor chart that was made from the previous year.</td><td>Launch: Teachers display the number line and place a dot. Teachers ask students to think about a number that would be too low, too high, or just right. Students defend their answers.<table><tr><th>Too Low</th><th>Just Right</th><th>Too High</th></tr><tr><td></td><td></td><td></td></tr></table></td></tr>
</table>

Gradual Release	LED
We do: Teachers and students work through 4 additional problems together using the rhyme demonstrated in the "I do" portion of the lesson. For each example (19, 75, 38, 82), the teacher calls on a student to describe each of the steps. Student 1 finds the tens place, while Student 2 looks next door to the ones place. Then, Student 3 decides if the digit is 5 or more. Student 4 writes the new number, recording the responses on the smartboard while the other students follow along on their whiteboards.	**Explore:** Students are tasked with finding a more accurate number that represents the dot on the number line. As students are working, they are given access to tools that might support their thinking, such as number lines and counters. The teacher circulates and monitors student work, asking questions based on what they hear and see students do. The teacher looks for ideas or strategies that can be selected for a whole-class discussion focused on rounding numbers to the nearest 10.
You do: Students (individually or in pairs) complete a worksheet with 10 problems. Students are careful to refer to the rhyme posted at the front of the room that serves as an anchor chart. They also show the underlined tens places and circled ones places, carefully copying the notation demonstrated earlier in the lesson.	**Discuss:** The teacher uses student work and strategies to teach rounding to the nearest 10. The class collectively makes a list of patterns that students notice. The teacher asks students to generalize a rounding rule and explain why it makes sense. Stories are elicited from students to apply this concept to their lives and communities. Students are also encouraged to consider ways that rounding may be used to advantage some and disadvantage others, thereby eliciting critical consciousness of how mathematics is used around them.

Activity 9.2 involves comparing these two lesson plans. Various number lines are presented for consideration because we want to acknowledge that these facets are rarely binary; instead, they fall on a continuum of possibilities.

Activity 9.2 Comparing Instructional Models

Compare and contrast the two lesson plans—gradual release and LED models—using the number lines below. For each number line, put a red dot where the gradual release lesson plan would fall on the continuum, and a blue dot where the LED lesson plan would fall. After you've placed the dots, what do you notice? What do you wonder?

◄──────────	──────────►
PRIORITIZES PROCEDURAL FLUENCY	PRIORITIZES CONCEPTUAL UNDERSTANDING
FOCUSES ON TEACHER THINKING	FOCUSES ON STUDENT THINKING

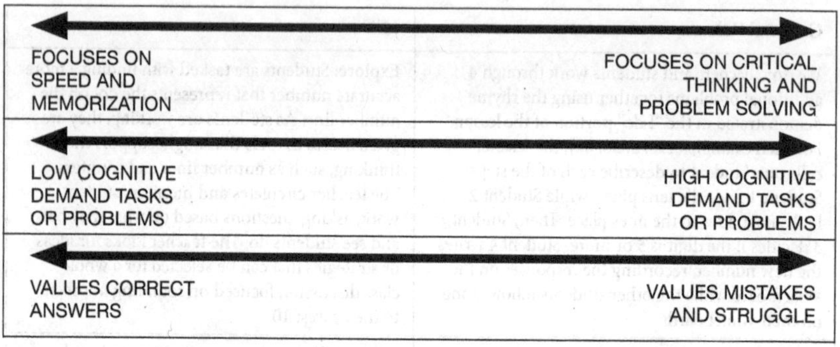

In summary, the LED instructional model uses student thinking to drive instruction through inquiry-based learning that has the potential to encourage academic rigor. Considering the cognitive demand of the task and the ways in which students have access from the start of the lesson is critical in our quest to design and enact equitable mathematics instruction for our students while simultaneously developing their conceptual understanding of identities around, and beliefs about mathematics. Tasks involving higher level questions that encourage students to investigate issues constitute a model for how students can develop their own questions about the world around them. As students explore societal issues, they can begin to problematize solutions that challenge inequities and disrupt the status quo. Through mathematics, students can see how diverse strategies, ideas, and experiences serve as the foundation from which we can make the world a better place, one that is inclusive for all.

Cultural Competence for Mathematical Thinking

Earlier, we noted that students often ask, "When am I ever going to use this in life?" When students ask such a question, they view the mathematics they're learning as disconnected from their lives and experiences. Consequently, recognizing and building on students' FOK is essential when creating curriculum and tasks that promote cultural competence and sense of belonging. Moreover, foregrounding students' diverse backgrounds and experiences in the classroom enables opportunities for students to learn more about themselves and the subject.

To explain this further, let's consider some examples of mathematics tasks that may mirror experiences you've had at home. Maybe you were in the kitchen baking chocolate chip cookies, hanging out with your sister and weaving her hair into braids, or outside in a park drawing with chalk. As you gathered the ingredients and measuring cups for the cookies, you wondered how much of an ingredient you would need if you wanted to double the recipe for your extended family gathering. You may have connected this to your learning of multiplying fractions. Or, if you were weaving your sister's hair into braids, you might have thought of the repeated patterns as the hair went over and under through your fingers. Or, as you drew a butterfly on the cement, you were careful to draw wings with colors and shapes that could be reflected over a line of symmetry, a concept like what you explored when you studied geometry.

Mathematical explorations in the classroom also may have provided opportunities for you to learn about your peers and their cultures. For example, maybe you looked up at a recipe for hamantaschen cookies. While considering the ingredients for a doubled recipe, you learned about the history of the triangular pastries called Hamantaschen served during the Purim holiday. Or, as you considered weaving a sweetgrass basket, you learned about the Gullah Geechee people, descendants of enslaved Africans who worked on rice plantations along the Lowcountry marshlands of the southeastern coast from Florida to North Carolina. Or maybe you studied strip patterns found in Ndebele beadwork from South Africa to talk about geometric symmetries and transformations.

Incorporating Funds of Knowledge in Mathematics

Next, we'll dive deeper into the power of using students' FOK. Let's say you're teaching students fraction division. Memories of "invert and multiply" might immediately crop up; you also may realize that you never fully understood fraction division yourself. By this point, you realize that, instead of teaching the same algorithm you learned, you want to draw from your students' FOK and help them develop conceptual understandings of what fraction division means to them. To do this, you look at your students' FOK chart, and you realize that several students noted that their interests and experiences include baking with family and friends. Drawing from this, you write the following problem:

> Quang is cooking Chuối Chiên (fried bananas) for his family. He needs to add ½ cup of rice flour but can't find his ½ cup measuring cup anywhere! Instead, he only has ¼, ⅓, and ⅛ cup measuring cups available. Which measuring cup should he use, and how many scoops will he need to make ½ cup?

When you analyzed this problem, you probably noticed a few things. First, the problem has a real-world application (by this, we mean real-world problems that many of us have experienced). We can personally tell stories of times when we couldn't find a certain measuring cup, or we didn't want to take the time to wash the one we needed. Second, the problem allows for student choice. Rather than assuming what students are capable of, we give them the opportunity to choose the measuring cup (or cups) that is right for them—or maybe even solve the problem multiple times!

Third, many students have either used measuring cups themselves or watched family members do so. Therefore, they can draw on those experiences to make sense of the problem. When students have a meaningful connection to mathematical concepts, they can maintain focus and interest in the mathematics they learn, thereby developing their mathematical thinking skills. Moreover, when teachers use a FOK chart to gather cultural insights from their students and make note of students' FOK in their instructional practice, they convey respect for the unique contributions and experiences that each learner brings into the classroom, while simultaneously supporting the development of self-efficacy and self-determination.

Finally, to see the true power of learning through problem-solving, take a few minutes to solve the problem on your own. You can solve it for one of the measuring cups or challenge yourself to solve it for all three! As you do so, carefully consider what you're thinking and what memories or experiences you're drawing on to make sense of the problem. Continue reading when you're done.

Now that you've solved the problem, consider what you pictured as you were doing so. Did you picture a kitchen that is familiar to you? Maybe you pictured measuring cups you've used in the past, or even drew a picture to represent the scenario. In any case, rather than reducing the problem to keywords, you used your rich experiences as powerful tools to make sense of the mathematics. This likely led to you developing deeper understandings of fraction division along the way. For example, imagine you chose the ¼ cup measuring cup. You likely figured out that it would take 2 scoops of the ¼ cup measuring cup to make the ½ cup. Maybe you figured this out using a picture. Maybe you thought about how there are 2 quarters in half-dollar. Or maybe you came up with your own creative way to make sense of the problem. No matter how you did it, you solved the problem! What you may not have realized is that the problem you solved can be expressed mathematically as ½ ÷ ¼ = 2.

If you're like us, you may remember being very confused as a child about how dividing two fractions could possibly result in a bigger number, let alone a whole number. What the problem is asking, in essence, is "how many ¼'s are in ½." Suddenly, the answer of 2 makes sense. The lightbulb moment didn't occur because you'd practiced inverting and multiplying hundreds of times. But when you drew on your own FOK to make sense of the mathematics for yourself, you were able to make connections to other mathematical ideas and think deeply and critically.

In Chapter 8, you explored how mathematical identities are shaped by the intersection of other identities such as race, class, ethnicity, gender, sexual orientation, immigration status, and religion. Hopefully, you now realize how these identities and experiences are intrinsically interwoven into the mathematics we teach. Consequently, as we strive to teach using culturally relevant pedagogy, it is imperative that mathematics tasks be developed in ways that allow students to use their backgrounds and experiences to learn more about themselves, others, the mathematics, and the world around them.

Using Mathematics to Enact Community Change

As discussed throughout this chapter, it's important for you, as a teacher of mathematics, to have critical mathematical literacy skills. To have a solid understanding of the critical aspect, we must first realize that mathematical skills and concepts are used to understand societal issues for purposes of developing critical consciousness. From global issues such as climate change and supply chain logistics, to local issues that may include voting access or crime reports, our view of the world is often filtered through the lens of mathematics. An awareness of critical consciousness, then, encourages you to critically examine these issues and consider ways to disrupt inequities and promote justice-oriented advocacy.

Using Mathematical Models to Disrupt Inequities

Let's take data gathered from statistical and mathematical models as an example. Data may be misrepresented in such models, or not used at all, to strengthen an opinion or position. An individual or a group of people may benefit, or the aim may be to provide political, financial, or other advantages to some groups while further disempowering oppressed groups through the spread of misinformation. Maintaining awareness that mathematics may be used to maintain power is a skill that involves recognizing mathematics for its historical importance to dominant ideologies that perpetuate systemic inequities—privileging some and marginalizing others. Those with a sense of critical mathematical literacy can critique the teaching and learning of mathematics, noting the ways that these approaches lead to inequitable access to, participation in, and outcomes in mathematics, especially for historically marginalized groups.

Thus, it is important for us to see how mathematics is intrinsically intertwined in the sociopolitical realm of the world in which we live if we hope to challenge the notion that mathematics is apolitical, and a subject driven by logic rather than culture or biases. We can help teachers and students understand this by using tasks like the one in Figure 9.1 to explore how mathematics can be used to examine societal structures. The tasks can spark conversation with students at all levels about how mathematics empowers people to become change agents who can leverage mathematics as a tool to advocate for productive changes within our society.

The local city council wants to propose the construction of a new airport in the area. While some residents are excited about opportunities to travel to new destinations and increase tourism that would benefit local stores and restaurants, other residents are concerned about how nearby communities would be affected. Communities near the planned site would need to contend with a multitude of injustices: destruction of land and ecosystems, forced housing evictions, and construction-related environmental and health impacts. A meeting is scheduled for residents in the surrounding area to share their input on (a) whether the airport should be constructed and (b) where the airport should be constructed if the proposal is approved. You plan to attend the meeting to learn about the proposal's next steps for a school assignment. Your mathematics teacher knows you're going and asks you to consider how mathematics is used during the meeting. You are asked to reflect on the following prompts: (1) What data are presented, if any, and how are they used to convey a message? (2) Who benefits from the data, and what purpose does this information serve? These questions involve consideration of the ways in which mathematics can be used to influence power while simultaneously disempowering other groups.

Figure 9.1. A Vignette: A Flight Toward Justice.

When reading the vignette in Figure 9.1, did you recall a similar task assigned to you during one of your mathematics classes? Unfortunately, we could not relate. But what if we had this task to encourage using mathematics to challenge and disrupt social justice issues? How encouraging would it be to spark interest and motivation in learning to use mathematics to address real-world problems? While we acknowledge that advocacy and awareness are only a piece of the larger challenges, given that many decisions are made on golf courses and behind closed doors, the skills gained from such a task could be applied to considering other injustices and problematize ways mathematics can be used to engage in justice-oriented political discourse.

You might be wondering how the vignette in Figure 9.1 can be used to engage in such discourse. Given its open-ended nature, the task allows students to generate numerous mathematical questions, such as *What is the area of the land that the airport will need?* Or *how many flights will land every day?* Take, for example, the question of where the airport should be constructed. At face value, the question may seem of little importance to the average resident. However, when one digs deeper, new facets of the issue surface. For example, it's worth considering the impact that the proposed airport would have on:

- The local environment
- The neighborhood housing and land prices
- Health and welfare of the local community
- Future opportunities to attract businesses or tourists to the area
- Local revenue streams

While the list of potential impacts is endless, they illustrate the broader point: Answering these critical questions requires mathematical data and analyses. Such projects would likely have both positive and negative impacts for the broader communities in which they are being built. On the one hand, access to airports allows for shorter travel times for those who travel frequently for work, more accessibility to commodities that are shipped via air freight, and increases in the number of jobs and tourists in the local area. On the other hand, a UCLA study of the Santa Monica Airport found that residents of the neighborhoods surrounding the airport faced numerous potential negative impacts, including hearing loss, increased exposure to carcinogens, increased rates of asthma and cardiovascular diseases, and even decreased IQ in children (see Castro et al., 2010). Consequently, one can easily imagine fierce debates raging in city council meetings as citizens lobby for or against the proposed sites for the construction of the airport.

Within this context, those who are able to leverage mathematical arguments to support their perspective wield far more power in terms of being able to advocate for policies and systems that benefit themselves or their communities. Conversely, those who have "math phobias" or have been afforded fewer opportunities to understand mathematics conceptually are more likely to be left out of the conversation altogether. Moreover, those on both sides of the argument are likely to present selective or misleading data to lobby public support for their proposals. Businesses may show graphs of projected increases in jobs and community revenue. Residents of the neighborhoods surrounding the proposed sites may present data on potential health concerns and the likely drop in housing prices. Therefore, being an informed citizen requires complex understandings of what the mathematics shows, what it doesn't show, and what all the data, taken together, mean for themselves and their community.

Mathematical Understandings for Critical Consciousness

As this airport proposal scenario demonstrates, mathematical understandings are intrinsically tied to the development of critical consciousness; while the scenario unpacks a single example, similar examples may be found in nearly every aspect of the sociopolitical realm. Table 9.2 has a couple of examples of tasks that may be of interest to elementary school students. Consider how each task in the table relates to standards that you teach. What other tasks might you pose to generate questions with your students?

Table 9.2. Tasks and Potential Questions for Elementary School Students

Task	Potential Questions
The mayor of your local area wants to build a new library. He has commissioned you to determine the number of libraries in each district, then make an argument for which district should receive the funding for the new library.	• Do all the districts have the same number of libraries? • What mathematics can be used to compare the number of libraries in a way that is as fair as possible? Are all libraries equivalent? • How is the number of libraries related to the racial and economic composition of each district? • Should all districts have the same number of libraries?
The president of the homeowners association (HOA) in your neighborhood has recommended that the community allocate funds to develop an empty field in the neighborhood. A wealthy, well-respected member of the community, who has five dogs, has pushed for the field to be turned into a dog park. However, some of your friends in the neighborhood have wondered why they wouldn't build a playground.	• Would the dog park or the playground get the most use? • How can mathematics be used to make an argument for one side or the other? • What are the potential impacts on the neighborhood (e.g., home values, community health)? • How do power and privilege impact the voices of community stakeholders?
After talking to your friend, you realize that each of you receives a different rate per hour for babysitting.	• How are babysitting pay rates related to the racial and economic composition of the neighborhood? • What mathematics can be used to compare babysitting pay rates? • Are differences in babysitting pay rates fair?
Your state is trying to find a fair way to determine the locations and number of voting sites per district.	• What data could you use to determine fairness in the number of voting sites and locations? • Do all voting sites currently have the same days of operation and wait times? • How are voting days and wait times related to the racial and economic composition of the areas? • Why might the accessibility of voting sites not be fair across the state?

These tasks are merely examples, but they demonstrate how teachers can design problems that allow students to use mathematics to better understand the world around them. In reviewing the tasks, you might have noticed that they are open-ended in nature. Writing the tasks in this way allows students to generate their own questions based on what they notice, wonder about, and are interested in. Moreover, doing so allows students multiple entry points into solving the problems. Take the babysitting task, for instance. One student might present data using tally marks, while another might create a bar graph, and still another might compute descriptive statistics, such as the mean, mode, range, or standard deviation. In other words, the tasks create a low floor, which gives all students the opportunity to solve them, but they also have high ceilings, allowing students to use complex mathematics if they wish to. Critically, using these problems also allows students to develop more holistic understandings of issues such as equality versus equity, to debate what is fair, and to become more aware of inequities that exist in their neighborhoods. In this way, students develop the ability to become change agents who can advocate for themselves and their communities.

Conclusion

Our world is increasingly driven by data—from the way we interact with technology, to the information presented to us through social media and news organizations, to the arguments presented in defense of opinions across the sociopolitical spectrum. Mathematics has become fundamental to making sense of our world and forming opinions on political, cultural, and economic issues. Moreover, many of the issues that persist in our lives and our society are complex and multifaceted, and they do not have straightforward solutions. Consequently, supporting students in developing their critical consciousness and gaining the knowledge necessary to use mathematics as a tool to understand and change the world is a critical component of teaching math. Our students deserve not only to imagine a better future, but also the opportunity to work toward the realization of that future. They deserve opportunities to ask hard questions about the inequities they face and to be able to leverage mathematics in support of their advocacy for a better tomorrow. Thus, it is important for us, as teachers, to reflect on how critical mathematical literacy informs instructional practices. In doing so, we consider the role of power and privilege that impacts who has access to mathematics, including one's participation in and experience of rigorous mathematics instruction.

As you read through this chapter, you considered three key ideas that are central to critical mathematical literacy and culturally relevant pedagogy. We looked at the need for teachers to develop students' conceptual understanding of mathematics and use inquiry-based learning to maintain academic rigor. In particular, you studied the LED model and how it offers a learning cycle that positions students as capable and competent while also facilitating the development of conceptual understandings of mathematical concepts through culturally relevant contexts. In the LED model, the teacher launches a task through an exploration of a mathematics problem. Students can make connections to the problem using their prior learning or life experiences, especially those that involve their FOK. Then, students can share their strategies and learn about various problem-solving approaches through discussion. Such a model presents opportunities for students to develop a deeper sense of meaning around mathematics by grounding it in real-world tasks, thereby promoting a conceptual understanding of mathematics that leads to rigorous, high-quality learning.

Building from this, you also looked at how students' FOK can be used to promote cultural competence. When students' FOK are used to guide instructional decisions and maintain a focus on their mathematical thinking, the learning of mathematics is meaningful and relevant. Students can build their mathematics knowledge alongside their cultural knowledge and use such interconnected knowledge to foster critical mathematics thinking and critical consciousness. In this way, teachers can connect students' racial and cultural identities and communities to forge relationships with students and community (Matthews, 2009). Students can also use these relationships presented through empowerment orientations, rather than deficit orientations, to develop their positive mathematical identities and critical agency (Matthews et al., 2022). Thus, the focus on student thinking empowers students with the knowledge and beliefs necessary to become change agents in their communities, leveraging mathematics in support of their advocacy for beneficial changes to societal structures.

Additionally, you learned that developing critical consciousness requires teachers and students to engage in tasks that use mathematics as a tool not only to better understand issues of social justice, but also to enact change in their communities. Encouraging problem-solving and having critical conversations about students' communities and the world around them equip students with the agency and knowledge necessary to make informed decisions about the social systems and structures that impact their lives and communities. We encourage you to consider these key ideas in your classroom to assist students in engaging and making sense of mathematics.

References

Bill, V., & Sherin, M. G. (2019). *The five practices in practice [elementary]: Successfully orchestrating mathematics discussions in your elementary classroom*. Corwin Press.

Carpenter, T. P., Fennema, E., Peterson, P. L., Chiang, C. P., & Loef, M. (1989). Using knowledge of children's mathematics thinking in classroom teaching: An experimental study. *American Educational Research Journal, 26*(4), 499–531.

Castro, A., Chen, L., Edison, B., Huang, J., Mitha, K., Orkin, M., Tejani, Z., Tu, D., Well, L., & Yeh, J. (2010). *Santa Monica Airport Health Impact Assessment (HIA)*. UCLA Community Health and Advocacy Training. https://www.pewtrusts.org/-/media/assets/2010/02/santamonicaairportfinalhia.pdf

Frankenstein, M. (1990). Incorporating race, gender, and class issues into a critical mathematical literacy curriculum. *The Journal of Negro Education, 59*(3), 336–347. https://doi.org/10.2307/2295568

Lappan, G., & Phillips, E. (2009). A designer speaks. *Educational Designer, 1*(3). http://www.educationaldesigner.org/ed/volume1/issue3/article11.

Matthews, L. E. (2009). Identity crisis: The public stories of mathematics educators. *Journal of Urban Mathematics Education, 2*(1), 1–4.

Matthews, L. E., Jones, S. M., & Parker, Y. A. (2022). *Engaging in culturally relevant math tasks: Fostering hope in the elementary classroom*. Corwin.

Rittle-Johnson, B., Siegler, R. S., & Alibali, M. W. (2001). Developing conceptual understanding and procedural skill in mathematics: An iterative process. *Journal of Educational Psychology, 93*(2), 346–362.

Smith, M. S., & Stein, M. K. (2018). *5 practices for orchestrating productive mathematics discussion* (2nd ed.). National Council of Teachers of Mathematics.

TEN

Science

Katie Lynn Brkich

I MAY NEVER HAVE SAT IN a P–12 science class with you, but I can envision what you've experienced. Most likely, the teacher introduced the content you'd be learning, gave you a lecture or presentation on the content, assigned you reading in preparation for answering questions and/or copying definitions, and then—if time and resources allowed—you conducted a "lab" demonstrating what you'd already been taught. Unfortunately, this is what science looks like for most K–12 students in America today—a primarily passive approach in which teachers project science content to their students rather than allowing them to discover and construct their own knowledge.

However, the science classroom doesn't have to be this way. In fact, it shouldn't be this way. We should be teaching science in ways that mirror how students learn.

Currently, there is a shift in science education toward all students having more equitable, inclusive, active, and engaged learning. This is an important shift because, despite numerous previous waves of reform, portions of the student population still are not consistently being engaged in high-quality, meaningful science instruction—specifically, students of color, students from low-income and under-resourced communities, and students whose first language is not English (Bang et al., 2017).

In this chapter, I will show how incorporating teaching methods that allow students to experience meaningful, challenging, and engaging science instruction—while addressing social justice and equity into your science instruction—can transform how science is learned and experienced in your classroom (see Activity 10.1). Specifically, I break down how the three core tenets of culturally relevant pedagogy (CRP; Ladson-Billings, 1995a, 2014) can be implemented in an elementary science classroom.

Activity 10.1 Teaching Inclinations

What do we naturally know about how children best learn about the world around them?

Imagine you're taking a young child—say, 4 or 5 years old—for a walk outside to the park or playground.

Do you do this?

a) Sit the child down and tell them everything they're going to see on their walk: "Today we're going to go on a walk to the park. You are going to see trees. They are brown and green things with leaves. Leaves are sometimes round or oval shaped, and they are how the tree gets energy from the sun to stay alive. You can't see them, but under the ground, there are roots that bring water into the tree up to the leaves. The leaves are usually green, but at other times of the year they might be various colors, like yellow, red, or orange, or you might see a tree with no leaves at all. On our walk, you also might see animals like squirrels or insects. Squirrels are often brown or gray . . . (and so on)."

Or do you do this?

b) Take the child on the walk. When they see something and ask, "What's that?" and point to the tree, you tell them, "That's a tree." When they say, "No, what's that?" and more energetically point to the top of the tree, tell them, "Oh, those are leaves." Then, perhaps you pick up a leaf and hand it to the child, or you allow the child to pick leaves and explore them—how they look, smell, and feel.

- Which option would you choose and why?
- What does this tell us about how children learn?
- What does this tell us about how we should be teaching science?

Positionality Statement

Katie Brkich (she/her)

I, like most elementary teachers in the United States, am a middle-class White woman who is cisgender, heterosexual, and able-bodied. Therefore, I have a lot of privileges—politically, socially, culturally, economically, and historically. My personal cultural history was taught in school, and my schooling almost always validated my privileges. I have White privilege and live in a world of White supremacy. All this privilege has led to my having a very biased and naive understanding of and outlook on the world in general, and education specifically. Knowing this, I must work hard to constantly check my privilege and biases when doing work in culturally relevant and sustaining pedagogy. I must consistently question my own attitudes, assumptions, values, prejudices, and thought processes to try and understand the complexity of interactions with others, especially those in marginalized communities. I have chosen to do this work because I truly believe it makes me a better teacher and a better human being. However, I struggle daily doing this work. I constantly make mistakes, and I never really feel confident in my decisions until enough time has passed to confirm that I didn't make another mistake. This chapter is my attempt to translate about 8 years of my purposeful growth toward being a culturally relevant/responsive/sustaining educator in elementary science education into a text that can be helpful to those seeking to also be a critical pedagogue.

Key Terms:

- **3-dimensional science:** that students should be able to demonstrate proficiency in disciplinary core ideas (DCIs), be able to use science and engineering practices (SEPs), and have a broader understanding of crosscutting concepts (CCCs).
- **5E model:** engage, explore, explain, elaborate, and evaluate are the steps for teaching and learning science.
- **Disequilibrium/cognitive dissonance:** the feeling associated with the idea that two competing concepts cannot both be true.
- **Socio-scientific issues:** problems that are informed by science, socially relevant, and are controversial.

Key Ideas:

1. ***Incorporating the 5E (or explore before explaining) model of lesson planning***, in addition to writing and teaching three-dimensional (3D)

science lessons, is the best way to align your teaching with culturally relevant pedagogical practices to maintain academic rigor.

2. ***You should include women, people of color, people with disabilities, bilingual or multilingual learners, and Indigenous populations in your planning and teaching about what is science and who does science.*** This lets students see those who look like them as scientists who have contributed to science knowledge. You should also consider the role of place, students' Funds of Knowledge, and your member properties to practice cultural competency.
3. ***To teach science for social justice, teachers must include connections to socio-scientific issues that align with awareness, empathy, and social engagement and/or participation around social inequities.***

Academic Rigor in Elementary Science

The first tenet of CRP, academic rigor, involves looking at addressing student learning and academic success based on high standards for all students (Ladson-Billings, 2014). In elementary science, this means that one's teaching focuses on equity in facilitating access to science for all students. Furthermore, academic rigor requires differentiation, meaning that everyone—those working above grade level and those working below—should have a challenging learning experience.

Currently, access to science is neither fair nor equitable. You may be aware of the well-documented and decades-long lack of access to science resources (updated science books, equipment, science materials, extracurricular science experiences, etc.) in under-resourced schools and those with high populations of Black, Multilingual learner, Indigenous, and Latinx students in both urban and rural settings (Oakes et al., 2003). Further, high-poverty urban students are disproportionately excluded from gifted programs that focus on powerful science content—and this exclusion is frequently based on behavioral and disciplinary factors rather than academic ones.

These are real issues, but they also make one incorrect assumption: that science is an objective and universal body of fixed knowledge, and that merely providing equitable access to that knowledge will allow all students to be successful in science. In fact, nothing could be further from the truth. Science is *not* objective.

When people think of science as an objective account of the world, we miss the fact that all knowledge has been constructed by humans who are influenced by external factors, personal biases, and social/political interests—all of which in turn influence their science. Claims of objectivity in science ignore these influences, giving it the illusion of perfect trustworthiness. Now, I'm not claiming that science *isn't* trustworthy. Rather, I'm claiming that we need to be aware of these influences and to acknowledge the effect of personal values, beliefs, and biases in the production of scientific knowledge. Similarly, as teachers, you may have the best intentions to be objective in your classroom and to be "fair" to everyone, but that doesn't mean you are necessarily being fair or objective—especially if you haven't acknowledged your biases and triggers and haven't yet learned productive ways to address them.

3D/Phenomenon-Based Science Instruction

In 2012, the National Research Council put out a new vision for science education in their publication, *A Framework for K-12 Science Education*. This vision of science education was based on the idea of 3D instruction: that students should be able to demonstrate proficiency in science content knowledge (disciplinary core ideas [DCIs]); be able to use the practices used by scientists and engineers (science and engineering practices [SEPs]); and have a broader understanding of concepts that cross traditional science content lines (crosscutting concepts [CCCs]). Used together, these dimensions create an integrated curricular framework to guide the teaching and learning of science (National Research Council, 2012).

Tepper (n.d.) helps us understand the importance of the three dimensions: "Imagine a world of one dimension, length without height or depth: our whole universe would be an impossibly thin, straight line. This is how many of us learned science." Most likely, your teacher had a lesson plan that taught science content based on reading a science textbook about that content. You were only learning one dimension—content—or, if you were lucky, you learned bigger concepts, known as DCIs, that helped you apply and understand the content.

Tepper continues, "Next, imagine a two-dimensional world, perhaps having length and height, but no depth." When I was an elementary school teacher, my students learned science ideas by reading about them and doing hands-on activities so they could experience the science they were learning about. I took what the textbook provided but then used school resources, often premade kits, or I used my own funds for resources to allow students to "do" something with the science they were trying to understand. We didn't call it that at the time, but we were using SEPs.

Finally, Tepper concludes the metaphor: "Now visualize a three-dimensional world, with length, height, and depth. Yes, students can still learn by reading and by doing, but now those ideas and practices are connected." This is where we bring in the CCCs, or ways of thinking about the world that help across all domains of science. CCCs allow students to be metacognitive about their own thinking using schema such as "systems" or "cycles." The interconnectedness of science is illuminated using CCCs.

Planning a Science Lesson

Pedagogically, there's one three-word phrase to remember about teaching elementary science in ways that best align with how people learn and in ways that are culturally relevant: "explore before explain." This simple phrase can transform how you teach science and how your students learn both science content and what science is as a content area. This notion is best exemplified by the 5E instructional model, which I detail next.

5E Model

One of the best ways I have found to help teachers plan lessons that are developmentally and culturally appropriate, while mirroring how people best learn, is the 5E instructional model (Bybee, 1990). In this model of lesson planning, rather than having direct instruction followed by guided practice and/or independent practice, the order of activities follows 5Es: engage, explore, explain, elaborate, and evaluate.

Engage is the start of the lesson and the chance for teachers to help students connect to what they already know about the topic/standard for the lesson. This can be prior science knowledge, and it can also be prior lived social and cultural experiences. When *engaging* with cultural relevance, make sure each student can talk about their experiences and ideas (at least in pairs or small groups), and call on a diverse representation of students to share their thoughts with the whole group. Also, it is vital that you don't tell students that any idea is "wrong" at this stage. Students are brainstorming what they think they know, and "correct" answers will come out in the explain stage.

Engage is also the part of the lesson during which you want common student misconceptions to come out—that is, to be presented by students as "true" or something they "know." The remainder of the lesson can be used to allow that student to experience disequilibrium, or cognitive dissonance, or the feeling we get when two competing ideas cannot both be correct.

The second stage of the 5E lesson is *explore*. This is when students do just that: They explore. The students are presented with a problem to solve, a situation to explain, or a task to complete, and they work together using their prior knowledge to experience the phenomenon being explored in that lesson. The explore portion can take on many different forms, but it will always include students making predictions and observations. *Exploring* with cultural relevance requires investigation that is relatable to the lives of your students. Also, allow students to work collaboratively to solve the problem or answer the question, and allow students' ideas and questions to guide how students explore the phenomenon being investigated.

The third stage is *explain*. This is the portion of the lesson most like direct instruction, but with one significant change: You'll use what students did in explore to teach any new content or vocabulary for your lesson, such as complete metamorphosis (4-stage life cycle).

During explain, you verbally and visually allow students to see the science explanations for what they just experienced. When *explaining* with cultural relevance, make sure you're creating a class community where all students' ideas—especially those historically marginalized in science (BIPOC, students with disabilities, LGBTTTQQIAA+, girls, lower income students, Multilingual Learner, etc.)—are heard, amplified, and valued. This is also a great time to incorporate into the conversation students' lived experiences, cultures, communities, and interests.

The fourth stage of a 5E lesson is *elaborate* (also called *extend*). This is when students are given the opportunity to try out using their new science content and/or vocabulary knowledge, which they just learned in explain, but with a new example of the phenomenon. Elaborate is somewhat like guided practice, in that you've just taught something to students, and this is their chance to try using it on their own without fear of failure or being formally assessed (yet). When *elaborating* for cultural relevancy, try to choose an example of the phenomenon that is authentic and relevant to students' lives. Also, be sure that collaborative problem-solving and decision-making are happening, and make sure all students are actively engaged.

Finally, the last stage of the 5E model is *evaluate*. This is representative of the individualized formative assessment you might give at the end of a traditional lesson, with a few small differences. This does not look like a true/false or multiple-choice assessment. Your assessment should allow for multiple ways of representing what students learned in the lesson. Students can write or draw to align with the SEP that goes with that lesson (e.g., make a model, construct an argument from evidence). Realistically, I know you're limited by both time constraints and what is developmentally appropriate for your students. Thus, this stage can be as simple as an open-ended ticket out the door, or as elaborate as having students write, for example, a poem, play, skit, or rap about the content from the lesson. Ideally, this is a time to allow students to choose from multiple types of assessment to show their understanding.

During the *evaluating* segment, to ensure cultural relevancy, make sure you hold high expectations for *all* your students, and connect your assessment with students' lived experiences, cultures, interests, and values as much as possible. This is a crucial juncture to check your biases and make sure the criteria for the assessments are clearly communicated to students.

Cultural Competence in Elementary Science

When you consider the current and ever-diversifying demographics of the United States' school-age population, providing an improved science education for all students is essential in ensuring educational attainment and that opportunity gaps do not further widen. Indigenous, Latinx, and Black people, who are vastly underrepresented in the fields of science, technology, engineering, and mathematics (STEM) and who make up only a small fraction of college-age science and engineering students, are collectively becoming a demographic majority in the United States. As students in the educational system become more diverse, teachers must learn to be culturally competent to meet those diverse student needs. A science teacher practicing cultural competency "has the ability to understand, communicate with, and effectively interact with students from different cultures, and successfully engage them in science learning" (Santiago, 2017, p. 3).

In a culturally sustaining classroom, cultural competence encourages, values, and amplifies students, inviting and making space for them not only to use their cultural practices from home in school, but also to maintain, unpack, and extend them. Cultural competence in elementary science requires an asset-based approach to cultural and linguistic differences. This is especially crucial when a student does not share the same personal characteristics or cultural background as the teacher and/or dominant group. The onus to increase awareness begins with the teacher, and it starts with self-awareness—knowledge of your own biases, triggers, ignorance, struggles, etc.

In science, this means that teachers draw attention to "the use of culture towards understanding cultural contexts that shape science" (National Association for Multicultural Educators, n.d.). This attention can be focused on who is doing the science, where the science is being done, and students' Funds of Knowledge (FOK). This also means that teachers present a form of science that is inclusive of non-Western, or nonmodern, ways of knowing the world—which leaves room to consider Native/Indigenous or traditional ways of knowing. Thought and planning for students with special needs and students who are linguistically diverse should also be part of the process.

To become better teachers of science, we need to examine our own ideas about what science is and who does science. Complete the "Draw a Scientist" activity (see Activity 10.2) before reading on.

Activity 10.2 Draw a Scientist

Get a piece of paper and writing/drawing utensils (pencil, markers, crayons, etc.).

Now consider this prompt:

Imagine a scientist. Think about where the scientist is and what the scientist is doing. Draw the scientist, where the scientist is, and what the scientist is doing. Then, add a caption (talk bubble) that says what the scientist might be saying about the work they are doing.

Now analyze your drawing, and answer the following questions:

- Who is pictured (race/ethnicity and gender)?

- What do they look like (hair, clothes, etc.)?
- Where are they working (in a lab, outdoors, in a museum, etc.)?
- What activities are they doing (mixing chemicals, studying fossils, observing animals)?
- What tools are being used (flasks, beakers, flames, googles, lab coats, etc.)?

If possible, compare your drawing with those of your classmates or peers.

- What similarities and differences do you observe?

Statistically, you most likely drew an older White male scientist with wild hair and wearing goggles or glasses. He is wearing a white lab coat, working alone in a laboratory, and is surrounded by test tubes or beakers with fire, smoke, or colored liquids (Farland-Smith, 2017). You may have changed one or more of these details, and the further your drawing is from this "stereotypical" image, the wider your conception is of who can do science. For example, if you drew a Latina marine biologist who is wearing a wetsuit and snorkel gear and talking about observing whales, you have demonstrated that you have an image of science beyond the stereotypical one.

The stereotypical scientist just described—one that has consistently been drawn by students over the last 40 years—indicates that we (teachers) are not doing a good job presenting other examples of scientists, and this is a problem. This is perhaps based on what science teachers and textbooks have chosen to teach about (see Activity 10.3).

Activity 10.3 How many scientists do you know?

Write the full or partial names of any scientists, inventors, or engineers you can think of.

Now think about the demographic identities of those you named.

- What gender are they?
- What race/ethnicity are they?
- What is their nationality?
- What is their sexual orientation?
- Do they have visible disabilities?

The problem is that your list was most likely composed of almost all White men. On its own, paying attention to scientists who are White men is not problematic. However, the problem arises when attention is paid to them to the exclusion of all others—such as BIPOC scientists, women scientists, scientists with disabilities, LGBTTTQQIAA+ scientists, and scientists from other historically marginalized groups. As recently as the early 1900s, people from these historically marginalized groups were denied entry into the fields of formal science and science education (e.g., Barona, 2013). This is not to say that they didn't contribute—just that their contributions were not recognized, or they were appropriated and uncredited. These scientists were left out of the story of science. An example is Alice Ball, an African American scientist who developed a tremendously successful method for treating leprosy. After her untimely death at the age of 24, her work was effectively stolen by her university's president. Unfortunately, this just one of many examples (Wong, 2022). Scientists from historically marginalized groups have experienced systemic exclusion and exploitation, which has perpetuated their underrepresentation in STEM fields. This has had the added effect of sustaining stereotypes of who is a scientist, contributing to imposter syndrome among those who are minoritized.

Therefore, culturally relevant teachers looking to improve their cultural competence must learn about the scientific contributions of non-White, nonmale scientists, inventors, and engineers to include in students' science instruction.

Practicing cultural relevance as a teacher means teaching beyond the standard, but not without it. Therefore, whatever content you're teaching, try to find some non-White males who work in that area and include them in your lesson. Without a doubt, your students will learn about the important contributions of White males through media representation and any traditional teacher. Your job is to add the legitimate and often unrecognized contributions of *Others*, too. You might bring in children's books or kid-friendly biography videos, or just display the scientist's picture as an example of someone who did (or is doing) work in the area you're covering. This small change can lead to diversifying students' view of who "belongs" in science/STEM, improve their understanding of how science works through increased engagement, and perhaps inspire them toward becoming scientists!

One note: Be sure you are respectful and inclusive as you talk about scientists who are not White males; often when they are mentioned, they are not given the respect that White male scientists are afforded. Just as you cannot be surprised when minoritized students excel academically, it is vital that you do not minimize, simplify, or patronize the achievements of minoritized scientists. For example, George Washington Carver is often just referred to as the "peanut man" or the "inventor of peanut butter," but his contributions to science and agriculture are vast and important. George Washington Carver was a botanist and teacher. He identified the need for farmers to improve their farming practices by rotating cotton planting, which depleted the soil of nutrients, with soil-enhancing, protein-rich crops like peanuts and soybeans. This taught farmers to be more self-sufficient and was a type of early conservation work. While he did invent more than 300 products from peanuts, his larger contribution was to the great economic improvement of the rural South, and George Washington Carver should be taught about in a way that reflects the magnitude of his impact, like we do for so many other American heroes.

When Moll et al. (1992) developed the Funds of Knowledge framework, they did so to show teachers how students' interests, activities, and social networks could be used to enhance in-class learning (see Activity 10.4). They found that students had access to a wide range of science-related ideas that teachers could draw on to help students make connections between school science and their everyday lives. Some student FOK they identified involved construction and vehicle/appliance repair, which can be connected to multiple science ideas, including physical properties of materials, force and motion, gravity, and electricity. They found that students' FOK about cooking helped them to understand chemical changes; FOK about medicine (contemporary and folk) helped them to understand how the human body works; FOK about mining helped when learning about rocks and minerals; and FOK about farming helped with understanding plants and soil.

Activity 10.4 Funds of Knowledge

A Vignette

I am observing a science lesson being taught in Mrs. Buchanan's fourth-grade classroom. She has just started a lesson on the water cycle. The day before, she introduced the idea with a class OWL chart (observe-wonder-learn). She read a picture book about water, and then the class worked together to develop a list of questions they had about the concept on a chart paper in the front of the room. Today, Mrs. Buchanan has asked students to "draw the water cycle" on a blank piece of paper. Students get out their crayons and markers and start to draw. As I walk around, I see most students drawing pictures with arrows between lakes, clouds, and rain. One student is drawing a pot boiling with steam. When Mrs. Buchanan gets to Sofía's table, she stops and looks concerned. By the time I get to the table as well, the teacher is reprimanding Sofía for "being off task" and "not following directions." Sofía had drawn a rectangle with a smiley-face inside. When the teacher walks away, I bend down to Sofía's eye level and softly ask her, "Can you tell me what you drew?" Sofía is upset about being reprimanded once again; she had tried her best to do what she thought the teacher had asked her to do. I tell her I understand her frustration, but I'm very interested in her drawing, so could she please tell me about it. She says, "It's like when you breathe on the bus window on cold mornings. It's condensation."

Questions for reflection:

- What science concepts did Sofía demonstrate she understood with her drawing?
- What might you have done differently if you were Mrs. Buchanan in this situation?
- What does this vignette tell us about how we can use questioning to get at students' ideas?
- What does this vignette tell us about learning about students' FOK?

Since then, teachers have come up with all sorts of ways to use students' FOK to help them understand science concepts. For example, one student of mine used her second-grade students' knowledge of and interest in Pokémon to introduce a lesson on animal habitats (Achieve, Inc., 2013, 2-LS4-1). Another used a student's interest in becoming an x-ray technician to teach a fifth-grade lesson on vertebrates and invertebrates using animal x-rays (CPalms, 2008, SC.5.L.14.2). I've seen teachers use Marvel movies to teach about balanced and unbalanced forces (Next Generation Science Standards, n.d., K-PS2-2) and witnessed students talking about food chains using a short video clip from Disney's *The Lion King* (Georgia Department of Education, 2016, S4L1b).

When teachers remember that students have complex multifaceted identities that extend beyond the classroom and into their homes, neighborhoods, schools, and communities, they can get to know their students as "whole people." Importantly, when teachers understand the intersectionality of student lives that are marred by systemic inequities, they can be more intentional in their approaches toward equity. Adopting this humanizing mindset allows teachers to use students' FOK to provide connections that promote student interest, helping them find deeper, personal meaning in science learning and positioning them as experts with respect to science content knowledge (McLaughlin & Barton, 2013) and SEPs.

Indigenous/Native Ways of Knowing

Just as traditional science content has undervalued traditionally marginalized groups' contributions to science knowledge, it has also undervalued or sought to exclude non-Western ways of knowing in science. This means that traditionally Indigenous or Native ways of knowing about the world have been not only excluded from how science is taught, but also purposefully targeted as "nonscientific."

Until recently, almost all science teachers were educated in systems that dismissed Indigenous knowledge and valued only Eurocentric knowledge as science. Further, they taught a hidden curriculum to assimilate Indigenous students into a Western science framework, which forced "some children to abandon their traditional ways of knowing" (Snively & Williams, 2018, p. 14).

I currently struggle to integrate Indigenous/Native ways of knowing into my science methods instruction, because for so long I was taught that these ways of knowing were irrelevant to modern science, and those topics were not included in any of my high school or college science courses or labs. Further, I taught elementary science in northern Florida and now teach elementary science methods in southern Georgia. Neither northern Florida nor Georgia has significant numbers of the Native populations that originated there, because those populations were subjected to genocidal removal at the hands of the federal and state governments. Consequently, I rarely, if ever, taught Native American elementary teachers or students—something that had caused me to think incorrectly that I didn't need to include this content in my instruction.

As Kendy (2018) explained, "Before teachers can become effective change agents in an educational system that has worked to assimilate First Nations, Métis, and Inuit peoples for over a century we must be able to change our way of thinking." This means that becoming aware of our preconceived ideas, thoughts, and judgments about Native science knowledge, especially those impacting our teaching practices, is imperative. This is a process that I am working through: coming to know myself and my biases.

As I see it, integrating Indigenous knowledge into the science curriculum serves at least two main purposes. First, it is good for all students to appreciate Indigenous knowledge for the history of science that it provides. The foundational knowledge of many areas of science originates from traditional knowledge and practices, including knowledge of agriculture, astronomy, botany, food technology, mathematics, medicine, physics, and pharmacology, among others (Pawilen, 2021).

Second, when teaching students from Native or Indigenous populations, it is important to bring in their FOK to help them make sense of Western science content. Native groups have cultural values and attitudes that align with scientific values and attitudes, including valuing the connection between people and nature, finding ways to creatively communicate new knowledge, and a general curiosity about nature and natural phenomena.

Critical Consciousness in Elementary Science

Critical consciousness is where CSP extends CRP the most. Critical work involves illuminating the cultural hegemony that sustains systemic oppression, marginalization, and minoritization. In other words, to be critical is to name and acknowledge the impact (by way of direct influence and authority) of dominant forces. Practicing critical consciousness does not require a specific demographic identity, but it does require sustained evaluation of self, society, systems, cultures, and others. It also requires refinement in approach and collective activism that centers the most marginalized among us. Critical consciousness requires acknowledging that you're not doing enough, and likely never can—however, you can do more if you're brave enough to bring about local change.

Goal for Moving Forward

My teaching does a good job of addressing the elements of elementary science related to the first two elements of CRP: academic rigor and cultural competence. Where I need to grow is in showing students how to create a classroom culture that includes discussions about and connections to social justice, or critical consciousness.

I'm not alone in this deficiency, and this is not unusual in teacher preparation programs and even in multicultural education courses. Gorski (2009) found that many courses and programs fell short of teaching critical consciousness after researching syllabi from 45 multicultural education courses in the United States. The third component of CRP is perhaps the most controversial, or debatable, regarding its inclusion in schools, particularly in science. This is because science is often thought of as a set of objective facts to be learned rather than a way of knowing the world that relies on observation and evidence but is still subjective, given that it is being performed by humans.

Personally, I have been hesitant to include these issues in our science course because they are so very different from how most of my students understand science. Also, I like for students to feel as comfortable as possible in my course, because so many of my college students come in either afraid of, or strongly disliking, science based on their K–20 science class experiences. But I know I need to do better, so I've looked for examples of what critical consciousness looks like in elementary science, especially lower elementary (K–3).

What It Might Look Like

In the book *It's Still Debatable! Using Socioscientific Issues to Develop Scientific Literacy, K-5* by Sami Kahn (2019), I found inspiration for what this might look like or include. While her book does not include issues of CRP or critical pedagogy, it does provide sample lessons that include social justice issues in 5E lessons for K–5 students. Kahn explains that work in science education around socio-scientific issues (SSI) is about providing students with opportunities to argue about scientific issues to prepare them to be informed, active citizens as adults. Work in SSI somewhat aligns with our work in culturally relevant science. Where it differs is that SSI does not delve into issues of students' identity (race, gender, class, religion, language, etc.) as affecting how they learn or how to differentiate to meet different students' needs and FOK. While Kahn (2019) is helpful for thinking about what social justice topics you might include in lessons for elementary schoolers and how you might incorporate them into a 5E lesson, teachers who are practicing being culturally relevant would need to add the missing cultural competency piece.

Conclusion

Many educators teach elementary school every day and never teach science. The few who do often do so in very problematic and outdated ways. To take up social justice in elementary science by practicing CRP is quite the undertaking. Surely, you will be in the minority—but so are Nobel Prize winners and people with verified Twitter accounts.

To teach science in culturally sustaining ways, you'll need to have extensive knowledge of the content, ample practice applying the concepts, and a broad cultural and discipline-based understanding of the curriculum. Just like your students, you'll have to know yourself, know your limits, and be resourceful and creative. You will fail. That is fine. We learn from failures. You'll also succeed—some students will come to love science because you made it engaging, accessible, and relevant. Others will achieve perhaps beyond what they could ever have imagined because they will be empowered. You'll work hard, but it will be worth it. In addition to being a better teacher, you will become a better person when you decide that no subject area can be taught without the identities, circumstances, and systemic context of your students in mind.

References

Achieve Incorporation. (2012). *2-LS4-1 Biological Evolution: Unity and Diversity*. Nextgenscience.org.https://www.nextgenscience.org/pe/2-ls4-1-biological-evolution-unity-and-diversity

Bang, M., Brown, B., Barton, A. C., Rosebery, A., & Warren, B. (2017). Toward more equitable learning in science: Expanding relationships among students, teachers, and science practices. In C. V. Schwarz, C. Passmore, & B. J. Reiser (Eds.), *Helping students make sense of the world using Next Generation Science Standards and engineering practices* (pp. 33–58). NSTA Press.

Barona, J. L. (2013). Women and science: Genealogy of exclusion. *Mètode Science Studies Journal, 76*, 51–55.

Bybee, R. W. (1990). Science for life and living: An elementary school science program from Biological Sciences Curriculum Study. *The American Biology Teacher, 52*(2), 92–98.

CPalms. (2008). *SC.5.L.14.2.* https://www.cpalms.org/PreviewStandard/Preview/1743

Farland-Smith, D. (2017). The evolution of the analysis of the draw-a-scientist test. In *Drawing for science education* (pp. 171–178). Sense.

Georgia Department of Education. (2016, March 31). *Science Georgia Standards of Excellence.* (S4L1b). https://www.georgiastandards.org/Georgia-Standards/Documents/Science-Fourth-Grade-Georgia-Standards.pdf

Gorski, P. C. (2009). What we're teaching teachers: An analysis of multicultural teacher education coursework syllabi. *Teaching and Teacher Education, 25*(2), 309–318.

Kahn, S. (2019). *It's still debatable! Using socioscientific issues to develop scientific literacy, K-5.* National Science Teachers Association.

Kendy, N. (2018). Transforming teacher thinking about Indigenous science through cultural experiences. In *Knowing Home: Braiding Indigenous Science with Western Science, Book 2.* https://pressbooks.bccampus.ca/knowinghome2/chapter/chapter-2/

Ladson-Billings, G. (1995a). But that's just good teaching! The case for culturally relevant pedagogy. *Theory Into Practice, 34*(3), 159–165. http://www.jstor.org/stable/1476635

Ladson-Billings, G. (2014). Culturally relevant pedagogy 2.0: aka the remix. *Harvard Educational Review, 84*(1), 74–84.

McLaughlin, D. S., & Barton, A. C. (2013). Preservice teachers' uptake and understanding of Funds of Knowledge in elementary science. *Journal of Science Teacher Education, 24*(1), 13–36.

Moll, L. C., Amanti, C., Neff, D., & Gonzalez, N. (1992). Funds of knowledge for teaching: Using a qualitative approach to connect homes and classrooms. *Theory into Practice, 31*(2), 132–141.

National Association for Multicultural Educators. (n.d.). *I teach science. Can I be a multicultural educator.* https://www.nameorg.org/learn/i_teach_science_can_i_be_a_mu.php

National Research Council. (2012). *A framework for K-12 science education: Practices, crosscutting concepts, and core ideas.* Committee on a Conceptual Framework for New K-12 Science Education Standards. Board of Science Education, Division of Behavioral and Social Sciences Education. National Academies Press.

Next Generation Science Standards. (n.d). *National Science Teaching Association.* (K-PS2-2). https://ngss.nsta.org/DisplayStandard.aspx?view=pe&id=26

Oakes, J., Joseph, R., & Muir, K. (2003). Access and achievement in mathematics and science: Inequalities that endure and change. *Handbook of research on multicultural education, 2,* 69–90. San Francisco, CA: Jossey-Bass.

Pawilen, G. T. (2021). Integrating Indigenous knowledge in the Philippine elementary science curriculum: Integrating Indigenous knowledge. *International Journal of Curriculum and Instruction, 13*(2), 1148–1160.

Santiago, A. (2017). Focusing on cultural competency in STEM education. *Informal Science,* 1–16. https://www.informalscience.org/sites/default/files/Focusing on Cultural Competence in STEM Education.pdf

Snively, G., & Williams, L. W. (2018). *Knowing home: Braiding Indigenous science with Western science, Book 2, 1-270.* ePublishing Services, University of Victoria Libraries.

Tepper, D. (n.d.). 3D science instruction in a 3D world. *Learning A–Z*. https://www.learninga-z.com/site/breakroom/3d-science-instruction

Wong, K. M. (2022, March 23). The trailblazing Black woman chemist who discovered a treatment for leprosy. *Smithsonian Magazine*. https://www.smithsonianmag.com/history/the-trailblazing-black-woman-chemist-who-discovered-a-treatment-for-leprosy-180979772/

ELEVEN

Social Studies

Ariel Cornett and Erin Piedmont

YOU MAY REALIZE THIS, OR you may not, and that's okay, because we're going to learn more about it in this chapter: You stand as curricular-instructional gatekeepers in your elementary classrooms (Thornton, 1989, 1991). What does that mean? Essentially, your frame of reference—that is, Funds of Knowledge [FOK], worldview, perspectives, lived experiences—impacts your day-to-day decisions in the elementary social studies classroom (e.g., how you define social studies, as well as how you plan for, instruct, and assess the subject). It is crucial that you be aware of your role as a curricular-instructional gatekeeper because it ultimately influences the learning opportunities that you adopt, adapt, and create for students.

Positionality Statements

Dr. Ariel Cornett (she/her)

I present as a White, able-bodied cisgender woman. These are my visible identity markers, which have afforded me several privileges throughout my schooling experiences. My invisible identity markers tell other aspects of my life's complex narrative—millennial, middle class, Appalachian. I have layers; however, I frequently have been viewed through a singular identity: the know-it-all teacher's pet. I benefited from this imposed identity because I was perceived as knowing all the answers and being the most helpful. I actively worked (and severely overworked myself) to maintain this stereotype because of the academic success and social status that accompanied it. I was proud when others associated identity markers such as "Type A," "perfectionist," and "overachiever" with me. While I have struggled (and continue to struggle) to distance myself from this stereotype, I have realized that this language and these perceptions have flattened my identity in some contexts. Even in my professional career (i.e., teaching in an elementary school and at multiple universities), my colleagues have stated, "Oh, she's got it—right?"

Well, what if I don't got it? Assuming that I have it each and every time has led to years of anxiousness around making sure everything is absolutely "perfect." In many instances, I believed there was only one correct answer, and I had to get it "right." I have worked to unlearn this notion. When I research and instruct on the teaching and learning of elementary social studies, I stress the importance of connecting the classroom with students' and families' communities—where there are various ways of knowing and being. I encourage teachers to draw on students' and families' Funds of Knowledge; this affords teachers the opportunity for increased awareness about the diverse ways in which students can engage with social studies inquiries.

Dr. Erin Piedmont (she/her)

I believe that social studies education is at the foundation of everything we teach; we are preparing the next generation of citizens, and I approach this work through an anti-oppressive lens. I identify as a middle-class, able-bodied White cisgender woman, among many other dominant social identity markers. I was raised in a small, rural agricultural town in Nevada that felt culturally homogenous regarding race, sexual orientation, and religious affiliation, and I did not experience diversity until I attended college in an urban city after I graduated from high school. My experiences in college—both academic and social—led to my realization that people lived vastly different lives from my own and that there were many ways of thinking, knowing, and existing in the world. College was the first setting where I had ever been pushed to recognize social inequality and consider my role as a citizen in helping to either maintain or dismantle oppressive structures. Having grown up on the lower end of the spectrum in terms of social class, I applied to complete my student teaching internship in a Title I elementary school where 86% of the population qualified for free or reduced lunch, hoping that I could connect with my students through this shared experience. I spent 6 years teaching at the same school with the most resilient students who overcame more adversity than I could have ever imagined. These combined experiences influenced how I perceived the overall purpose for education—to prepare enlightened and empowered citizens—and, more specifically, my passion for social studies education.

These visible and invisible identity markers have provided (and will continue to provide) us with a certain set of privileges in society. These privileges impact us personally; however, they also influence our professional decisions as curricular-instructional gatekeepers of undergraduate and graduate elementary social studies methods courses.

Key Terms:

- **Anti-oppressive approach:** acknowledges, addresses, and dismantles injustice.
- **Curricular-instructional gatekeeper:** an individual (teacher) who controls access to the curriculum.
- **Democratic citizen:** critically conscious citizens who have the knowledge, skills, and dispositions to challenge the status quo and disrupt oppressive structures.
- **Place:** serves as a "lens" that you, as a teacher, can utilize to inform your social studies curricula, instruction, and assessment (Cornett, 2022).

Key Ideas:

1. ***To promote academic rigor with elementary students in social studies, you must critically evaluate curricula to ensure that you are personalizing learning experiences (instruction and assessments) in ways that are relevant and responsive to your students' needs and interests.*** Academically rigorous curricula and associated learning experiences should be rooted not only in state standards (social studies content knowledge, understandings, and skills), but also in students' and families' (and potentially your) communities.
2. ***To practice cultural competence with students in social studies, you must reflect on the influence of your own culture and identities on the ways in which you learn and teach the content.*** Additionally, you must strive to learn more about the lived experiences, cultures, and identities of your students, their families, and their communities. Then, it is important to document this information in a place such as FOK chart to connect to social studies content in the curriculum as well as to inform and enhance your social studies instruction and assessments to be more culturally competent.
3. ***To promote critical (sociopolitical) consciousness with elementary students in social studies, you must provide interdisciplinary learning***

experiences (i.e., history, geography, economics, civics) that guide students to problem-solve social issues in their many communities. To engage as critically conscious citizens, your students must develop the knowledge, skills, and dispositions to challenge the status quo and disrupt oppressive structures.

The Impact of Policy

Local, state, and national policies shape the content we teach, how we teach it, when we teach it, and the extent to which we teach it. Since the passage of No Child Left Behind and the reauthorization of Every Student Succeeds Act, the marginalization of social studies has continued. This marginalization has led to reduced instructional time for social studies in elementary classrooms and an accountability context that has witnessed the disappearance (i.e., complete or partial removal) of social studies from state curricula in favor of subject areas such as English language arts and mathematics. Currently, social studies are held under a magnifying glass in several state legislatures and local boards of education as stakeholders make their respective cases for the five Ws and H (*what* and *who* should be taught in the curriculum, as well as *how, when, where*, and *why* particular content is taught). Largely, BIPOC (Black, Indigenous, and People of Color) voices are being minimalized, or completely dismissed, during these discussions. We, along with the National Council for the Social Studies, support the "accurate and truthful representation of historical events" for students to "learn about the experiences and viewpoints of people of color and America's legacy of racism" because it is "critical to feeling connected and equally valued in a participatory society" (National Council for the Social Studies [NCSS], 2021, para. 6) (see Pause & Reflect 11.1).

Pause & Reflect 11.1

Have you observed the marginalization of elementary social studies? If so, in what ways? What is the status of social studies teaching and learning in your state, local school district/division, school, and grade level? Reflect on your experiences in the classroom. What daily decisions highlight your role as a social studies curricular-instructional gatekeeper?

A Rationale for Social Studies Education

The field of social studies (see Figure 11.1) comprises "history, economics, geography, civics, sociology, anthropology, archeology, and psychology, [which] are rich, interrelated disciplines, each critical to the background of thoughtful citizens" (NCSS, 2016, p.181).

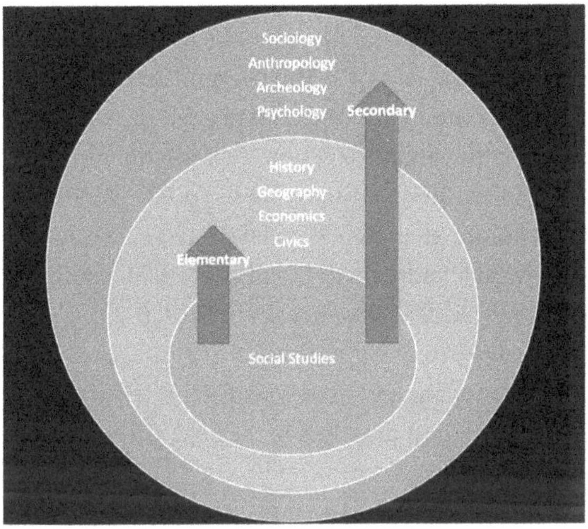

Figure 11.1. The Olive: Social studies diagram.

In many state standards documents across the United States, elementary social studies focuses on four primary disciplines—history, economics, geography, and civics (see Figure 11.1)—and students explore key content knowledge and understandings associated with each. Furthermore, some states include disciplinary skills standards alongside content knowledge and understandings (e.g., Virginia), while other states create stand-alone documents. For example, the state of Georgia has stand-alone social studies standards documents that outline information processing skills, as well as map and globe skills. Still other states do not include any standards that address disciplinary skills (e.g., Alabama). Professional organizations and scholars have called for the use of best practices in social studies curricula and instruction, which should be meaningful, integrative, value-based, challenging, and active (e.g., Anderson, 2014; Bauml, 2016; Curry, 2010; NCSS, 2009, 2016). We also believe that powerful and purposeful social studies instruction at the elementary grade levels should be culturally relevant (Ladson-Billings, 1995a). More recently, scholars (Rodríguez & Swalwell, 2022) have also urged the field to shift to an anti-oppressive approach.

We advocate for the use of culturally relevant pedagogies (CRPs) and anti-oppressive pedagogies in elementary social studies, which includes making critical and inclusive decisions about what knowledge, skills, and dispositions to include and exclude, as well as which narratives to place in the foreground and background. One addition we'd like to make to the Rodríguez and Swalwell (2022) quotation in Table 11.1 is the recognition of elementary social studies assessment as the third mechanism (i.e., in relation to elementary social studies curriculum and instruction) that is "either invested in reproducing oppression or committed to disrupting it" (p. 28). We believe that teachers must critically examine elementary social studies curricula, instruction, and assessment to avoid "inadvertently send[ing] problematic and mixed messages about the social world" (Gallagher et al., 2019, p. 217). Thus, throughout this chapter, we bring attention to those three mechanisms in social studies—curriculum, instruction, and assessment—and the ways that you can ensure they are aligned with best practices in the field, CRP, and anti-oppressive pedagogies.

The NCSS characteristics (best practices), as well as culturally relevant and anti-oppressive pedagogies for powerful and purposeful social studies, are defined in Table 11.1.

Table 11.1. Characteristics of Best Practices in the Field, CRP, and Anti-Oppressive Social Studies

Characteristics	Definition
Meaningful	"Instruction focuses on social studies knowledge, understandings, and skills through a variety of ways to meet students' diverse needs, capitalize on their interests, and encourage connections" (Cornett, 2020, p. 5).
Integrative	"Instruction occurs throughout the school day and explores social studies curricular concepts across disciplinary boundaries (e.g., integrating history, geography, economics, and civics) as well as subject areas (e.g., social studies and English Language Arts) in order to integrate students' knowledge, understandings, and skills with authentic action" (Cornett, 2020, p. 5).
Value-Based	"Instruction involves students in the ethical dimensions of topics as well as controversial issues, promotes critical thinking as well as informed decision-making, and addresses core democratic values (e.g., freedom of speech, equality of opportunity) as well as the common good" (Cornett, 2020, p. 5).

Characteristics	Definition
Challenging	"Instruction fosters debate, discussion, research, decision-making, problem solving, as well as issue analysis and provides opportunities for students to critically investigate, question, evaluate, and challenge sources" (Cornett, 2020, p. 5).
Active	"Instruction supports students as they consider new ideas in relation to their background knowledge, modify misconceptions, and evaluate multiple perspectives. Additionally, instruction facilitates student discovery as well as engagement through a variety of formats, teacher actions, and materials" (Cornett, 2020, p. 5).
CRP	"(a) students must experience academic success; (b) students must develop and/or maintain cultural competence; and (c) students must develop a critical consciousness through which they challenge the status quo of the current social order" (Ladson-Billings, 1995a, p. 160).
Anti-Oppressive	"An education that explicitly addresses the functions and impacts of oppression as well as the courageous and inspiring struggle against it—*as a means of disrupting oppression* [emphasis in original]. For the record, there is no 'non-oppressive' teaching. Because teaching entails making infinite choices about what to include and foreground, as well as what to exclude and background, there is no escaping it. As educators, our curriculum and instruction are either invested in reproducing oppression or committed to disrupting it" (Rodríguez & Swalwell, 2022, pp. 27–28).

Note. CRP = culturally relevant pedagogy.

Let's dive, run, walk, roll, electric slide, TikTok dance—come in whatever way you choose to present yourself—into the rest of this chapter! We will explore the overarching question, what are the foundational understandings at the intersection of elementary social studies education and CRP? We will employ the three tenets of CRP—academic rigor to promote student learning, cultural competence, and critical-sociopolitical-consciousness (Ladson-Billings, 1995a, 1995b)—to showcase the ways in which anti-oppressive elementary social studies can be taught in meaningful, integrative, value-based, challenging, and active ways.

What does it look like to teach elementary social studies to further academic rigor?

Student learning is the ultimate purpose of education, regardless of the content area (e.g., social studies, science, mathematics, English language arts). For social studies, you should establish high expectations for all students during academic experiences. You may ask, "What do high expectations look like for students in social studies?" For us, the best practice characteristics outlined in Table 11.1 embody high expectations in our discipline: meaningful, integrative, value-based, challenging, and active. When providing opportunities for students to engage with social studies learning in these ways, you must also steadily increase the rigor of those academic experiences. Rigor means that students have the "ability to read, write, speak, compute, pose and solve problems at sophisticated levels—that is, pose their own questions about the nature of teacher- or text-posed problems" (Ladson-Billings, 1995b, p. 475). For example, if students have been asked to create a map of the school and answer the question, "What story does your map tell?" students should be able to create their maps in whatever format they choose (e.g., two-dimensional drawing, three-dimensional diorama). Then, they should be able to present (e.g., their map and their answer to the question) to their peers and teacher through writing (e.g., essay, poster, brochure) or speaking (e.g., presenting PowerPoint slides, reading poetry, rapping).

To ensure rigor within social studies, teachers must be critical designers and consumers of curricula. The emergence of websites such as Teachers Pay Teachers (TPT) and Pinterest has made this a challenging endeavor because many unit and lesson plans shared on these sites promote mere fact retention. Learning experiences that reflect best practices for elementary social studies education are largely excluded (Rodríguez et al., 2020). Additionally, many of the curricular materials found on TPT and Pinterest are quite problematic, misrepresenting cultural backgrounds and experiences and perpetuating generalized stereotypes of different social groups. It is essential that teachers learn to "[pin] with pause" (Gallagher et al., 2019, p. 217) and critique the curricula they use to teach social studies to teach with rigor that is culturally relevant and anti-oppressive.

Academic Rigor Activity 1 (see Activity 11.1) provides an opportunity to critique a social studies inquiry design model (IDM) blueprint, housed within the C3 Teachers' curricular library (C3 Teachers, n.d.), for academic rigor. As you review the IDM blueprint, pay close attention to the major components of the blueprint, such as the compelling question (Do we still need paper maps?), staging of the compelling question, standards, featured sources, supporting questions, formative performance tasks, the summative performance task, and the suggestions for taking informed action. Once you have familiarized yourself with the curriculum, begin your critique using the guiding questions in the activity. Ultimately, the objective is to determine whether you believe the curriculum is rigorous regarding elementary social studies (meaningful, integrative, value-based, challenging, active, culturally responsive, and anti-oppressive).

Acitivity 11.1 Academic Rigor Activity 1: Critical Consumerism

Critical Consumerism

Guiding Questions

- Is the curriculum *meaningful*? *Integrative*? *Value-based*? *Challenging*? *Active*? *Culturally relevant*? *Anti-oppressive*? Reference the definitions of those best practice characteristics in Table 11.1.
- What are the curricular material's strengths and weaknesses?
- How might you revise and/or supplement the curricular material to make it more rigorous?

Kindergarten Map Inquiry

Do We Still Need Paper Maps?	
Georgia Performance Standards & C3 Framework Indicator	SSKG2: The student will explain that a map is a drawing of a place and a globe is a model of the earth. D2.Geo.1.K-2. Construct maps, graphs, and other representations of familiar places.
Staging the Question	Students watch a video in which a boy talks about a time he got lost and have a discussion about what they have done when they have gotten lost.

Supporting Question 1	Supporting Question 2	Supporting Question 3
Understand	Understand	Understand
How do maps help us find what we are looking for?	How can we use maps to show others where things are?	How do electronic maps make finding some places easier?
Formative Performance Task	Formative Performance Task	Formative Performance Task
Explain how each map helps people find something they may be loooking for.	Create an electronic and paper map of their home, classroom, school, or neighborhood.	Use a GPS mapping site to get directions from student's address to school and participate in a discussion of ways this can make finding the school easier.
Featured Sources	Featured Sources	Featured Sources
Source A: Map of Zoo (example) Source B: *My Map Book* Source C: Google Maps or MapQuest	Source A: *The Cat in the Hat Can Map This & That* Source B: National Geographic MapMaker Tool	Sources from SQs 1 and 2

Summative Performance Task	ARGUMENT Do We Still Need Paper Maps? Construct an argument supported with evidence that addresses the compelling question.	
	EXTENSION Students record their arguments for presentation to their peers.	
Taking Informed Action	ASSESS Determine which type of map would help a school visitor find their classroom. ACT Create a school map in the chosen medium to share with school visitors.	

How does it feel to be a critical consumer of social studies curricula? We hope you feel empowered to closely examine and critique the curriculum you are currently using in your classroom, whether you have curated it from an online platform, or your district has purchased it from a developer. We also want you to be a critical *designer* of curricula. This means that you can design the curricula to be academically rigorous from the beginning instead of adjusting curricula that someone else designed to be more academically rigorous for your students. One way to do this is to remember that students' academic experiences occur inside and outside the elementary classroom in social studies. Your context—your *place*—matters. Place serves as a "lens" that you, as a teacher, can utilize to inform your social studies curricula, instruction, and assessment (Cornett, 2022). It is also a lens that students can use to "make sense of themselves and their surroundings" (McInerney et al., 2011, p. 5) and as a resource for "[their] education, entertainment, nourishment, inspiration, and lifelong learning" (Clark & Glazer, 2004, p. 1). As learning spaces, communities should be just as academically rigorous as the four walls of a classroom.

For Academic Rigor Activity 2 (see Activity 11.2), you'll explore the ways in which you can create academically rigorous social studies field trip experiences in the communities of your students and their families. Keep in mind that this may or may not be the community that you call home; it may be the community in which you teach. Thus, if you're a visitor in a community, be respectful of the place and space. The objective is to reflect on and learn more about the ways that you can create academically rigorous social studies field trip experiences. The first part of this activity is a reflective exercise on planning engaging experiences that occur before, during, and after field trips, while the second part includes a hands-on experience for you to go out and learn in the community on your own.

Activity 11.2 Academic Rigor Activity 2: Social Studies Rigor in Your Community

Social Studies Rigor in Your Community

Part 1: Let's foster rigorous (meaningful, integrative, value-based, challenging, active, anti-oppressive) field trip experiences! Have you ever gone on a field trip as a student (or planned a field trip as a teacher) that's simply a "one-off" experience? That is, you go because your grade level always goes there, it's not aligned to standards, and/or it's just for fun? More than likely, the answer is begrudgingly yes. And that's okay, but we want to avoid this in the future. We want to create more purposeful and powerful learning experiences for students in social studies. Complete the following table, reflecting on how you can engage in before, during, and after planning for meaningful field trips.

I'm planning for our ______________________________ grade (fill in grade level) field trip to ______________________________ (fill in field trip location). It happens during ____ (fill in the time of the school year).

	What can you do, as the teacher, to prepare for the field trip experience?	What can students do during the field trip experience (e.g., research, documentation, presentation)?	How can we ensure that the field trip experience is meaningful? Integrative? Value-based? Challenging? Active? Culturally relevant? Anti-oppressive?
Before			
During			
After			

Part 2: Now, we're going on a field trip to a place in our community! Remember, just observe and stay safe.

- **Civic action field trip**—Engage in a new civic action (e.g., volunteer for a political party or interest group, observe a board of education or city council meeting, participate in a community related organization).
- **Historic site field trip**—Visit a historic site (e.g., museum, state park, local monument). After researching the history and origins of its creation, funding, and so on, enlist the aid of docents and/or guides, as well as websites and

archival materials (if applicable), to understand the significance of the site to the larger community.

- **Cultural geography field trip**—Inquire about a group in society that you are unfamiliar with. Identify resources (e.g., literature, school library, local expert) to help you study the group's culture. Then, interview a member of that group to understand their views on a current issue in society. If appropriate, visit a restaurant, museum, exhibit, church, synagogue, temple, cultural association meeting, or school to complement your research/interview.
- **Economic decision-making field trip**—Visit a location where you can observe economics in action, such as a bank, grocery store, restaurant, clothing boutique, car dealership, or flea market.

While on the field trip, document your experience with field notes. Following are some questions to guide your note-taking:

- Make note of how you show up in the space. Did anything (or anyone) trigger you in some way (i.e., struggle groups, biases, etc.)?
- You chose to enter this space—what made you choose this field trip?
- Did you consider other places? If so, why did you decide against them?
- How does your field trip experience connect to state social studies standards?
- Now, complete Part 1 of this activity for this field trip.

Note. Part 2 is adapted from Dr. Patrice Preston-Grimes's assignment in her Elementary Social Studies Methods course at the University of Virginia (Broome & Preston-Grimes, 2009).

How was that experience? We hope it was #fieldtripgoals. A field trip is one way to help students make connections among the disciplines that comprise social studies (e.g., civics, history, geography, and economics) in academically rigorous ways. It allows them to apply what they have learned in class to real-life situations (see Pause & Reflect 11.2). Get out there and start planning field trip experiences for your students. We believe in you—you got this!

Pause & Reflect 11.2

Key Idea 1: To promote academic rigor with elementary students in social studies, you must critically evaluate curricula to ensure that you are personalizing learning experiences (instruction and assessments) in ways that are relevant and responsive to your students' needs and interests. Academically rigorous curricula and associated learning experiences should be rooted not only in state standards (social studies content knowledge, understandings, and skills), but also in students' and families' (and potentially your) communities.

After reading Key Idea 1, do you:

- Have the skills necessary to critically design and consume social studies curricula? If so, what skills have you learned?
- Know how to personalize academically rigorous learning experiences to make sure that they are relevant and responsive to students' needs and interests?
- Have strategies in mind to ensure that they are *meaningful*? *Integrative*? *Value-based*? *Challenging*? *Active*? *Anti-oppressive*? Do your strategies address state standards and consider students' and families' (and potentially your) communities?

What does it look like to teach elementary social studies to practice cultural competence?

As an elementary teacher, you practice cultural competence in your classroom through the social studies curricular, instructional, and assessment decisions that you make. For example, intentionally adjusting the curriculum to incorporate untold narratives, such as the stories of marginalized peoples (e.g., BIPOC), is a culturally competent approach. Most important, your students, their families, and their communities should be able to see themselves (i.e., their identities and cultures) in the curriculum and feel that their voices are represented. In Chapter 2, we learned that our identities consist of fundamental aspects such as our "size, neurodiversity and ability, citizenship status, language, education, gender, social class, age, location and place, sexuality, race and ethnicity or indigenous status, political orientation, and religion" (pg. 30 & 31). Power differentials within and among cultures, our own and others', influence the social, historical, and political ways in which we construct our identities. Through examining your own culture, you have the potential to develop a deeper awareness of your own identity as a culturally competent elementary social studies educator. Culturally competent educators find comfort in the discomfort (i.e., where you learn and grow). The following activities will require you to be vulnerable and trusting as you reflect on how your cultures, identities, communication, and perceptions of the world impact the way you (re)learn content, enact change, and, ultimately, teach social studies.

You can regularly inquire about students' lived experiences to practice cultural competence before, during, and after social studies instruction. You might ask, how do I do this? Take notes when students write about a pet, mention a favorite food they eat during a particular holiday, or invite you to a dance recital, for example. Survey students and families at multiple points during the school year, not just at the beginning. Go to community events if invited. Documenting as much as you can about students, their families, and their communities will allow you to have information to draw on for subsequent experiences in your classroom. Also, don't be afraid to share your own lived experiences; students will be responsive to learning more about their teacher (see Figure 11.2).

I fondly remember a first-grade classroom conversation that I facilitated on outdoor recreation. I will never forget the shocked look on a student's face when I shared that I cannot ride a bike. The student could not believe that his teacher had the same lived experience that he did. He was not ashamed when he shared with his peers that he didn't know how to ride a bike, either. He confidently mentioned that he preferred soccer as a form of outdoor recreation, anyway; I confidently mentioned that I prefer hiking for outdoor recreation.

Figure 11.2. Dr. Ariel Cornett.

Dialogue—student to student, teacher to student, and student to teacher—will support connection-making among shared and differing lived experiences. These connections may not be related to topics taught in school (like riding a bike); however, they could be related to your content area. That dialogue could foster content bridges to the history, geography, economics, and/or civics/government topics that you are exploring in social studies. You could even see opportunities to build interdisciplinary content bridges between lived experiences, your content area, and another content area (e.g., science, mathematics, or English language arts). Relatedly, with your assessments, you can promote cultural competence through varying the ways in which students can demonstrate their social studies content knowledge, understandings, and skills; they should be able to showcase what they have learned in ways that align with their FOK.

In Cultural Competence Activity (see Activity 11.3), you'll use the classroom FOK chart (see Appendix). Read the content-bridging scenarios, which are focused on elementary social studies instruction and assessments that you'll face (or are already facing) daily in the classroom. How would you respond to these scenarios? (Or how have you responded to these scenarios?) The objective is to analyze these scenarios and apply to them what you have learned about being a culturally competent elementary social studies educator—that is, how your own culture and identities interact with the cultures and identities of your students, their families, and their communities.

Activity 11.3 Cultural Competence Activity: Content Bridges

Content Bridges

Social Studies Content Bridges:

- **History**—You're teaching about Indigenous Peoples' contributions in your state (e.g., tools, clothing, homes, ways of making a living). What are the relationships between your cultures and identities?
  - Instruction: In what ways could you recognize and honor Student 15's Creek ancestry in your lessons? How would you discuss these ideas with Student 15 and Student 15's family?
  - Assessment: You want the summative assessment to be a presentation highlighting one of the contributions that students have studied. You assign students a contribution, and they are asked to complete further research. You want to have several presentation format options. What format might Student 8 (who enjoys calligraphy and painting) choose? What format might Student 13 (who enjoys story writing) choose? What format might Student 14 (who likes hip-hop music) choose?

- **Geography:** You're teaching about topographical features (e.g., continents and oceans) of the earth's surface. What is the relationship with your own culture and identities?
  - Instruction: In what ways could you bring in students' geographic backgrounds (e.g., ancestral homelands)? For example, Student 2 visits Hanoi, Vietnam, every summer, and Student 7 is Guatemalan.
  - Assessment: You want one of the formative assessments to include making a physical map of the continents and oceans using recyclable materials (Students 1, 3, 9, and 15 will be very excited). Once students have built the maps, you want them to explain their work verbally via a form of technology. How might you bring in technology options for this portion of the assessment? What types of technology do your students have background knowledge in and experiences with? (Hint: Check out the FOK of Students 3, 5, 6, 7, 9, 10, 12, and 15.)
- **Economics:** You're teaching about opportunity costs and how those relate to making saving or spending choices. What is the relationship with your own culture and identities?
  - Instruction: In what ways could you bring in students' interests as examples of opportunity costs? For example, one opportunity cost prompt for your class could be, "Would you rather buy a K-pop or hip-hop album?" Student 12 is going to say K-pop; thus, Student 12's opportunity cost is hip-hop. However, Student 14 is going to say hip-hop; thus, Student 14's opportunity cost is K-pop. Write a few example opportunity cost prompts based on the FOK chart.
  - Assessment: The formative assessment for this lesson is that students will pair up with a partner and write their own opportunity cost prompts to use with the class, based on what they know about their peers. You want students to share their prompts like on a game show (e.g., *The Price Is Right* style). How might you give Student 11 (an aspiring economist) an opportunity to shine during the sharing portion of this assessment?
- **Civics/Government:** You're teaching about citizenship and how and why rules are made. What is the relationship with your own culture and identities?
  - Instruction: In what ways could you apply students' interests to places and situations where rules are explicitly written or verbally communicated? For example, Student 2 loves basketball—how are basketball rules communicated? Student 11 enjoys the beach—how are rules communicated at the beach? Student 14 enjoys hiking—how are rules communicated in such

places as local, state, and national parks? Look at the FOK chart: What other students are connected with places where rules are explicitly written or verbally communicated?
- Assessment: Your summative assessment for this unit is revising classroom rules (i.e., expectations, norms, etc.). Students will make these suggestions in small groups. Based on the FOK chart, how could you adjust the ways in which students provide these suggestions for classroom rule revisions?

Well, culturally competent elementary social studies educators: Are you scenario'ed out? We hope not, because we're pretty sure there are more scenarios throughout this book. Reflecting on scenarios like these allows you to link theory to practice. You're linking culturally responsive pedagogy to best practices in social studies. Our goal is to walk alongside you as you envision how to translate your learning experiences from this course into culturally competent learning experiences that you create for your future students (see Pause & Reflect 11.3).

Pause & Reflect 11.3

Key Idea 2: To practice cultural competence with students in social studies, you must reflect on the influence of your own culture and identities on the ways in which you learn and teach the content. Additionally, you must strive to learn more about the lived experiences, cultures, and identities of your students, their families, and their communities. Then, it is important to document this information in a place such as a FOK chart to connect to social studies content in the curriculum as well as to inform and enhance your social studies instruction and assessments to be more culturally competent.

After reading Key Idea 2, do you:
- Feel confident in reflecting on how your constantly evolving culture and identities influence your learning and teaching of social studies?
- Have strategies in mind to learn more about the lived experiences, cultures, and identities of your students, their families, and their communities?
- Know how to connect information learned about students, families, and communities to social studies content found in the curriculum as well as how to inform and enhance your social studies instruction and assessments?

What does it look like to teach elementary social studies to advance critical (sociopolitical) consciousness?

Though social studies education is rooted in the development of democratic citizens, it has always been a contested field (Ross, 2017; Westheimer & Kahne, 2004). Scholars continue to ask controversial questions, such as, who is considered a citizen? What makes a "good" citizen? And, thus, what kind of citizens should teachers prepare the next generation to be? Teachers of social studies must consider these questions when developing classroom curricula because our ideologies and perspectives about the world greatly influence what we choose to teach and how we choose to teach it (Knowles, 2018): #curricular-instructional gatekeeper (we know, we know—we can't get enough of that phrase).

For Critical (Sociopolitical) Consciousness Activity 1 (Activity 11.4), we want you to grapple with your own ideas about what it means to be a democratic citizen, particularly in the United States of America. The objective of the activity is to self-reflect and consider how your perceptions impact your pedagogical approach in preparing young learners to engage as citizens. As teachers, we are lifelong learners, so consider your perceptions as baseline data that you will broaden and build on throughout your career.

Activity 11.4 Critical (Sociopolitical) Consciousness Activity 1: Democratic Citizen

Democratic Citizen

What does it mean to be a democratic citizen? Grab a piece of paper and define "democratic citizen." Feel free to use written language (singular words, hashtags, sentences) or imagery (drawings). Some guiding questions to consider as you complete this portion of the activity:

- What should democratic citizens know? What specific knowledge about our society—past and present—should they have (e.g., people, events)?
- What should democratic citizens understand? What broader themes about society should they have an awareness of?
- What should democratic citizens be able to do? What skills should they possess?

- What should democratic citizens value? What attitudes should they exhibit?

If possible, compare your list with those of your peers.

- What similarities or differences do you observe?
  - Why do you believe that you have similarities with your peers?
  - Why do you believe that you have differences with your peers?

K–12 classroom research has shown that good democratic citizenship has been taught to students as an amalgam of personally responsible civic actions such as paying taxes, volunteering, and following laws. Relatedly, Westheimer and Kahne (2004) argued that such civic characteristics are helpful and uplifting to a democracy—however, they are not enough in a multicultural society that is deeply steeped in inequity. Social issues continue to plague the United States, including racial injustice, unequal access to voting, climate and environmental injustice, economic injustice, and gender-based violence, among many others. For this reason, it is essential that the next generation of citizens envision a more equal and just society and engage in ways that transcend personally responsible civic actions. Society demands critically conscious citizens who have the knowledge, skills, and dispositions to challenge the status quo and disrupt oppressive structures.

What does this mean for social studies pedagogy? If we, as teachers, are to prepare students to be critically conscious citizens, we must design interdisciplinary (i.e., history, geography, economics, civics) learning experiences that foster an understanding of and commitment to issues of social justice. Such instruction should include, but is not limited to, the following components:

- Critical analysis of unequal and oppressive power structures in society
- Explorations of counternarratives that elevate the voices and experiences of groups often marginalized or omitted in society and in mainstream social studies curricula
- Discussions that challenge implicit biases, stereotypes, and overgeneralizations of people
- Authentic experiences that guide students in problem-solving issues of social injustice in their many communities (i.e., local, state, national, global)

History labs are one example of a learning experience that can be designed to prepare critically conscious citizens. Learning about the past helps to inform the democratic decisions we make today and thus can aid in everyday citizens' reconstructing society to be a more equitable and socially just place for all (Martell & Stevens, 2021). History labs focus on essential questions, such as, what does it mean to be a citizen? They support students' development of analysis and interpretation skills like those of professional historians as they engage in the exploration of primary and secondary sources and reconstruct narratives of the past. To foster critical consciousness, history labs should center counternarratives that elevate the voices and experiences of groups often marginalized and/or omitted in mainstream curricula while guiding students' exploration of citizens who have organized and influenced social change throughout time.

For Critical (Sociopolitical) Consciousness Activity 2 (see Activity 11.5), we detail an example of a history lab appropriate for upper elementary students (Grades 4–6). The example illuminates the narratives of children during the American civil rights movement as they engaged in civil disobedience to enact social change. The objective of this activity is to foster critical consciousness about what it means to be a democratic citizen via historical inquiry. We hope you will enjoy this powerful learning experience and see the potential for using it in the classroom. It offers a great opportunity for young children to recognize the contributions of citizens their own age and the ways in which they have impacted—and can impact—social change.

Activity 11.5 Critical (Sociopolitical) Consciousness Activity 2: History Lab

History Lab

Essential Questions: How did children engage as citizens during the American civil rights movement? How can we use this knowledge to guide us as citizens today?

Historical Source Work Activity

1. This activity can be implemented with individual students or small groups.
2. Distribute copies of the two primary sources to the student(s).

Primary Source #1:

(Image from Gottesman Libraries, Columbia University)

1. Guide your student(s) in the analysis of the primary source by asking these document-based questions (DBQs):
   - **Literal level:** *What do you observe in the photo?* (i.e., children are walking in a single-file line; police officers are watching the children march; the children are Black; the police officers are White)
   - **Interpretive level:** *Why do you think the author of the source took this photo? What story do you think the photo is telling, and what evidence do you have to support your thoughts?* (i.e., the police officers are arresting the children)
   - **Evaluative level:** *What questions would we want to further explore that are left unanswered by this source? What have we learned about citizens in a democratic society from this source? What have we learned about social change?*

Primary Source #2

1. Read aloud the oral history of *Debra V. Powe Brown* on the Kids in Birmingham 1963 website.[1]
2. Guide your student(s) in the analysis of the primary source by asking the following DBQs.
   - **Literal level:** *Where did Debra live in 1963? What is her race? What is her gender? Did she share any other elements of her identity? What were her experiences as a child during this time period?*
   - **Interpretive level:** *How did her identity and experiences help shape her thoughts, feelings, and actions during this time period?*
   - **Evaluative level:** *What questions are left unanswered by this source that we would want to further explore? What have we learned about citizens in a democratic society from this source? What have we learned about social change?*

Reflection

1. Come full circle with the learning and reflect on the essential questions.
   - *How did children engage as citizens during the American civil rights movement?*
   - *How can we use this knowledge to guide us as citizens today?*

Note. Analysis levels and questions adapted from Obenchain and Morris (2015).
1. See https://kidsinbirmingham1963.org/an-account-of-growing-up-in-birmingham-in-1963/#more-1312

Teaching about social issues such as racism can be challenging and should be approached in developmentally appropriate ways. In our experience teaching lower and upper elementary learners, we have found that students are very interested in discussing such issues because they witness and experience them firsthand. If you or anyone you know has ever said, "They're too young to talk about racism!" know that silence about this issue is harmful to society. Talking about race and racism is the only way to both acknowledge our country's difficult past and better reconstruct its future. Figure 11.3 and Pause & Reflect 11.4 can help you navigate teaching about the social issue of racism and address many others with children.

Pause & Reflect 11.4

Key Idea 3: To promote critical (sociopolitical) consciousness with elementary students in social studies, you must provide interdisciplinary learning experiences (i.e., history, geography, economics, civics) that guide students to problem-solve social issues in their many communities. To engage as critically conscious citizens, your students must develop the knowledge, skills, and dispositions to challenge the status quo and disrupt oppressive structures.

After reading Key Idea 3, do you:

- Understand the need to broaden our definitions about what it means to be a democratic citizen to include critically conscious knowledge, skills, and dispositions?

- Have strategies in mind to engage young learners in the examination (past or present) of social issues, such as racism?
- Know how to center content and historical narratives that challenge the status quo?

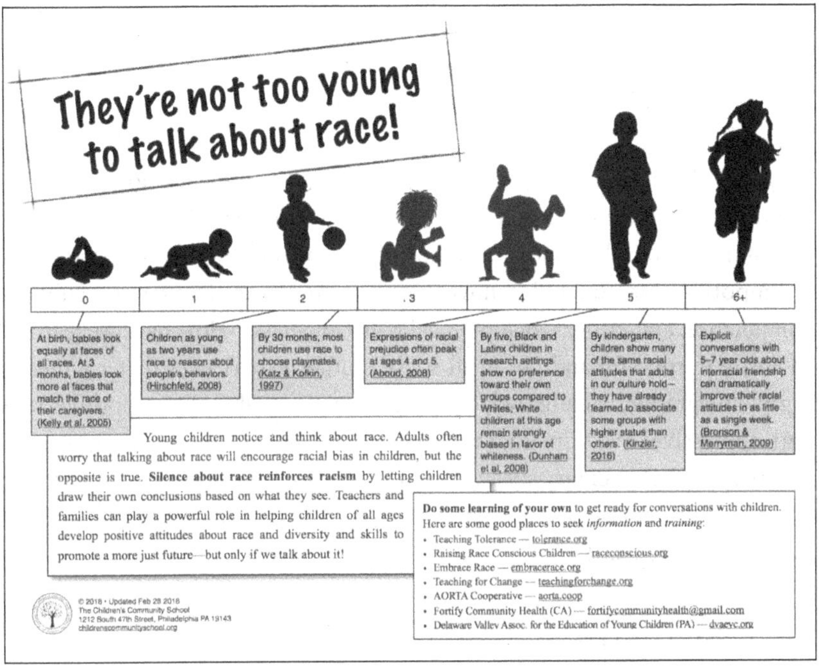

Figure 11.3. Social Justice Infographic. http://www.childrenscommunityschool.org/social-justice-resources/. Reprinted with permission.

Note: Infographic created by the Children's Community School, based in part on information and ideas from Jillian Addler at FirstUp, Lori Riddick at Raising Race Conscious Children, and kiran nigam at the Anti-Oppressive Resource and Training Alliance. © 2018.

Conclusion

To conclude this chapter, we want to leave you with a poem we've written. It began as a form of procrastination and work avoidance when we were supposed to be writing the chapter, but it evolved into a productive creative writing experience (you've probably been there and done that too—we're all human). Hopefully, the poem will take us full circle with this chapter. Imagine this poem sung to the tune of "Part of Your World" from *The Little Mermaid* (Benson, 1989).

I've got reading and writing a-plenty.
I've got science and mathematics galore.
You want social studies?
Just 10 to 15 minutes, occasionally.
But why does that matter?
It's actually a huge deal.
They (*your students*) need more.

As you look back on your own experiences (past or present), do you understand why we need increased instructional time for social studies at the elementary level, rather than continued marginalization? Why is social studies important for student learning (i.e., in regard to academic rigor, cultural competence, and critical sociopolitical consciousness)? How have we learned to create purposeful and powerful social studies experiences that are meaningful, integrative, value-based, challenging, active, culturally responsive, and anti-oppressive? We hope that this chapter has helped you to recognize the importance of elementary social studies and, more important, the importance of linking elementary social studies with CRP and anti-oppressive pedagogies (see Pause & Reflect 11.5).

Pause & Reflect 11.5

After you've read this chapter, consider these questions: What do you believe are the foundational understandings at the intersection of best practices in elementary social studies education, CRP, and anti-oppressive pedagogies? How will you work these foundational understandings into your classroom? In what ways can you advocate for these foundational understandings throughout your school, district/division, state, and nation, as well as our world?

Go out and change the world, culturally competent elementary social studies educators! And as Rodríguez and Swalwell (2022) advocate, make it a better world.

References

Anderson, D. (2014). Outliers: Elementary teachers who actually teach social studies. *Social Studies, 105*(2), 91–100. doi:10.1080/00377996.2013.850055

Bauml, M. (2016). Is it cute or does it count? Learning to teach for meaningful social studies in elementary grades. *Journal of Social Studies Research, 40*(1), 55–69. doi:10.1016/j.jssr.2015.02.001

Benson, J. (1989). Part of your world. On *The Little Mermaid: An Original Walt Disney Records Soundtrack*. Walt Disney.

Broome, J., & Preston-Grimes, P. (2009). "Doing" community civics: Connecting pre-service teaching and social studies standards to study local problems. *Social Studies Research and Practice, 4*(1), 169–177.

Clark, D., & Glazer, S. (2004). *Questing: A guide to creating community treasure hunts*. University Press of New England.

Cornett, A. (2020). *Elementary social studies teaching and learning in a standards-based multi-age classroom* [Unpublished doctoral dissertation]. University of Virginia. https://doi.org/10.18130/v3-395d-m660

Cornett, A. (2022). Family as an extension of place: Finding (and interrogating) your roots. *Hollywood or history? An inquiry-based strategy for using film to acknowledge trauma in social studies*, 189–200. Information Age.

C3 Teachers. (n.d.). *Inquiries: Join the adventure*. https://c3teachers.org/inquiries/

Curry, K. (2010). Beyond MIVCA: How social studies student teachers negotiate the National Council for the Social Studies' (NCSS) curriculum guidelines for powerful teaching and learning. *Social Studies Research & Practice, 5*(1), 24–44.

Gallagher, J. L., Swalwell, K. M., & Bellows, M. E. (2019). "Pinning" with pause: Supporting teachers' critical consumption on sites of curriculum sharing. *Social Education, 83*(4), 217–224.

Knowles, R. T. (2018). Teaching who you are: Connecting teachers' civic education ideology to instructional strategies. *Theory & Research in Social Education, 46*(1), 68–109.

Ladson-Billings, G. (1995a). But that's just good teaching! The case for culturally relevant pedagogy. *Theory Into Practice, 34*(3), 159–165. http://www.jstor.org/stable/1476635

Ladson-Billings, G. (1995b). Toward a theory of culturally relevant pedagogy. *American Educational Research Journal, 32*(3), 465–491. doi:10.3102/00028312032003465

Martell, C.C., & Stevens, K. M. (2021). *Teaching history for justice: Centering activism in students' study of the past*. Teachers College Press.

McInerney, P., Smyth, J., & Down, B. (2011). "Coming to a *place* near you?": The politics and possibilities of a critical pedagogy of place-based education. *Asia-Pacific Journal of Teacher Education, 39*(1), 3–16. doi:10.1080/1359866X.2010.540894

National Council for the Social Studies. (2009). Powerful and purposeful teaching and learning in elementary school social studies. *Social Studies and the Young Learner, 22*(1), 31–33.

National Council for the Social Studies. (2016). A vision of powerful teaching and learning in the social studies. *Social Education, 80*, 180–182.

National Council for the Social Studies. (2021). *A response to the attacks on social studies education in state legislatures and local boards of education*. https://www.socialstudies.org/current-events-response/response-attacks-social-studies-education-state-legislatures-and-local

Obenchain, K., & Morris, R. (2015). *50 social studies strategies for K-8 classrooms* (4th ed.). Pearson.

Rodríguez, N., Brown, M., & Vickery, A. (2020). Pinning for-profit? Examining elementary preservice teachers' critical analysis of online social studies resources about Black history. *Contemporary Issues in Technology and Teacher Education, 20*(3), 497–528.

Rodríguez, N. N., & Swalwell, K. M. (2022). *Social studies for a better world: An anti-oppressive approach for elementary educators*. W. W. Norton.

Ross, W. E. (2017). *Rethinking social studies: Critical pedagogy in pursuit of dangerous citizenship*. Information Age.

Thornton, S. J. (1989, March 27–31). *Aspiration and practice: Teacher as curricular-instructional gatekeeper in social studies*. Paper presented at the annual meeting of the American Educational Research Association, San Francisco, CA.

Thornton, S. J. (1991). Teacher as curricular-instructional gatekeeper in social studies. In J. P. Shaver (Ed.), *Handbook of research on social studies teaching and learning* (pp. 237–248). Macmillan.

Westheimer, J., & Kahne, J. (2004). What kind of citizen? The politics of educating for democracy. *American Education Research Journal, 41*(2), 237–269.

TWELVE

Literacy

Kara M. Taylor

IN THE EDUCATION RESEARCH REALM, researchers grapple with the continuous task of how to operationalize the term "literacy." Historically, a common definition of literacy highlights an individual's "ability to read and write" (American Speech-Language-Hearing Association, n.d.). However, on closer examination, this term holds many more complexities that have been explored through continuous literacy research. What are the many facets of literacy other than reading and writing? How can literacy reflect our changing society? How is literacy equitably measured to account for the diversity of students? Who is silenced and empowered with current perceptions of literacy? Despite these uncertainties and the complex nature of literacy, it is continuously utilized to assess competencies, trajectories, success, and opportunity in the 21st century.

This chapter functions under the understanding that literacy is dynamic and evolving based on the shifts in our 21st-century society. I acknowledge the pluralistic nature of literacy that seeks to sustain the lifeways of students raised with literate practices of a mother singing in the kitchen while straightening hair at the stove, to honoring the literacy of maneuvering Lebron James down the court in NBA2K12 (Ladson-Billings, 1995a; Moll & Gonzalez, 1994; Monson et al., 1994; Paris & Alim, 2017; Yopp & Singer, 1994). For the sake of this chapter, I will focus attention on a single second-year literacy methods course within the urban education program. This course challenges preservice teachers (PSTs) to examine their beliefs and assumptions about teaching literacy and their past experiences learning literacy. PSTs are prompted to reflect on how learning occurs for their future students and how young children develop their concepts and beliefs. This course calls for us to use research-based understandings of the development of children 8–12 years old as we explore intermediate literacy through multiple perspectives. All the content for this course is taught through a culturally relevant lens that intersects with the lens of critical literacy instruction.

Positionality Statement

Kara M. Taylor (she/her)

I am Dr. Kara M. Taylor.
I am Dr. Kara M. Taylor who is a Black womxn.
I am Dr. Kara M. Taylor who is a Black womxn educator.
I am Dr. Kara M. Taylor who is a Black womxn educator dedicated to being a public intellectual.
I am Dr. Kara M. Taylor who is a Black womxn educator dedicated to being a public intellectual activist.
I am an artist.
I am a wife.
I am a sister.
I am a friend.

The best way I can introduce myself to you, as readers, is to discuss my relationship with literacy over time. All my formative experiences with literacy were born in the Black church, from reading scripture in front of the congregation and filling the aisles with Psalms and Lamentations, to me and my schoolteacher-mother bonding over reading books of adventures we could not reach outside of our imagination. Literacy then nurtured me through life, teaching me that my Black was beautiful and why my hips did not fit any old jeans. Literacy became my good friend, and writing became my diary. I fostered a radical imagination through my literate practices to explore what equity looked like to me and to call out the oppression I carried, reluctantly, on my back. I used this radical imagination to begin my work as a middle school literacy educator, curriculum designer, and coach on Chicago's South Side for several years. Literacy became a lifeline for me to learn from my students and for them to learn from me. My classroom career was centered on creating a critical healing space around reading the word and world through my culturally sustaining literacy instruction and curriculum. Through my teaching and research, I hope to provide space for the stories that need to be told, spotlighting the Funds of Knowledge (FOK) that students carry to the classroom—stories of students that explain the prefix *micro-* by the microbraids in their hair. Personally, for me, literacy became a tool to kickstart my work of activism. I wrote letters advocating for the justice of my Black body and my students' bodies. These various literate practices cultivated literate spaces and experiences developed in classroom teaching and helped me expand my impact by becoming a clinical assistant professor of literacy at Indiana University Purdue University Indianapolis. My experience with literacy shifted to narrative inquiry research, a vehicle to spotlight the voices of silenced and marginalized populations. My teacher education classrooms explored literacy's dynamic nature through critical reflection, media analysis, field experiences, and curriculum design. I learned from narratives of PSTs like Emma who examined her Whiteness when her mother married a Haitian man. Literacy again became a lifeline for me as junior faculty at a predominantly White institution (PWI). My hope has always been equity and justice.

I present myself as a Black and able-bodied cisgender womxn first and foremost. This chapter is written through the lens of my specific experiences of oppression and privilege linked to my identity. I use the privilege of my educational background as a platform to discuss my equity work. While I am a Black womxn, I do understand that this chapter is told from a unique perspective grounded in my lived experiences. Everything about my teaching, learning, and experiences with literacy is based on how I presently interact with the world, and my life history. What drives my equity-oriented culturally relevant literacy work is my need to explore the power of literacy beyond just reading books and writing essays. With all equity work, the first step toward change is interrogating one's own bias and relationship to justice (see Pause & Reflect 12.1).

Pause & Reflect 12.1

- What is your relationship with literacy?
- How has your relationship with literacy evolved? Think of specific formative experiences you can call upon.

Key Terms:

- **Activism:** intervening through action and policy to effect social, political, economic, or environmental change.
- **Critical literacy:** the ability to discern and interpret power dynamics in text.

- Lifeways: the customs, values, and practices of a culture.
- Literacy: ways of thinking about, doing, understanding or expressing knowledge.

Key Ideas:

1. *Academic rigor in culturally relevant literacy classrooms requires preservice teachers to explore their relationship and understanding of academic content introduced within state standards before they can create effective learning opportunities for all students.*
2. *Cultural competence in culturally relevant literacy classrooms requires preservice teachers to examine their own relationships with literacy and culture before they can design similar learning experiences for their students.*
3. *Critical consciousness in culturally relevant literacy classrooms requires preservice teachers to engage with the media to critique the world around them and learn about the lives of their students.*

What Is Culturally Relevant Literacy Instruction, and How Does It Intersect with Critical Literacy?

Culturally relevant pedagogy (CRP) can be broadly defined as a conceptual framework that promotes the value of students' cultural and linguistic backgrounds, interests, histories, and lived experiences in all aspects of teaching and learning in classrooms, as well as in schools (Ladson-Billings, 1994, 2009; Milner, 2017). The sustenance of the cultures and histories of students and their communities can be achieved through promoting students' various lifeways in instruction (Paris, 2019). In conjunction with the preservation of cultures, CRP can improve student engagement and achievement, and college readiness and success for all youth, particularly for youth of color. CRP offers a teaching approach that empowers students socially, emotionally, academically, and politically by using cultural referents to impart knowledge, skills, and attitudes (Ladson-Billings, 1994, 2009). Gloria Ladson-Billings (1995a) proposed three interconnected tenets of CRP: (1) student academic rigor through a commitment to learning and achievement; (2) students' turning their gaze inward through cultural competence; and (3) the facilitation of a sociopolitical/critical consciousness through allowing opportunities to critique inequities within educational and social institutions. Literacy is viewed through the framework of culturally relevant instruction in this literacy methods course.

Culturally Relevant Literacy Instruction

The 2020 "What's Hot in Literacy" report revealed that almost a quarter of the respondents ranked highly "emphasizing culturally responsive curriculum and instruction" (Cassidy et al., 2021, p. 10). The big overarching question is: What is culturally relevant literacy instruction? The core of my course is grounded in the belief that literacy and education are intrinsically culturally relevant. Teaching and learning are shaped by culture. But the question is, whose culture? Culture is defined by a group of people's lifeways, linguistic repertoires, values, habits, and common understandings—all the things that are recognized as membership and belonging within this group of people (Bomer, 2017). In-service teachers typically draw on their own cultural experiences and dominant cultural understandings to plan instruction, and interpretation and predictions of student responses are seen through the lens of the teacher's social experiences. In the case of the PWI I work with, most of my PSTs are White women functioning with a White gaze (Bomer, 2017). A culturally relevant literacy instruction framework disrupts the habit of merely projecting PSTs own culture onto the students they teach. Literacy, as a subject matter, is fertile ground for this framing because reading, writing, and signing are grounded in people's interactions within a culture together. Though we expect our students to have the minds and habits of the culture we are familiar with, they come with their own identities and cultural background that are sometimes outside the majority. The sad reality of the cultural disconnect between teachers and students seems to be true of any teacher; however, it is most prevalent among White women because they occupy most of the teaching force. I, as a Black womxn, possess a unique experience as a former teacher in Chicago Public Schools from the South Side of Chicago, which frames how I teach my methodology courses, how I taught my middle schoolers, and how I view literacy broadly; however, I do not expect my PSTs to view the world through my unique lens as a person of color (POC). Though my instinct is to plan my methods course through my experience, to reach my White PSTs in a class, I had to adjust my instruction and tasks. This required me to learn along the way because I am no expert. A big aspect of CRP is the necessity for adaptation, and this applies to both teachers and students.

A common definition of literacy is reading, writing, listening, and speaking. Culturally relevant literacy instruction seeks to bridge the gap between students' lives inside and outside school through the lens of their own culture to meet the needs of all students (Shealey & Callins, 2007). In other words, students read the word to read the world around them—with the option of writing themselves into the world if they do not see depictions of themselves. Literacy is varied based on the cultural lenses that students bring (see Pause & Reflect 12.2).

Pause & Reflect 12.2

- What social and cultural experiences do you bring to your teaching? What potential biases are attached to these experiences?
- How can literacy connect cultural identities across classrooms, schools, and society?

How does culturally relevant literacy instruction look in action?

A common misconception when engaging in CRP is the belief that success in teaching is measured by knowing the right things to do. Culturally relevant literacy teaching is not formulaic and does not come with a prescribed manual to follow. The truth is, success in teaching relies heavily on how we, as teachers, think about our students, the communities to which they belong, and our critique of the social structures that exist in the schools we teach and in the world. Coming into a PWI as a Black womxn scared me because I was hyper-aware of the oppression that research revealed I might face. However, viewing all my students as "impenetrable" because they are White would not serve a purpose. I turned my attention to facilitating opportunities to examine social structures of White supremacy in schools and society. CRP was not an "add-on" or something I sometimes did; it had to be the foundation of my methodology course and inform every aspect of our practice. What I use is not part of a list of specific strategies or checklists; it was gathered through trial and error, unique to the experiences, communities, and histories of students enrolled in my courses, as well as my own. Though my assignments and tasks rely on my outlook on literacy and the experiences of my PSTs, a common element within my course and that of any culturally relevant classroom is the focus on the three tenets of culturally relevant instruction: academic rigor, cultural competence, and critical/sociopolitical consciousness. Not every tenet of CRP may be achieved in every assignment, but I strive to have well-rounded assignments.

What does academic rigor look like in a culturally relevant literacy classroom?

The first pillar of CRP is academic rigor. This tenet contends that part of the teacher's role is to stimulate the minds of students academically. I had an obligation in this course to have PSTs explore, and become thoroughly familiar with, the content for literacy for Grades K–5, as well as research-based methodological practices of how to teach literacy in an inequitable way. This looks like holding high transparent academic expectations scaffolding instruction from where students are. My role as a culturally relevant teacher educator was to teach content, know the learners in the class, model strategies that they too can carry over into their future classes, and provide explicit instruction on how to teach and learn content for themselves and future learners. Reflexivity and vulnerability were key concepts to rehearse by all members of our classroom community. The aspects of this course that exhibited academic rigor were covered in an assignment called "Unpacking the Standards."

Unpacking the Standards

The goal of state standards is to define the skills and knowledge of students. This concept seems easy enough. I used to read the standards, look for key literacy vocabulary in the standards, and teach the skill in whatever way I found fitting to my PSTs. However, I learned in my fifth year of teaching in professional development that standards are more than just a list of skills;

each standard provides a road map of essential skills that must be taught, and how they should be taught. Standards guide the goals of educators. This assignment is a result of my purposeful focus on creating space for students to slow down and critically view literacy standards and how they are perpetual and instructive nature.

State standards seem to be the enemy for many classroom teachers because they are considered "restrictive" in a system steered by standardized tests; however, I introduce state standards as a road map that allows both creativity and autonomy in my course. Yes, skills that need to be mastered for each grade level are introduced within standards, and sometimes the methods used to teach these skills need to be addressed, but concepts like texts and activities are the teacher's prerogative. The broadness of the standards allows for the culturally relevant work of teachers. Often, academic success is one of the most forgotten in CRP.

Activity 12.1 Unpacking Standards

Unpacking Standards

Task: Pre-service Teachers (PSTs) were asked to dissect a group of standards across K–5 grades.

For each standard, PSTs will operationally define each term in Grade K–5 student-friendly language as they understand it, write all objectives associated with the standard, note necessary prerequisites, and describe how this skill shows up in our everyday lives.

Value

PSTs must know the content that their students are required to learn and how the state perceives it to be taught. This allows a refresher on content, and this is a live document and resource to be used throughout the semester. Also, the connection between academic content and the world is drawn through the examples.

Understandings

- We must know content before teaching, and it's okay to refresh our memories on content at any time.

- Content is viewed in more specific ways than we are used to knowing.
- We use literacy skills in our everyday life.

Components

1. **Close reading:** The PSTs will read through the standards and annotate them one by one, circling the verbs and underlining the nouns. This practice reminds students to slow down and read the standards for what they are.
2. **Looking at the what and how:** The PSTs remove all the nouns and verbs from the standards. Students will work to operationally define the nouns that are representative of the skill and list the verbs representative of the method in which the skill is achieved. This offers PSTs a safe space to reacquaint themselves with content before teaching.
3. **Put it all together:** The PSTs then will create objectives using the frame "students will be able to ________ (verb) ______________(skill) using __________". This closing statement allows the teacher to assess the effectiveness of their pedagogy.
4. **Turning your gaze out into the world:** The PSTs will provide real-world examples in which this literacy skill appears. This creates a deep connection between content and the world around them.

Example:

Describe characters in a story (e.g., their traits, motivations, or feelings) and explain how their actions contribute to the plot.

Characters: a character is a person, animal, being, creature, or thing in a story.

Story: an account of an incidence or events.

Trait: character traits are aspects of a person's behavior that are valued by the community or society around them.

Characterization

Direct: narrator explicitly/directly describes a character.

Indirect: character traits are revealed through actions that the reader must infer.

S.T.E.A.L. Method Mapping Model

- Speech
- Thoughts

- Effect on others
- Actions
- Looks

Objectives Student Will Be Able To (SWBAT):

- Describe characters in a story using traits, motivations, and feelings by the STEAL Method Mapping.
- Explain how character actions contribute to plot using a plot map/story mapping.

This assignment was framed from my experience serving as a literacy coach and as a middle school literacy teacher (see Activity 12.1). In my conversations with teachers I coached, and from my own lesson planning, I often found myself addressing the skill of characterization, or any other skill, solely to cover the state standards using whatever method(s) I chose. In my early years of teaching, I derived strategies/resources from websites designed specifically for teachers, by teachers, like Teachers Pay Teachers. Through observation, I discovered that teachers spend more time on the identity aspects of CRP than on the responsibility we must apprentice students into the content. My students expressed the necessity they had in common to familiarize themselves with literacy concepts for grades as early as kindergarten to complete the assigned task. There is a particular beauty in my PSTs coming to understand that, as teachers, we are not experts. I am no expert, and, as their instructor, I sometimes find myself going through the same process they experience (see Pause & Reflect 12.3).

Pause & Reflect 12.3

- What is your relationship with the state standards? What are the values of the state standards for you?
- An intern turned in the following assignment. They are struggling to find real-world connections to this state standard. What examples would you suggest to this student?

What does cultural competence look like in a culturally relevant literacy classroom?

The second tenet of CRP is cultural competence. Cultural competence requires teachers to journey inward and take critical looks at their own linguistic and cultural histories in education on a personal level. Teachers are better able to take responsibility for facilitating the learning about their students' culture and community as they interrogate their own identity, culture, biases, and privilege to critically assess and strengthen their instructional practice (Ladson-Billings, 1995a). Ideally, instruction that reflects cultural competence would be full of mirrors reflecting the lifeways of students and teachers, and windows into new understandings across the cultures of others. The teacher, using students' culture as a basis for instruction, helps students honor their own culture while accessing and learning about the rest of the world around them. In my course, one important way to accomplish this was through critical interrogation of self through narrative writing.

I firmly believe that literacy holds the power to heal, and, as individuals in the world, we are walking texts. This assignment has always been situated toward the middle or end of my course because it relies so heavily on a classroom culture of trust and safety. To prepare for this task, smaller discussions generated through quick-write assignments were used to build rapport and trust. Asking PSTs to reflect and "describe a time in which you felt 'otherness'" seems much more feasible and approachable than the personal narrative task. PSTs traveled through many different ideas and scenarios, searching for the right event to elaborate on with clarity of the intended purpose. I was aware that questions about life stories are not often something asked of PSTs, classroom teachers, or students, but everything that is taught or learned should reflect on who we are as people (see Figure 12.1).

Personal Narrative

Preservice teachers (PSTs) are asked to write about and discuss the first time they realized they were __________[insert race here] or why they chose to work in urban education. PSTs choose one event to chronicle using elements of plot, etc., and attach a critical reflection on new outlooks. Students go through a workshop process with drafts, analyzing dialogue, plot, descriptive language, character, reflection, etc.

This assignment allows PSTs to engage in critical reflection to interrogate bias, identity as racial beings, privilege/oppression, and formative experiences that drive their philosophy of teaching. Essentially, this is necessary because we teach who we are.

Understandings

- We all bear race and culture that comes with privilege and oppression.
- Teachers must reflect on more than just our practice.
- Our beliefs are embedded heavily in our experiences.

Examples: Some PSTs of color reflect on their experiences witnessing racial aggression

It was towards the end of my Junior English course when the topic of race came up. My professor, Mrs. Embry, a short middle-aged White woman with brown shoulder-length curly hair, stood in the middle of the white-walled oval-shaped classroom. She began explaining the roadblocks African Americans faced when trying to obtain a job. "Right when they get on the phone, they deal with discrimination. Right when the employer hears their voice, they're automatically judged by the sound of it. Some do not even get a call based on their name on their application." Kierra, an African American student with shoulder-length black hair and a Nike long-sleeve sweater, began to touch on her oppressive experiences: "I walk into a store in the mall and I feel people staring at me. Not asking if I am okay, but just following me to make sure I am not stealing." "Mmmmm" and head nods began to fill the room. I kept quiet with my legs mushed together and my elbows resting on my desk. Sitting near the back of the classroom staring out at my classmates, some whose faces showed frustration as their eyebrows began to form a V shape and some displaying acceptance as they nodded their heads but showed no emotion on their faces. I related to the individuals who showed acceptance. I related to their casual response to the situation at hand. I knew the world had a lot of fixing to do, but what was I going to do at 15 years old? My eyes began to shift to a square table full of four White male students. Their eyebrows furrow with their anticipation on the rim of breakage. One male, in particular, began to stomp his foot in place. He raised his hand ready to state his clause. Mrs. Embry, turning her attention away from the chatter, made eye contact with the young man. "Kyle?"

The buildup of words spewed out of his mouth, "That does not happen," and he began shaking his head profusely, with all eyes on him. Mrs. Embry started to pace with her head down and said, "Honey, it's systematic racism. Why do you feel this does not happen?" Kierra, whose eyebrows now resembled Kyle's, shifted her seat towards him and said, "But how do you know?" Bloodshot red Kyle now turned his seat to face his desk and began to start back up his therapeutic foot taps.

Another example illustrates critical reflections of a PSTs' internal struggles with their own identity:

Being a Mexican American woman, a minority, will not make or break me, it will not be the definition of who I am. It will always be a part of my identity, but it shouldn't be the only thing people see. I want to use my position to show the ones who pushed me down that I can get back up just fine by being who I am. My mama is White, has green-blue eyes, dirty blonde and straight hair, and very thin and light eyebrows. When you look at me you don't see white at first sight, you see Mexican. I have very dark brown hair with some waves and curls. My eyebrows are very thick and dark, and my facial hair in general is darker. Being one of the only two Mexicans in an almost all-White school, and one Black family, was one of the rudest awakenings to me when it comes to racial injustice.

Being in eighth grade, having some type of social studies class is a requirement, and mine was a difficult class to be a part of, especially when we talked specifically about the history between Mexico and America. We were learning about immigration and how it has affected American culture, this topic came after learning about the Mexican-American war. One of my peers, Brogan, asked the question, "Why is it okay for Mexicans to keep coming over to the United States?" All my teacher could say was, "I don't know, but it needs to start happening the right way."

I knew what he meant by his statement. After that particular conversation between my teacher and my peer, all I got were daggering stares! All of these were so piercing, that they made me feel sick to my stomach.

Alternative prompts

- A prompt to address otherness

Describe a time in which you felt otherness.

- A prompt to address relationships to language

Write a metaphorical letter to language discussing your relationship to it. This letter should chronicle a formative experience that is indicative of your relationship.

- A prompt to address PSTs' purpose for teaching

Describe a formative moment that has impacted your purpose for becoming a teacher.

Figure 12.1. Critical Reflection.

I am aware that this assignment is very personal, but also very necessary. In the profession of teaching, I was never asked how I knew I was culturally affiliated with the community with which I identified, nor had I ever asked anyone this. And rarely was I asked about how I was doing outside of classroom performance. My hope was to normalize vulnerability among teachers. Many White PSTs felt discomfort with this assignment because fragility and privilege had to be addressed within their narratives. Some told stories of the oppressions they may have caused or witnessed as a bystander. This is a very early course in the urban teacher education program sequence, so exposure to critical conversations was novel to many of the students. My PSTs of color tackled emotions of trauma and disappointment in their stories of being oppressed, or witnessing other marginalized populations being oppressed. PSTs discussed why activism and bravery were important in their stories to bring about change for future students they wished to teach (see Pause & Reflect 12.4).

Pause & Reflect 12.4

- What cultural communities are you a part of? What bias may you be bringing into your teaching as a result of your personal and cultural experiences?

What does critical (sociopolitical) consciousness look like in a culturally relevant literacy classroom?

The last tenet of CRP is critical/sociopolitical consciousness. Critical/sociopolitical consciousness requires that teachers actively engage in personal and sociopolitical issues that impact their students and facilitate opportunities for their students to critique the world around them. Teachers must acquaint themselves with relevant issues and structures of oppression that plague the communities' students that come from, and maintain an awareness about what is going on in the larger world. This is mostly achieved through discourse in which students challenge norms and name systems of oppression for what they are. Students are encouraged to see themselves as agents of social change and transformation. Students are therefore empowered to think and act in ways that challenge the inequitable status quo among people, within communities, and in society at large. In my course, I designed an assignment called "While We Were Gone News." This assignment was a response to students' admission that they do not engage with the media or news beyond their own social media interactions.

My PSTs, and many people around me, avoid the news because they say it's "just too sad"; however, discussing the news provides opportunities to rehearse critical discourse and critique the world around us. The construct of this assignment was rehearsed many times as a class because of the discomfort my PSTs expressed with the "name it" section. Terms such as "bullying" or "injustices" were used to describe the occurrences, as opposed to specifically calling out types of oppression such as ableism, racism, and sexism. This is important to address because as advocates for students in our classroom and marginalized populations in the world, individuals must be willing to name and call out injustices specifically (see Figure 12.2).

PSTs are required to pull and present a news story centered on oppression and inequalities in schooling spaces and the world. PSTs must summarize the event, present multiple viewpoints through Twitter/Facebook, name and explain the injustice, and lead a class discussion every week. PSTs are given opportunities to overtly call out injustices and oppression and see how it is addressed in the world. PSTs are forced to look at the implications of events in the world on the PSTs in the classroom and themselves.

Understandings

- World events impact schooling spaces.
- We all have positions and views—even as teachers.
- Oppression surfaces in many forms: implicit and explicit.
- Each of us must be an activist for our students and injustices in the world.

Step 1: PSTs list the title of the article, a picture of the event, and a summary of the event. This step allows PSTs to work on their ability to objectively summarize crucial details of the story.

Summary: A high school teacher from Virginia was fired in December for refusing to use the preferred pronouns of a transgender student. After being fired, the terminated teacher from West Point High School filed a lawsuit against the school district. Peter Vlaming, who was a French teacher, stated that he refused to utilize the pronouns of a female-to-male transgender student because it "violated his conscience" and cited religious beliefs. In his lawsuit that he filed on Monday, October 1st, he accused the school board of violating his right to free speech. Vlaming stated that he was eventually given an ultimatum by school administrators. He could either choose to use the male pronouns when addressing the transgender student OR he could lose his job. The lawsuit states, "Mr. Vlaming's conscience and religious practice prohibits him from intentionally lying, and he sincerely believes that referring to a female student as a male by using an objectively male pronoun is telling a lie." He is requesting $1 million in damages. There is also an online petition that has more tham 1,000 signatures titled "Don't terminate Mr. Vlaming."

Step 2. PSTs will gather various viewpoints from social media platforms and the article itself showing how the public is addressing the issue. This step provides PSTs with multiple viewpoints apart from their own on the social issue.

Viewpoints:

Peter Vlaming was punished for remaining silent.
So citizens can remain silent during the Pledge of Allegiance, but this Christian teacher cannot remain silent when school officials demand that he pronounce a false pronoun?

Sound of Silence: Teacher Fired over Trans Pronouns Sues School
frc.org

Madeline Marsanne
@MadelineOnMars

Remarkable how a religious prohibition on [some ostensible] lies requires people to tell different lies, isn't it?

Mr. Vlaming teaches French. He's cynically counting on other people's ignorance.

Pronouns are just a start! Did he manage to avoid using verbs and adjectives too?

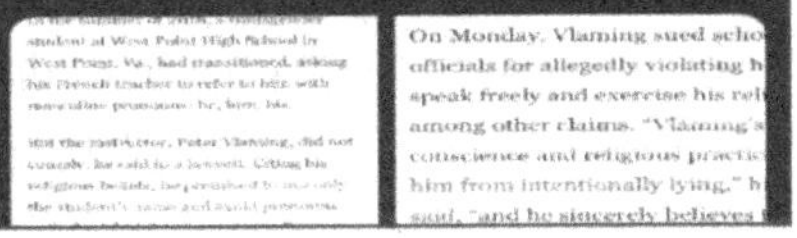

Claire Lankford
Man. As a teacher I can absolutely say he is an embarrassment to the profession. Personal religious/political beliefs have no place in the classroom. Our job is to create this supportive environment for our students and anyone who is not capable or willing to do that should not be teaching. Of all of the things our students have to go through, especially students that are part of the LGBT community, the classroom should be the last place where students feel targeted and disresepcted.
Like Reply 35

Erin Tate
What a hateful stance. This child's right to human dignity is not a lie - it is objectively their truth if they say it is their truth. This man clearly does not have religious beliefs surrounding compassion and respect for others.
Like Reply 45

Step 3. PSTs name the system of oppression and explain why they named the issue as such. Finally, PSTs will facilitate a class discussion regarding this news occurrence and its impact on the class. Naming a structure of oppression allows PSTs a safe space to practice engaging in critical discourse.

Social Injustice: Heterosexism

het·er·o·sex·ism

noun

1. discrimination or prejudice against homosexuals on the assumption that heterosexuality is the normal sexual orientation.

This article represents heterosexism because Mr. Vlaming deliberately ignored the child's wishes to be properly generated and be addressed by the correct pronouns. By ignoring the student's wish to be gendered properly, Mr. Vlaming is devaluing this student and his identity. Mr. Vlaming is discrediting this student who is part of the LGBTQ+ community based on his personal beliefs and religion.

Questions:

1. As a religious teacher, what limits should be taken to not allow religious influences and ideologies to affect the treatment of students?
2. What's more important: the separation of church and state or constitutional right?
3. How would you approach a situation where there may be a religious student who may not want to acknowledge another student who is a part of the LGBTQ+ community in your classroom?

Figure 12.2. While We Were Gone News.

This assignment fostered an interesting result from my PSTs , who confidently approached previous task. The project, While We Were Gone News, centers racism, ableism, heterosexism, and classism. When I asked the class what brought about the narrowing in on these two forms of oppression—racism and classism—they responded that it was due to their lack of knowledge about and relationship to other oppressive practices. This heightened my awareness of the necessity of presenting more varied news content in my courses to generate critical discourse (see Pause & Reflect 12.5).

Pause and Reflect 12.5

- How often do you watch or read the news? Why?
- When did you last engage in a critical conversation?

Conclusion

The journey toward culturally relevant literacy instruction is constantly shifting with the times and innovations of society. However, fostering opportunities for future teachers/educators to build critical dispositions centered on the three large tenets—academic success, cultural competence, and critical/sociopolitical consciousness—could have a tremendous impact on building equity in the field. In literacy education, these tenets work together to allow both future teacher educators and students to read the word (text) so they can critically engage with the world.

References

American Speech-Language-Hearing Association. (n.d.). Reading and writing (literacy). Retrieved July 5, 2022, from https://www.asha.org/public/speech/development/literacy/#:~:text=Literacy%20is%20your%20ability%20to,at%20work%2C%20and%20at%20home

Bomer, R. (2017). What would it mean for English language arts to become more culturally responsive and sustaining? *Voices From the Middle, 24*(3), 11.

Cassidy, J., Ortlieb, E., & Grote-Garcia, S. (2021). What's hot in literacy: New topics and new frontiers are abuzz. *Literacy Research and Instruction, 60*(1), 1–12.

Ladson-Billings, G. (1994). What we can learn from multicultural education research. *Educational Leadership, 51*(8), 22–26.

Ladson-Billings, G. (1995a). But that's just good teaching! The case for culturally relevant pedagogy. *Theory Into Practice, 34*(3), 159–165. http://www.jstor.org/stable/1476635

Ladson-Billings, G. (2009). *The dreamkeepers: Successful teachers of African American children* (2nd ed.). Jossey-Bass.

Milner, H. R., IV. (2017). Race, talk, opportunity gaps, and curriculum shifts in (teacher) education. *Literacy Research: Theory, Method, and Practice, 66*(1), 73–94.

Moll, L. C., & Gonzalez, N. (1994). Lessons from research with language-minority children. *Journal of Reading Behavior, 26*(4), 439–456.

Monson, R. J., Monson, M. P., & Harste, J. C. (1994). Literacy as inquiry: An interview with Jerome C. Harste. *The Reading Teacher, 47*(7), 518–521. http://www.jstor.org/stable/20201312

Paris, D. (2019). Naming beyond the White settler colonial gaze in educational research. *International Journal of Qualitative Studies in Education, 32*(3), 217–224.

Paris, D., & Alim, H. S. (Eds.). (2017). *Culturally sustaining pedagogies: Teaching and learning for justice in a changing world.* Teachers College Press.

Shealey, M. W., & Callins, T. (2007). Creating culturally responsive literacy programs in inclusive classrooms. *Intervention in School and Clinic, 42*(4), 195–197.

Yopp, H. K., & Singer, H. (1994). Toward an interactive reading instructional model: Explanation of activation of linguistic awareness and metalinguistic ability in learning to read. *Theoretical Models and Processes of Reading, 4*, 381–390.

THIRTEEN

Arts

Alexandra J. Reyes

Arts Integration as a Tool for Humanization

When people mention the arts in schools, what comes to mind? Do you think of those "specials" classes: art and music? Do you smell the paint? Can you feel the wooden rhythm sticks in your hands as you alternate patterns of tap-tap-ruuuuuuub? Or are you reminded of the time you dressed up as a historical figure and told your audience about your life and accomplishments? Perhaps you were really into making dioramas, like I was.

Each of these experiences is a part of the arts as students experience them in schools. The first two examples are reminiscent of discrete arts classes (i.e., arts education), while the last two describe arts-integrated curricular activities. In this interactive chapter, we'll focus on the latter—arts as an integral part of learning content. More specifically, we'll focus on how we can integrate arts and literature across the curriculum to create humanizing learning experiences that promote rigor, advance cultural competence, and foster critical consciousness within a frame of culturally relevant pedagogy.

Arts integration refers to the intentional use of the arts—literature, visual art, music, dance/creative movement, drama, and media arts—as a teaching methodology to engage students in learning content. Silverstein and Layne (2010) defined arts integration as "an approach to teaching in which students construct and demonstrate understanding through an art form. Students engage in a creative process, which connects an art form and another subject area and meets evolving objectives in both" (p. 1). Arts integration may also be called arts-infused curriculum or swept under the broader umbrella of interdisciplinary or multidisciplinary studies.

Positionality Statement

Alex Reyes (she/her/ella)

Hi! I'm Alex Reyes. I am both Latina and American—ethnically ambiguous and with an accent in Spanish that is uniquely that of a Latinx kid who grew up in the States ("de aquí"). I have features just dark enough to make some view me as "exotic," and for similarly mixed folks to recognize the "Other" in me (see Figure 13.1). I am a cisgender middle-aged, able-bodied woman. I am fat and working to unlearn my internalized fatphobia and ageism. I have U.S. citizenship and can speak English without a "foreign" accent, although my Spanish surname "gives me away" as Other. Alternately, I experience the anxiety of so many bicultural people—am I Latina enough? I share all of this to say: I simultaneously have many privileges and exist at the intersection of multiple marginalized identities.

I credit my diverse schooling experiences, along with my early exposure to different cultures and disparity, for my lifelong interest in multiculturalism, justice, and the arts. Or perhaps it's just that I was born a Libra. Either way, my early exposure to people, religion, art, and music from different backgrounds gave me a view of potential ways of being and knowing. My pedagogy stems from my understanding that culture, language, and diversity are assets to be shared and that the arts provide opportunities for everyone to be heard, seen, and celebrated.

Figure 13.1. Alex Reyes.

Key Terms:

- **Arts integration:** using various art forms to deepen the understanding of teaching and learning.
- **Critique:** a four-step process that includes describing, analyzing, interpreting, evaluating, and judging a piece of art.
- **Curation:** the process of selecting of pieces of art for an intentional purpose such as teaching or for an exhibit.
- **Soft skills:** interpersonal characteristics that help you effectively interact with others.

Key Ideas:

1. ***Incorporating the arts into instruction increases academic rigor and engagement, as well as a host of other important soft skills.***
2. ***The arts are for everyone.*** Art can be integrated into the curriculum to help us learn about and understand different perspectives, showcase diverse voices, and celebrate multiple cultures. Learning about ourselves and others advances cultural competence.
3. ***Reflecting on our arts practice can help us interrogate our beliefs about what is worth studying and knowing.*** Arts integration can help foster critical consciousness and be a force for increasing accessibility and equity in schools.

The Arts Are at the Heart of the Human Experience

The arts have likely been around for as long as humans have existed. Approximately 12,000 years before the Common Era, our ancestors were making artistic choices and telling stories through visual art (just look at the cave paintings at Altamira!). Archaeologists and anthropologists have unearthed pottery, jewelry, and other practical artifacts that show decorative patterns and images from prehistoric sites all over the world. Figurative representations have been found dating back some 45,000 years in Indonesia, and abstract decorations from South Africa may be as old as 100,000 years (McDermott, 2021). To me, this is clear evidence that art is central to being human. Art is intentional and creative, and it aims to either evoke or provoke a response from the viewer. Ancient carvings show people wearing jewelry, makeup or paint, and decorative clothing—none of which are biologically necessary to human survival. The desire for aesthetics is proof that humans are made to create and consume art. As Merryl Goldberg explained (2021), "the arts are fundamental to education because they are fundamental to human knowledge and culture, expression, and communication" (p. XV).

Reflecting on Our Arts Experience

Did you have art and music classes when you were in grade school? Increasingly, high stakes standardized testing is crowding out "enrichment" classes, and funding cuts are threatening arts education. As a result, the arts access gap between students in well-resourced schools and those in underfunded schools continues to grow (Goldberg, 2021). Currently, eight states don't even require elementary schools to offer arts education instruction (Arts Education Partnership, 2021)! These trends mean that more burden is placed on comprehensive classroom teachers to fill those gaps and provide arts education to students. In many schools, our students won't get any exposure to the arts unless we provide it. To prepare ourselves to integrate the arts into our teaching, we must not only learn about arts integration, but also practice arts integration by creating artworks and lessons that will deepen our understanding of teaching and learning. Additionally, we need to critically reflect on how and why (certain types of) art and (particular) artists are respected by society and/or end up in the canon, while others remain undervalued.

As we dive into arts integration, we'll learn what arts-integrated teaching is, discuss why we should do it, and explore how to implement it in our own practice. We will investigate questions like: What is literature? What are the elements and principles of visual art? Why should we use music in our teaching? Why is media literacy important? How do we integrate drama into our lessons? How can we use movement to assess student learning? We will engage these questions through hands-on activities that will mirror what you can do in your own teaching. We'll also reflect on how (and why) we select the art and artists we include in our lives. We'll consider all of these through a lens of critical pedagogy and cultural responsiveness.

On the first day of class, I like to have my students do a reflection activity (Pause & Reflect 13.1). Please join in.

Pause & Reflect 13.1

Read the following prompt and then close your eyes as you call on your memory:

Think of a specific positive school experience from your (K–8) childhood. Picture it in your mind with as much detail as you can.

What were you doing in the memory? ______________________

Who was involved in the memory? ______________________

What were you learning during that memory? ______________________

I've never had a student respond that their positive school memory was about taking a standardized test. Students get excited to tell me about how their social studies teacher had the class hold a mock trial, or how they performed Macbeth in their English class. Students light up as they describe learning songs to memorize facts in science or math, and how they still remember all the steps to the dance they made up to explain mitosis. Was your memory an arts-integrated activity?

What Arts Integration Contributes to Academic Rigor

While many may dismiss art as "just coloring" or a "filler" activity, engaging with the arts has numerous benefits for students, ranging from improved learning and achievement across subject areas to increased empathy, persistence, and self-discipline. The arts are more than a "bonus"— they act as a motivator for students and foster key 21st-century skills (i.e., critical thinking, creativity, communication, and collaboration). You can check out Claudia Cornett's (2015) or Merryl Goldberg's (2021) texts for in-depth discussions of specific research findings related to these and other arts-integration outcomes (e.g., increased engagement, improved test scores, higher education attainment) if you're interested. I'd like to focus on some specific ways we can engage the arts to deepen our understanding of our roles as educators and lifelong learners.

Brainstorm!

Think about what makes a good learner (not a good *student*). Then think about what makes a good teacher. Use the T-chart in Activity 13.1 to make a list of the traits of a good learner and those of a good teacher. List as many traits as you can for each.

Activity 13.1 Brainstorm!

Good Learner	Good Teacher

Now look at the lists you made. What types of traits did you write down? If you're anything like the students in my class, you said that a good learner is "persistent," "curious," and "present" (or similar). You probably said that a good teacher is "kind," "open-minded," and "patient." You probably didn't list anything about test scores or standards. Both good teaching and good learning are about being curious and open to deep engagement. The arts allow us to teach all kinds of important soft skills (e.g., creativity, collaboration, problem-solving, reflection) while providing alternate paths to mastering hard skills (a.k.a. "content"). An arts-integrated curriculum demands higher order thinking, as students learn to analyze and evaluate options and then create solutions to meet their inquiries. Maybe my favorite thing about art is that the process is just as valuable as the product.

The Arts Domains

Before we go any further, let's make sure we have a working understanding of the arts. There are many types of art, but in this chapter, we'll focus on literature (literary art), visual art, dramatic art, music, and dance/creative movement. The media arts will also be mentioned in passing; typically, they are used in combination with other arts domains.

Please recognize that there is often overlap in arts domains, depending on the nature of a specific work. Each domain can be categorized based on how art is created, shared, and consumed. For example, visual art is created using some medium (e.g., oil paint, pastels, collage, clay), displayed, and taken in by sight. Some museums are moving toward greater accessibility and including tactile versions of visual arts that blind and visually impaired patrons "see" with their hands. Music, dance, and drama are all performing arts that are meant to be performed and consumed in real time. Music can be created with instruments, voices, or everyday objects and is consumed aurally. Deaf and hard of hearing people also enjoy music, typically through sensing sound vibrations. Dance and dramatic arts use the body as the instrument; dance is often accompanied by music, and dramatic arts often rely on written dialogue (a form of literary art) and visuals (e.g., costumes, set, props) to convey the narrative. Media arts are generally technology-assisted and may combine several different art domains.

Arts Literacy

In schools, we tend to focus on literacy as it pertains to the written word. Often the emphasis is on comprehension of canonical texts, or "learning to earn" (Duncan-Andrade & Morrell, 2008), with little attention to critical literacy. True literacy goes beyond identifying main ideas, retelling, and sequencing; it is "an interchange where [one's] understanding of the world allows them to better understand the word, and the word allows them to better understand their world" (Duncan-Andrade & Morrell, 2008, p. 27). Critical literacy requires us to understand what we take in and be able to respond to it in meaningful and appropriate ways. Within the arts, we must understand the elements and principles of each art domain to appreciate their role in each work.

Critique as Practice

One way to practice literacy across contexts is to conduct critiques. I teach art critique as a four-step process:

1. Describe. What is the title of the work? Who is the artist? What media were used? When was it created? What do you see in the painting? What is the plot of the play? What instruments do you hear in the song? How many dancers are on the stage? What is the poem about? Be specific.
2. Analyze. How is the work organized? What elements and principles are in use? How do they work together? Use discipline-specific vocabulary.
3. Interpret. What is the artist trying to communicate/what is their goal? How are the elements and principles being used to achieve that goal? How does any background knowledge or context inform our understanding? Make connections between the goal and the form.
4. Evaluate/judge. Do you like the piece? Is it effective in meeting the artist's goal? Use evidence from Steps 1–3 to support your evaluation.

Art Critique

Now, find any piece of art you enjoy (visual, dramatic, music, literary, or dance) and practice critiquing it using the four-step process just outlined. To make sure you're working from a frame of critical pedagogy, consider the following: Who is the artist? What are their privileged and oppressed identities? Who is the intended audience? What were the relevant social or political issues that the artist faced at the time of their creation? (How) Is the sociopolitical context showing up in the work? Use the guide in Activity 13.2 to answer these questions.

Activity 13.2 Practicing Critiquing

Step 1. Describe. Be specific.	**Step 2. Analyze.** Use specific vocabulary.
Step 3. Interpret. Make connections.	**Step 4. Evaluate.** Support your judgment.

In using this critique activity with students in your own elementary class, it may be helpful to allow students to select a work of art that they enjoy or find meaningful. The skills used in the art critique process will reinforce their skills in the areas of observation, application, supporting claims with evidence, making connections, evaluation, and communicating ideas. These skills are used across content areas and at all levels of schooling. Depending on how students present their critiques (orally, in written form, or using technology), this assignment can strengthen their presentational and/or writing skills as well. Allowing students to choose their focus piece can provide space to draw on their Funds of Knowledge. Encouraging students to critique works by artists from marginalized backgrounds can also contribute to cultural competence and critical consciousness.

Arts integration also supports academic rigor across content areas by providing multiple avenues for students to learn, practice skills, and demonstrate understanding. For example, a music-loving student who may struggle to write an essay could show what they know about a topic by writing a song about it. Similarly, students who have test anxiety may better demonstrate their understanding by creating a piece of visual or dramatic art. By making learning more engaging, fun, and creative, we extend academic rigor to all students.

Why Arts Integration Improves Cultural Competence

Cultural competence requires individuals to be fluent in their own culture, as well as in the other cultures and in the culture of power. The arts provide the perfect opportunity for students to share and learn about their own cultures and others'. Integrating the arts to foster cultural competence means looking beyond high (i.e., prestigious, mainstream) culture and embracing cultures that may be marginalized or overlooked. It also means understanding the deeper levels of culture by examining the cultural products, such as art, music, and literature. In art, there is truth and reflection. Art can be a means for embodying, transmitting, or communicating histories and cultures (Goldberg, 2021). The arts connect families and reinforce identity.

The representative nature of art can provide insight to practices, perspectives, and products that distinguish a given culture. The creative aspect of art can suggest potential and alternative futures for that culture. Educators can incorporate the arts into their teaching in several ways: They can teach with art, about and in art, or through art (Cornett, 2015). Teaching with art often involves using the artwork as a companion piece to illustrate some point in the main content. Teaching about or in art treats the artwork as a text to be interpreted. Teaching through art occurs when the core content and arts objectives are balanced. Each of these approaches to integration has uses and benefits, especially in building cultural competence. Cultural competencies can be nurtured through the intentional use of diverse arts, artists, and themes.

In schools, the arts are an excellent way to present different perspectives, showcase diverse voices, and validate and celebrate various cultures, and cultural practices and perspectives. Arts integration creates spaces for classroom teachers to draw on their students' Funds of Knowledge. Students can share art from their own backgrounds and call attention to artists in their communities. Art has the power to transcend languages and borders. Conscientious educators can provide multicultural learning experiences to all students through arts integration, which extends Rudine Sims Bishop's (1990) essay, "Mirrors, Windows, and Sliding Glass Doors."

Activity 13.3 Arts Inventory

Think about all the various arts you engage in either as artist or as viewer. Are you just gazing in the mirror, or are you looking out different windows and walking through those sliding glass doors? Here, I would like for us to take an inventory of all our arts engagement and consumption.

Literary Arts: What do you read? Do the authors and subjects share your background? Do they represent a variety of backgrounds? Are protagonists from marginalized backgrounds portrayed positively? Are minoritized protagonists represented in works other than biographies and historical literature? Do you read books that are written in more than one language?

Visual Arts: What type of visual arts (paintings, drawings, collage, sculpture) do you enjoy? Who are the artists, and who are the subjects? Do they share your background, or do they represent a variety of backgrounds? Do they portray diverse geographic, historic, and cultural themes?

Dramatic Arts: If you are watching dramatic productions (including TV and movies), are the actors and writers from diverse backgrounds? Are you watching stories that feature a variety of themes, cultures, and communities?

Dance/Creative Movement: What are your attitudes toward dance? What kinds of dance do you enjoy? Are you familiar with multiple genres and cultural traditions?

Music: What kind of music do you listen to? Do you include a variety of genres and artists in the rotation? What kinds of music do you value?

Even though I'm bicultural, I realized a few years ago that a lot of the art I was consuming was very hetero-White-Anglo-centric. So, I made a point of diversifying my arts intake. I started to seek out art and content created by and about queer, BIPOC (Black, Indigenous, and People of Color), and non-English-speaking people. I have discovered amazing music, television, podcasts, poetry, and books. I have also expanded my understanding of different cultures, genres, and ways of life. More important to this conversation, I have discovered so many amazing resources to use in my teaching.

It's important for you, as a teacher, to (1) integrate art into your teaching and (2) consider how the art you use in your teaching reflects or does not reflect your students' experiences and backgrounds. It's also important to make sure you're choosing art that provides multiple windows and sliding glass doors for them to learn about other cultures. Modeling an appreciation for different cultural traditions will help students recognize and appreciate the value of their own cultures and those of others.

How Arts Integration Can be Empowering and Facilitate Critical Consciousness

Arts Inventory Reflection

Return to your arts inventory in Activity 13.3. For each resource you identified, ask yourself the following:

- Who is being uplifted? Who is being dehumanized? Who is being ignored?
- What messages am I receiving from these works of art?
- When do I consume art?
- Where will I make space for my students to bring in art from their lives?

- Why do I choose the art I take in?
- How do I select the art I consume? How can I include more voices and perspectives?

We can be intentional about the art we consume in our personal lives, as well as the art we use in our teaching. We can do this through honing our skills of curation. Including diverse artists and art forms in our teaching is a great first step. The next step is to interrogate what art we have been including, how we have been selecting it, and what messages we have been sending our students, intentionally or not, through their inclusion or exclusion. Reflection is where we are encouraged to think about our own thought process, feelings, and reactions, and how the assignment fits into the course. When we explicitly think about our problem-solving and decision-making approach, we learn about ourselves and become more empowered to make sense of the world and change it for the better. Activity 13.4 will help us practice and reflect on our decision-making and allow us to move past self-consciousness to creatively problem solve.

Self-Portrait Page

A huge piece of curation is decision-making and reflection. Activity 13.4 will help you practice your decision-making and reflection skills. Ideally, you'll need to work with a partner and a timer (I just use my cell phone). You should also have a variety of writing and drawing materials available. Please follow along, adhering strictly to each step of the process. If you're working with a partner, read each step (Steps 1–5) aloud to your partner.

1. You'll use each of the boxes in the template to complete a different task. Each task (also known as each "round") will be slightly different and will be timed.
2. Okay, pick one box for this first round. When I say "Go," you'll draw a self-portrait in that box.
   a. [Set the timer for 3 minutes.]
   b. [When you're ready, say "Go," and start the timer.]
   c. [When the timer goes off, call "Pencils down!" or "Stop!"]

3. Take a moment to shake out your hand. Now, focus on another box. This time you'll have 2 minutes to write as much as you can about yourself.
   a. [Set the timer for 2 minutes and repeat Steps 2b and 2c.]
4. Now pick another box. You'll have 1 minute to draw another self-portrait.
   a. [Set the timer for 1 minute and repeat Steps 2b and 2c.]
5. Last one! For your final self-portrait, you'll have 30 seconds.
   a. [Set the timer for 30 seconds and repeat Steps 2b and 2c.]

Activity 13.4 Self-Portrait Page

Self-Portrait Page	
Round 1	Round 2
Round 3	Round 4

After you and your partner have finished your self-portrait pages, reflect on the experience. In my class, students are encouraged to share their pages at their tables. There are usually giggles and smiles as they share and admire each other's work. Then we discuss the creative process, how we felt during the activity, and what we noticed when we shared our self-portrait pages. Respond to the following questions:

1. Describe how you approached each phase of the activity.

   ____

2. How did you feel during the various phases of the self-portrait activity?

   ____

3. What did you notice about your partner's portrait page?

   ____

4. How do you see this activity connecting to your courses?

Did you change your approach from one phase to the next? In my experience, most people do. For example, even though the first round provides the longest time limit, it is most often the least complete. Some may start out using color and trying to include a lot of detail. Once they have experienced the first drawing and writing rounds, they have a better sense of how long a minute last. They often stick to a single color and eliminate extraneous details in subsequent rounds. The process of thinking through the approach to the task, as well as articulating that approach, helps improve metacognition and can help strengthen self-confidence.

Forwarding Critical Consciousness in the Classroom: An Anecdote

I task preservice teachers (PSTs) in my arts and literature across the curriculum class to select an artist whose work is meaningful to them. PSTs research the artist's life, explore the context of the time in which they were creating their art, and select three or four works for analysis. They then develop a microlesson that integrates a content standard with an arts activity inspired by their chosen artist. After giving a brief presentation about their artist and sharing some of the artist's work with the class for context, PSTs lead the class in an arts-integrated microlesson. Classmates engage in the arts lesson and then keep their artifact as a sample to inspire future lessons. After completing the presentation and microteaching, everyone reflects on the experience. They are evaluated on the completeness of the task, the alignment of their standards and content matter, the creative engagement of the activity, and the depth of their reflection.

Recently, a PST researched Banksy, the elusive graffiti artist, for their project. After teaching the class about the artist and explaining that Banksy's work often has political or social commentary, the student had classmates work in groups to create "graffiti" using acrylic paint on sticky-backed poster papers hung around the classroom. Basing the assignment on a fifth-grade social studies standard, the PST instructed classmates to imagine they were graffiti artists in the 1960s creating activist art to oppose Jim Crow laws. The PST enforced a time limit by reminding their classmates that in this scenario, graffiti is unlawful, so they would have to work quickly to avoid being discovered by the police. The class created art that called for an end to Jim Crow, declaring "No justice, no peace," and "Together as one." Another used multiple colors to spell "Justice" with the message "F*** Jim Crow" underneath.

Students were not only learning about a street artist and engaging with visual art as a medium of expression; they were also role-playing activists during the civil rights era. This required a knowledge of the social and political context of the period and necessitated perspective-taking skills that would allow them to imagine how they would have felt in that time. It forced students to consider the roles of the government, the public, and activists in enforcing unjust laws. The activity provided academic rigor while building empathy, collaboration, creativity, and critical consciousness.

The arts provide the perfect vehicle for challenging the status quo and encouraging critical consciousness. Art serves many purposes, including as sociopolitical commentary. Examining and creating art can be powerful means to engage with complex curricular, social, and political concepts. The arts have long been used to explore social change, promote activism, and indicate protest (Donahue & Stuart, 2010; Greene, 1995). Public art and community art can provide windows into communities—they highlight what is valued or reveal what concerns exist.

Challenges and Opportunities

The biggest barriers to successful arts integration are lack of confidence on the part of the teacher, space in the curriculum, and access to resources. The first is easily overcome by recognizing that in art, the process and product are equally valuable, so you don't have to "be an artist" to implement arts integration in your classroom. Young children love to draw, sing, dance, and tell stories! Self-consciousness is learned, and children lose interest in the arts and certain school subjects once "being good" at them is prioritized over creativity and self-expression. Emphasizing the importance of the artistic process (rather than the product) can help build confidence. Collaboration can also ease some of the anxiety around your own artistic skills. Community members, local artists, university faculty, and colleagues may be able to act as visiting artists in your classroom. Model collaboration. Remember: You don't always have to be the expert!

The second concern is legitimate; more content is being squeezed into the curriculum, and more days are taken up by scripted curriculum, standardized testing, and test prep. Even so, content standards typically have broad objectives at their core. An English language arts standard may require students to identify elements of a story or write a persuasive essay. The standards don't typically dictate which stories must be read, or which specific essay topics need to be addressed. Bring in diverse authors and topics! Being able to add and subtract whole numbers is not dependent on completing soulless drill worksheets—make math relevant! You can implement effective art-integrated instruction in your classroom with a little creative problem-solving.

The last barrier, however, is not as easily removed. Under-resourced schools, which students from marginalized backgrounds are more likely to attend, offer arts opportunities less often than well-resourced schools do. "Real" art supplies can be costly, particularly because they are often consumable (i.e., they can't be reused). Lack of financial resources or administrative support can hinder arts-integration efforts. That said, reclaimed and recycled art supplies may be obtained with some effort. Many stores donate supplies to teachers or offer grants. Collaborations with area businesses, galleries, museums, and theaters may also be fruitful. Yes, I'm talking about collaboration again.

Conclusion

I have worked in schools where students who did not meet reading proficiency benchmarks were denied world language classes, art classes, and music lessons. Despite decades of research that indicates otherwise, many schools continue to treat the arts as disposable luxuries. As Rabkin and Redmond (2006) declared, "It's time to stop thinking about the arts as fluff" (p. 60). Arts education is important for all students, not just those who can afford private music lessons or who plan to attend college. The arts can mitigate factors that otherwise present barriers to academic achievement and educational attainment. Catterall (2009) found that students who had more exposure to arts education consistently scored better on the SATs, had higher academic achievement and attainment, earned better grades in college, worked at better paying jobs, and were more engaged with their communities than those with lower levels of arts exposure. Miller (2015) found that students who lacked arts education were at a disadvantage in college and career readiness.

In addition to leveling the field for students from under-resourced communities, arts integration can create more equitable learning experiences for members of other marginalized groups. The arts can be integrated in schooling to improve learning for special education students, students in gifted programs, deaf students, neurodivergent students, and emergent bilingual students, among others (Brouillette et al., 2021; Catterall, 2009; Goldberg, 2021). Because arts integration is multimodal, it offers students various opportunities for success. Content can be presented in multiple ways, and students can demonstrate understanding through the arts. This accessibility can be especially meaningful for students with cognitive disabilities or communicative barriers that may inhibit their ability to communicate through traditional (written or oral) means.

The arts provide the perfect vehicle for challenging the status quo and encouraging critical consciousness. Art serves many purposes, including as sociopolitical commentary. Examining and creating art can be powerful means to engage with complex curricular, social, and political concepts.

In making schools transformative spaces of possibility, we can look to the arts. Arts integration aligns with a critical pedagogical perspective in that it promotes rigor, supports cultural competence, and fosters critical consciousness. Implementing an arts-integrated curriculum increases accessibility and equity while helping students to develop crucial skills. Above all, art helps us understand what it means to be human. If schools and teachers truly want to do what's best for their students, they will find ways to promote and integrate the arts in their teaching.

Action Plan: Next Steps

I hope that you've found the activities in this chapter to be useful, fun, and thought-provoking. The exercises were all designed to help us think more deeply about what it means to engage in meaningful arts integration. Now that we've discussed the benefits of arts integration and its potential for increasing rigor, facilitating cultural competencies, and empowering critical consciousness, let's make a plan!

1. Name three specific ways you can be more intentional about integrating diverse art into your life and teaching.

2. Identify three areas in which you can be intentional about which voices, perspectives, and identities are prioritized in your classroom.
3. List three specific ways to advocate for more arts access and opportunities for students in your community.

References

Arts Education Partnership. (2021, March 29). ArtScan at a glance. https://www.ecs.org/artscan-at-a-glance/

Bishop, R. S. (1990). Mirrors, windows, and sliding glass doors. *Perspectives: Choosing and Using Books for the Classroom, 6*(3), 9–11.

Brouillette, L., Grove, D., & Hinga, B. (2021). How arts integration has helped k-2 teachers to boost the language development of English-language learners. *Journal of School Leadership, 25*, 286–312.

Catterall, J. (2009). *Doing well and doing good by doing art: The effects of education in the visual and performing arts on achievements and values of young adults*. Imagination Group/I-Group Books.

Cornett, C. E. (2015). *Creating meaning through literature and the arts: Arts integration for classroom teachers* (5th ed.). Pearson.

Donahue, D. M., & Stuart, J. (Eds.). (2010). How does art connect to social justice? In *Artful teaching: Integrating the arts for understanding across the curriculum, K–8* (pp. 31–41). Teachers College Press.

Duncan-Andrade, J. M. R., & Morrell, E. (2008). *The art of critical pedagogy: Possibilities for moving from theory to practice in urban schools*. Peter Lang.

Goldberg, M. (2021). *Arts integration: Teaching subject matter through the arts in multicultural settings* (6th ed.). Routledge.

Greene, M. (1995). *Releasing the imagination. Essays on education, the arts, and social change.* Jossey-Bass.

McDermott, A. (2021). What was the first "art"? How would we know? *Proceedings of the National Academy of Sciences of the United States of America, 118*(44), e2117561118. https://www.pnas.org/doi/10.1073/pnas.2117561118

Miller, C. C. (2015, October 16). Why what you learned in preschool is crucial at work. *The New York Times*. https://www.nytimes.com/2015/10/18/upshot/how-the-modern-workplace-has-become-more-like-preschool.html

Rabkin, N., & Redmond, R. (2006). The arts make a difference. *Educational Leadership, 63*(5), 60–64.

Silverstein, L. B., & Layne, S. (2010). *What is arts integration?* Kennedy Center for the Performing Arts. https://www.kennedy-center.org/education/resources-for-educators/classroom-resources/articles-and-how-tos/articles/collections/arts-integration-resources/what-is-arts-integration/

FOURTEEN

Physical Education

Deborah A. Garrahy

TEACHERS, REGARDLESS OF AREAS OF expertise, are duty-bound to create learning environments where students feel welcomed, valued, represented, and heard. The purpose of this chapter is to provide elementary classroom teachers, current and future, with information on the power of incorporating positive physical activity (PPA) into their daily learning environment. PPA is a term I use for educators, parents, and adults who work with children to emphasize that not all physical activity is PPA. PPA involves movement-oriented experiences that are inclusive of all children and lead to a lifelong enjoyment of movement. Let me share what PPA is not. It does not include movement experiences that humiliate, bully, or demean a human being. For example, a ridiculous game such as dodgeball, in which the focus is on hitting a classmate, is nothing more than sanctioned bullying by the teacher and has no place within a school building or playground. PPA should be a component of physical education, but I am not naïve; not all physical education experiences are positive. I want to acknowledge that I'm aware that your own experiences with physical activity and physical education may enhance or diminish your interest in this chapter, which is one of the reasons I'll have you revisit your movement experiences as a young learner.

In this chapter, I hope to convey the benefits of an academically rigorous elementary physical education/PPA program and the interconnections of movement integration with classroom subjects, cultural competence, and the ability to develop critical consciousness via physical activity. I have always believed that education should never be compartmentalized, meaning that the learning of reading, mathematics, and science does not just occur in a primary school classroom—it must occur in every classroom. The same is true for the movement skills found in a quality elementary physical education program. Classroom teachers can use movement as an extension of their daily lessons, while enhancing the movement experiences of their elementary children. Student learning should be a cross-integrational experience between classroom subjects, physical education, art, and music. For decades, I have integrated classroom subjects into my physical education lessons. Please understand that I'm not asking you to teach physical education; that must always be taught by a licensed physical education teacher. Chances are, as a classroom teacher, you're not accustomed to managing 25+ moving bodies, usually with some type of equipment. As your interest in adding PPA into your teaching develops, never hesitate to contact your physical education teacher, or visit one of the resources provided in this chapter.

Increasing the gross motor movements (large muscles of the body) of your students leads to their increased ability to concentrate, less fidgeting, and improved motivation and engagement, to name a few benefits (Centers for Disease Control and Prevention, 2022). Children are natural movers, but for much of their day, including the school day, they are sedentary—at a desk, watching TV, or using technology—engaging in activities that do not include using the large muscles of their bodies, nor increasing their heart rate. Therefore, it is imperative that we all find ways to increase the PPA levels of our children, which may also increase our own movement abilities.

Physical education is often marginalized based on stereotypes, misperceptions ("How hard could it be to teach physical education?" "Wow, you get to play all day with kids?," and so on), and positive or negative personal experiences. There are outstanding physical educators and those who are a disgrace to my profession. This is true with any school subject, not just physical education. However, when done well, physical education provides children with foundational skills needed to instill a love of movement that can lead to a healthy lifestyle.

Physical Education

Physical education, taught by a licensed physical educator, is the only school subject that consistently teaches within the psychomotor, cognitive, and affective domains. Quality physical education programs help students to develop motor skills that assist them in developing a healthy lifestyle and should provide individuals with physical literacy. Physical literacy is defined as "the ability, confidence, and desire to be physically active for life" (Aspen Institute, 2015, p. 9)

Young learners complete their physical education lessons in the gymnasium, which is a very public space. There are no desks or nooks in which to privately complete lesson tasks. Classmates can observe young learners' successes and frustrations. Given all this, for learning to occur, creating a movement environment built on trust, safety, inclusion, and acceptance is of the utmost importance, in the elementary classroom generally or the physical education classroom specifically.

At the elementary level, physical education and PPA should always focus on the learning and implementation of basic movement concepts (BMC) and fundamental motor skills (FMS). BMC and FMS are the foundations on which all other movements are based. Like elementary mathematics, reading, and writing, elementary physical education and PPA provide opportunities to use basic movement concepts (how the body moves, where the body moves, etc.) and the fundamental locomotor (hopping, skipping, jumping, etc.) and manipulative skills (tossing, throwing, striking, kicking, etc.). These basic forms of movement transition into more complex movements such as dance, racket sports, swimming, rollerblading, and team and individual sports. Students develop their likes and dislikes based on their experiences. Physical education and physical activity are no different. A love of physical activity must be instilled early on; it's a major component to leading a healthy life.

According to the U.S. Department of Health and Human Services, children 6–17 years old should have at least 60 minutes of moderate to vigorous physical activity each day (U.S. Department of Health and Human Services, 2018). Of course, physical education programs should provide a significant portion of this 60-minute requirement, but that is not the case: Only 15% of school districts in the United States provide elementary students with physical education three times per week (National Physical Activity Plan Alliance, 2018). This is a major problem. An issue related to the lack of access to quality physical education is its marginalization as an academic subject. The devaluing of physical education exists in every school district in this country, and this is exemplified when principals and superintendents either completely remove elementary physical education from the curriculum or bastardize it by placing a non–physical education teacher in the role. Even if, as an elementary education teacher candidate, you were required to complete a 2- or 3-credit-hour course in physical education, this in no way would prepare you to assume full-time responsibilities as a licensed physical educator. I am always concerned when I hear or read about districts placing the responsibility of physical education goals and outcomes on classroom teachers, especially regarding the safety of children.

While I will be focusing on incorporating PPA into your classroom routine, please note that I am not talking about recess types of activities. Although it plays a role in promoting active play for elementary students, recess does not always involve students' being physically active, nor is it always positive. Recess should be left as unstructured time for children. Currently, only 62% of school districts provide children with regularly scheduled access to recess (National Physical Activity Plan Alliance, 2018). Finally, the Aspen Institute, through its Project Play initiative, identifies the following groups of children as having the greatest need to increase their daily physical activity: Black and Brown students, girls, children with different abilities, children from low-income families, youth in the South, and American Indian and Alaska Native youth (Aspen Institute, 2015).

For this chapter, I'll focus on how PPA, outside of the physical education classroom, can be integrated into daily lessons to enhance not only your students' physical health, but their cognitive and affective abilities as well.

Positionality Statement

Deborah Garrahy (she/her/hers)

I am a female, gay White first-generation academic, born and raised in New York City, and I have spent my entire professional career in the Midwest. Throughout my 36-year career, I have taught kindergarten through graduate school and served 7 years as an administrator. My first 7 years had me teaching in the Ohio Public Schools in Central (Hilliard) and Northern Ohio (Lakewood), where I taught adapted (physical education for K–12 students with disabilities) and general physical education in Grades K–5. The remainder of my career has been with physical education-teacher education programs at Indiana University and Illinois State University. I have been at Illinois State University for 25 years. During this time, I earned the rank of full professor within the School of Kinesiology and Recreation and served 7 years as the director of the Cecilia J. Lauby Teacher Education Center, overseeing 28 undergraduate teacher education programs with 4,000 teacher candidates across five colleges. I returned to teaching in January 2020 and currently teach undergraduate courses in motor development and instructional methods, and our senior seminar. At the graduate level, I teach Sociocultural Perspectives in Physical Education Pedagogy. Additionally, I am a qualitative researcher. I include these details because as a gay citizen, a woman, a physical educator, and a qualitative researcher, I have experienced years of personal and professional marginalization. Using one example, during an on-campus interview for a tenure-track position, I was told by a faculty member that "qualitative research will not earn you tenure." I proved them wrong.

My positionality as an educator has always included the lens of a lifelong learner, especially with a focus on cultural humility—my own and assisting my teaching candidates with theirs. I am a work in progress as a teacher and a human being. For instance, in discussing White privilege with my seniors, I let them know that it was only during the last few years, after much reading and listening, that I truly comprehended what White privilege meant. It did not, as I originally thought, have to do with the following: "I worked and paid my own way through four college degrees, cleaning bathrooms during the summer as an undergraduate and working full time during advanced degree studies. Nothing was handed to me." As we should know, that is not what White privilege is about. It's about the institutional benefits I have been afforded and as a White person: experiences with law enforcement, having teachers who looked like me, books and TV shows that represented my race, neighborhoods, and so on. All of this is to say, we teachers (parents, guardians, all humans, actually) must continually examine our beliefs, because what a teacher believes becomes their teaching practice. We are socializing agents for the children we interact with each day. They are watching, listening, and learning from us.

Key Terms:

- **Lifelong learning:** dedication to being a pro-active student throughout life.
- **Physical education:** learning that encourages physical literacy, psychomotor control, and a healthy lifestyle.
- **Physical literacy:** "the ability, confidence, and desire to be physically active for life" (Aspen Institute, 2015, p. 9).
- **Positive physical activity:** movement-oriented tasks and experiences that lead to a lifelong enjoyment of exercise.

Key Ideas:

1. ***How does integrating positive physical activity promote academic rigor across the curriculum?***
2. ***What does physical activity have to do with cultural competency?***
3. ***How can positive physical activity promote critical consciousness?***

Before we begin, let's have you reflect on your own movement experiences. Please don't focus on organized sports, because sports are not inclusive for all children. Think about how you physically played as child—running, jumping, swimming, throwing, bike-riding, skateboarding, and so on—your physical education experiences. What did you enjoy? What did you not enjoy? What are your physical activity habits now? Do you wish you had different physical activity habits? If so, what are they? Our past experiences shape our beliefs, and as teachers, we must be aware of how we can pass those beliefs on to our students.

Activity 14.1 is a modified version of an assignment I use in my motor development class with my physical education-teacher education candidates.

Activity 14.1 Physical Activity Autobiography

Describe your personal gross motor development/physical activity based on the developmental levels that follow. If possible, speak with the adults in your life who witnessed your movement progressions. During your infancy and early childhood years, you may have had activities that you enjoyed, or you may have joined sports or movement teams. How are you physically active now?

Provide your information for the developmental levels included in the following list, including future projections for middle and older adulthood.

- Infancy
- Early childhood (preschool years)
- Late childhood (elementary school years)
- Preadolescence (middle school years)
- Adolescence (high school years)
- Young adulthood (college years)
- Middle/older adulthood (your projected future)

How does integrating positive physical activity promote academic rigor across the curriculum?

All of us teachers, regardless of our expertise, must help children experience learning beyond our classroom door thresholds. Teaching and learning need not be compartmentalized, such as math only happens at 10 a.m.; science is taught by Ms. Smith; and physical education is MWF. Having put this belief into my teaching practice, I never felt that I "lost" physical education content and time, nor did my first-grade colleague reduce her reading time by integrating other school subjects into my lessons. Here's an example. Through a small reading grant, I purchased 30 copies of *Albert the Running Bear's Exercise Book* (Isenberg & Jaffe, 1984) for our school library and first-grade classrooms. My students were familiar with the movements used in the book because I read the story aloud numerous times as we completed each exercise "just like Albert." Such a simple act of cross-curricular integration provided my students the chance to see their teachers through different lenses. I recall a child telling me "Ms. Garrahy, I didn't know you could read," and "Ms. Garrahy, did you know that Ms. F. (classroom teacher) can do physical stuff?"; out of the mouths of my first graders. On the days they did not have physical education, their teachers would read the story aloud and complete the movements with them. I did this with math, science, and spelling, to name a few. Did *every* colleague join me? No, but that was their choice. Learning to move and learning through movement positively impact the psychomotor, cognitive, and affective domains for each child in your care.

Over the course of decades, physical education teachers have developed and implemented movement tasks that incorporate classroom subjects. I wrote about this in a 2001 journal article entitled, "To Integrate or Not to Integrate? That Is the Question" (Garrahy, 2001). It may be a newer concept for some classroom colleagues to infuse movement into their teaching, but it is not in the physical education realm. Researchers have documented that when teachers integrate physical activity with mathematics, science, reading, and languages—and vice versa—there is a positive influence on the learner.

To incorporate PPA into your classroom, start small. Try movement tasks that can be completed next to a child's desk or anywhere you deem appropriate, and they should last no more than 5 minutes. Whatever you select, please remember that no one should be eliminated or embarrassed by participating.

If you're not sure where to begin, speak with your physical education colleague—I know they would love to assist you.

Positive Physical Activity Ideas

- Have developmentally appropriate music ready to go! In fact, many music selections for young children incorporate movements.
  - For instance, Hap Palmer's song "Sally the Swinging Snake" is a classic for young learners. My students loved this! Each student has a sock, jump rope, or piece of string that represents Sally. When they hear the words used in the song, the movement replicates the word. For example, when they hear "Shake," the students shake their "snake."
- Five-minute dance party: Choose two of student's favorite songs and dance!
- Balloon taps and spelling out the word of the day: Find a balloon of your choice and blow it up. Once it is inflated, toss it in the air and keep it in the air with hand taps. For each tap on the balloon, spell out the word of the day. A tap for each letter. Have students try it again using a different body part, keeping the balloon in their self-space. Save the balloon in a large trash bag for another day—perhaps for a lesson on addition or subtraction.
- Animal charades: Write the names of animals on a small piece of paper and place them in a hat or box. Have students take turns pulling names out of the container and then use their body to act out the shape and actions of the animals, for other students to guess.
  - This could be adapted to incorporate superheroine/ superhero poses. Additionally, it reinforces neuromuscular skills through mirror and balance activities.
- Silly 8s (instead of "Crazy 8s" because "Crazy" is ableist language): Have the students move through the following sequence: 8 arm circles, 8 jumping jacks, 8 high-fives to a partner, etc.
- Spelling: Bring various items into the classroom that are appropriate for tossing and catching (tote bags, clean socks rolled in a ball, skirts, gloves, scarves, etc.). Then, toss them to students and have the student who catches the item, spell it.
- Cooperative musical hoops—like musical chairs, but the only items eliminated are the hoops, and the students stand inside the remaining

hoops. At the very end of the game, one hoop is left in the center of the room, and the entire class must fit into it.

- Frozen shoe tag: Remove one shoe and balance it on a body part named by the teacher. Children move about the classroom. When a student's shoe falls off, the only way back into the game is for a classmate to pick up the shoe, while balancing their own, and place it back on the student.
- Human knot: This is a cooperative task for students in third grade and up and involves groups of no more than five. Students reach across and hold the hands of two different classmates. Once the group is joined, they must untie their human knot without letting go of hands.
- Partner tag: One partner is the "tagger", and the other student avoids their partner. When tagged, the new tagger spins around in a circle and then takes off to chase their partner. It involves constant movement for both students.

As your confidence increases (and as your day permits), consider moving to a larger space—perhaps the cafeteria, a multipurpose room, or the playground. Larger spaces give you more room to have students work with assigned partners and use larger muscles of the body for increased physical activity. A few considerations:

1) Smaller groups of students are always better because this provides more opportunities to participate. Keep groups to no more than four children.
2) When adding equipment, be sure there is enough equipment for each child and that no one is waiting a turn or in a line because this defeats the purpose of PPA.
3) Use the start/stop signals used by your physical education colleague because your students will be most familiar with this routine management expectation.

The Society of Health and Physical Educators (SHAPE; https://www.shapeamerica.org/) posts a monthly Elementary Health and Physical Education Activity Calendar with suggestions for activities to do in the classroom or at home for each day of the month, along with interesting health-related suggestions and historical facts. Calendars are available in Spanish and English. For example, the activity for June 26, 2022, is "Walk and Talk: Take a walk with your parents or an adult who takes care of you and talk about what to do if you are bullied or see someone being bullied."

What does positive physical activity have to do with cultural competency?

The choices we make as teachers impact every aspect of a child's day. Children complete physical activities within the public space of their classroom, multipurpose area, or playground. There isn't a private space, such as a classroom desk, to privately complete work. Teachers provide foundational experiences in developing a child's confidence when they handle activities in a developmentally appropriately way.

Cultural competency within PPA must focus on movements that are for every body (body confidence) and everybody (inclusion)! I'll reiterate this later in this section. Body shaming in the United States is horrifically alive and well, including in the primary grades. In American society, we have moved away from realizing that children are learning to move and moving to learn. Not everything must be about "winners and losers." For any human being to repeat a task, it must be enjoyable, otherwise they won't do it. Teachers must create a PPA atmosphere of belonging and safety to develop a sense of trust in students that will allow them to try a new movement task—even if the task lasts for less than 5 minutes.

Working within a cultural competence mindset reminds us that we don't know what we don't know, and we have implicit and explicit biases especially regarding the diversity of humanity. As teachers, we need to be willing to admit this to ourselves and our students, whether they are in kindergarten or graduate school. My teacher candidates learn early on that they are responsible for knowing about not only the students currently in their classrooms, but also the people in their communities and beyond their geographic location. Teachers and, therefore, their students must look beyond the lens of their immediate surroundings in the hope of developing a wider circle of knowledge—therefore I focus on cultural humility. It's not possible for me to truly believe that I can learn all there is to know and be deemed culturally competent. Cervantes and Clark (2019) defined cultural humility as

> the lifelong process of self-reflection, self-awareness, and transformation of one's attitudes, values, and beliefs towards people from diverse cultures and

> how these belief systems (e.g., our own assumptions, biases, values, traditions) affect our interactions with people who come from other cultures, ethnicities, or social classes. (p. 59)

When incorporating PPA in their classroom, teachers must realize that physical activity is for everybody and every body! (I told you I would repeat it!) We live in a country where people use visible traits—skin color, (dis)abilities, physical appearance, and zip codes—as prejudgments in determining interactions and access. Some of these people are teachers. In the physical activity/movement realm, additional stereotypes, modeled by adults and imitated by children, include notions of what girls and boys should or should not "do," and they affect access to extracurriculars, to name a few.

Physical education, physical activity, and sports have long been considered "male domains." While Title IX, an educational amendment, has opened many doors, inequities remain. The intersectionalities of gender, race, socioeconomic status, and abilities, and the constraints that each place on physical activity participation, go beyond the scope of this chapter. However, I'd like to share a few examples and an activity that exemplifies this point. An offshoot of physical education and physical activity should be students' taking what they learned in school and applying it to recreational and youth sports opportunities. (I use the term "recreational" to reflect an unorganized form of participation not governed by fees, parents/adults, and referees.) These types of physical activities are self-governed by children and perhaps incorporate motor skills and games learned in physical education. My goal as an elementary physical education teacher was for my students to find physical activities they enjoyed and use them beyond the walls of my classroom. Youth sport is a formal venue for applying physical skills, but its purpose has vastly changed over the last 30 years. Youth sport participation is a billion-dollar-a-year industry that focuses on the "haves" but not the "have-nots." Children as young as 6 years old are being "cut" from youth sport teams. Ridiculous, isn't it? This should be the place where children continue to learn and apply developing skills. Additionally, many adults/parents use youth sports as their pipeline to their child's future college education. However, the bigger issue with youth sports relates to socioeconomic status. Let's look at one example of how a parent's income determines who gets to participate. For some families, extracurriculars are financially out of reach. Here's the baseline cost to participate in softball, as an example:

- Registration fees: ~$50 or higher (depends on community). This does not include tournament play.
- Individual equipment: Bat bag ($40), bats ($50–$500). Gone are the days when the coach brought the equipment for players to share.
- Softball glove: $80
- Cleats: $50–$100
- Helmet: $30–$70
- Tournaments/travel fees for family, including hotel, food, and gas: variable cost
- Weeknight practices and weekend games

Such costs apply to any youth sport program, not just softball. High fees eliminate children. Think of all the talent automatically eliminated because of one's socioeconomic status. Fees exist for any of the "extra"-curriculars that enrich our souls—music, art, theater, dance, and sports—thereby excluding many talented children.

I hope that your classrooms are rich in diversity, yet there are no guarantees. However, unless you teach in a private school, I can write with certainty that you will always have girls and boys in your classrooms. Activity 14.2 is one that I have used for many years with my teacher candidates (I believe it originated at the University of Massachusetts). I am including this gender-focused activity to ask you to reflect on the messages you learned about what it has meant to be "female" and "male" throughout your lifetime. Educational researchers have written about the hidden curriculum (which is not limited to gendered teaching) for decades, yet, regardless of school subject, the hidden curriculum remains alive and well in each school. What gendered messages do you explicitly or implicitly send to your students?

Activity 14.2 Act Like a Woman/Act Like a Man

This is an assignment I complete with my students in my motor development course. It is the *only* time teacher candidates are segregated into female and male groups (no more than four to a group) to examine how society's gendered messages impact each of us.

1) Create a list of all the gendered stereotypes you have heard, read, observed, or experienced to date. For example:
    - Females will list what they have learned about what it means to "act like a woman."
    - Males will list what they have learned about what it means to "act like a man."
2) When developing your extensive list, consider messages from your environments: family members, teachers, colleagues, administrators, friends, coaches, groups you belong(ed) to (this includes all extracurriculars), social media, movies, etc.
3) Because we are focusing on physical activity, be sure to included gendered messages regarding movement—for example, "You throw like a girl," "Boys don't dance."
4) The examples on your list do not necessarily represent your personal beliefs, but messages you have read, heard, or experienced to date.
5) Select a female and male recorder to document answers from each group (notice I didn't use the word "secretary").
6) Have the class come together and share items that represent their sex, which are listed on the board, alternating between female and male preservice teachers/in-service teachers.
7) After sharing is completed, debriefing occurs regarding what has been noticed about both lists.
8) Discuss the societal messages that females and males/girls and boys receive on a daily basis.

How can positive physical activity promote critical consciousness?

> "If I love you, I have to make you conscious of the things you do not see."
>
> *–James Baldwin*

Diversity in our K–12 public school population is growing. The U.S. Department of Education predicts that by 2024, 56% of our public-school population will be students of color, with Hispanic students representing 29% of our total enrollment. Additionally, the *New York Times* published on June 10, 2022 reported that "1.6 million people in the United States now identify as Transgender, and 43% of them are younger adults and teenagers are White" (Azeen, 2022).

It is imperative that all teacher education programs and school districts interweave the fibers of cultural competency and critical consciousness throughout the tapestry of their professional development requirements for preservice and in-service educators.

Restrictions of chapter space prevent detailed information regarding the ongoing and decades-long research on social justice within physical education and physical education-teacher education. Research outcomes and practical applications center on multilingual learners, gender, body, (dis)ability, Indigeneity, self-identity, race, religion, sexual identity, social class, and bullying (Walton-Fisette, 2019). The activity I selected for this section leads us to examine the privileges we take for granted and possibly ignore their absence for others.

When reflecting on the systems of oppression within the physical activity realm, I am drawn to several areas—all reflect on the choices physical education teachers and classroom teachers make regarding activities that eliminate children, their use of inclusive versus exclusive language, and the opportunities they provide or do not provide for student representation within educational settings.

PPA in any classroom, especially physical education, must always be inclusive. When teachers design tasks that eliminate learners, multiple messages are communicated to the child, such as, "You're not good enough." For instance, I wrote earlier about the traditional format of "tag"—a child is sidelined if they are tagged out. Usually, the children eliminated are those who would truly benefit from the physical activity, yet the teacher designed the task that eliminated the lesser skilled children—in this instance, those who were "not fast enough." Additionally, children who are not comfortable with physical activity find ways to have themselves sidelined so they are not embarrassed by being eliminated. PPA focuses on including and valuing each student in your class. An example of negative physical activity is the repulsive game of dodgeball. Dodgeball is nothing more than teacher-sanctioned bullying and has been in the Physical Education Hall of Shame since 1992. If you cannot eliminate the elimination from your task, find a different activity that engages all your learners. Children should never be sidelined, embarrassed, or used as human targets when it comes to physical activity. No excuses. No discussion.

Importance of Person-First Language

Teacher beliefs have been researched for decades, and here is what is known. Regardless of the subject area, teachers enter classrooms with more than a teaching degree, curriculum guide, and lesson plans. Based on their own educational experiences, they enter their classrooms with embedded notions of the abilities of the students sitting before them. My research on gender and teacher beliefs began with an interaction with one of my third-grade students in 1992. One day after class, Kara asked me, "Ms. Garrahy, why do you call us 'guys? I'm not a guy." Kara was intuitive enough to know that my choice of slang omitted her presence in my class. Many will say "it's just slang," or "it represents girls and boys." Thus, our implicit and explicit beliefs manifest themselves in numerous ways, especially through the language we use in our classrooms. Are we using asset-based language? Gender-inclusive language? Person-first language? How we speak influences the learning experiences of students. Studies that examined the use of teacher language with young children revealed that girls and boys believe that the teacher is only referring to males when they hear the words "you guys." For years, I have shared with my teacher candidates that if it's "not that big of a deal," let's transition to "you gals . . . since you think it's generic, in place of 'you guys.'" That, they thought, was ridiculous, yet when they were made aware of their use of slang, they became more aware of their choice of words. Language remains one of our most powerful platforms, and how we use it tells those we are speaking with what we believe. A person-first perspective puts the student at the forefront. For instance, the "student with Down syndrome," versus "my Down syndrome student" reveals that the teacher sees the student first.

My seconds-long interaction with Kara many years ago led me to rethink what I said to my students and directed my research for many years, beginning with my dissertation focus. I spent 4 months within three elementary classrooms and one physical education classroom, studying teachers' beliefs about the influence of gender at the elementary school level. Despite my transparency with the focus of my study, each teacher worked from a gender-blind position, claiming that they didn't see girls or boys— "just children"—meaning that each believed they did not treat girls and boys differently. However, their interactions revealed otherwise. This outcome paralleled the color-blind perspective discussed when teachers declare, "I don't see the color of a child's skin, I just see a student." In both situations, teachers are diminishing and ignoring the gendered and racist experiences that children bring to our classrooms and the impact that those experiences have on their learning experiences.

We must continually look to infuse materials and examples that remove stereotypes because education is not color-blind, gender-blind, ability-blind, or socioeconomic-blind.

All children must be able to see themselves through your mentoring, including PPA. For instance, you might incorporate visuals of the following:

- Girls playing ice hockey
- Boys dancing
- Senior citizens participating in cycling, walking, or pickleball
- Muslim girls playing on a basketball team
- Students of color swimming
- Body confidence versus body shaming: Omit any visual of the false narrative about the "ideal" body image in American society.
- Remove sexist comments, such as "You throw like a girl," "Boys don't jump rope," or "Girls are better at reading/boys are better at math."

Mindful language and representation are imperative in classrooms. As a teacher, I have always redirected students, even college-age students, when they would comment about what they can't do. Instead of accepting their "I can't do that," I'll have them restate, "I can't do that yet." I also long for the day when there are no "firsts," such as in these examples:

- In advertising: In 2019, Huggies, the company known for their diapers, used a Black father and daughter in its packaging for the first time.
- In professional sports: In 2020, Chris Nikic was the first athlete with Down syndrome to complete the IRONMAN triathlon, and Kim Ng, the first female general manager in Major League Baseball.
- In the highest federal offices in the United States: In 2022, Justice Ketanji Brown-Jackson was sworn in as the 116th associate justice and the first Black female justice on the United States Supreme Court.

When we heighten and continually reexamine our own critical consciousness, we are inherently doing the same for our students.

Activity 14.3 How Privileged Am I?

I have selected a few examples from the How Privileged Am I? workshop from Arizona State University (Terrill & Correa, 2014). Please read through these and reflect:

- I have never been discriminated against because of my skin color.
- I have never been mocked for my accent.
- I am heterosexual.
- I never doubted my parents' acceptance of my sexuality.
- I still identify as the gender I was born in.
- I've never been denied an opportunity because of my gender.
- I've never been homeless.
- I've never had to worry about making rent.
- I graduated from college.
- I do not have any physical disabilities.
- I can afford medication if/when I need it.
- I have never been shamed for my body type.
- I have never been called a terrorist.
- I have never been bullied as a child.
- There is a place of worship for my religion in my town.
- I've never been told I "Sound White."
- My parents pay some of my bills.
- I don't rely on public transportation.

Concluding Thoughts

Whether you read this book as an obligatory assignment or to potentially improve your teaching, I want to thank you for considering how you can actualize the humanization of yourself and Others. Thank you for wading through our genuine attempts to do the same. If you get nothing else from this text, consider our argument that across all subject areas, the best way to teach someone is to center their humanity.

We're asking you to assess your initial perception and think again. When a student is late, is always frustrated, or is not performing at grade-level standard, rather than concluding there is an inherent deficit in them (one that we usually associate and align with the stereotypes of our society), consider if their basic needs are being met or if your instruction was clear, explicit, thorough, or simply interesting enough.

No matter their sexuality, political affiliation, gender, ethnicity, ability, dominant language, race, or geographic background, students have their own perception of schooling that is influenced by socialization. It is neither your fault nor theirs if teaching and schooling have been negatively framed by media, their family and friends, history, society, or their personal experience. Your responsibility—your professional obligation—is to counter and disrupt those ideas. Humanize your students, their communities, and differences to help restore hope.

I beg you to embrace the challenge of figuring out how to make your curriculum reflect student diversity in all its humanity. If you're nervous, great! You need that energy to make sure you're doing it well. That same energy should also have the capacity to allow you to humanize yourself and apply grace. You will mess up! Whether it's your first year of teaching or your 25th, you will continue to mess up. The goal is to mess up less frequently, less impactfully, and never the same way. You need to grow from your mistakes.

If you are a person of color, I'll leave you with a reminder that being culturally relevant is not limited to race and being born a person of color does not give you inherent cultural competence and pedagogical gifts. You are more than your race, ethnicity, class, age, sexuality, faith, geographic origin, upbringing, and other social locations that shaped your identity. Please do not assume that a student who looks like you has had the same lived experiences as you. The advantage you have—that anyone with a cultural parity has—is the potential for greater trust and expedient rapport. If your cultural identity does overlap with that of your students, that can be an excellent advantage if you master pedagogical skills and pedagogical content. Use your knowledge and skills of the curriculum and your knowledge and skills from your shared cultural background to your students' advantage by amplifying the assets of your shared culture and illuminating the connections between the curriculum and their lives. Do it all with an appreciative and humble approach.

If you are a White person, I'll leave you with a reminder that being culturally relevant is not limited to race and being born White doesn't mean that you can't develop cultural competence and pedagogical gifts that can meet the needs of non-White students. Moreover, White children with whom you share cultural parity stand to benefit from cultural competence in the same way that any other human being does. So, when teaching BIPOC students, you have the work of developing your cultural competence just as much as you need to develop pedagogical skills and content knowledge. If your cultural identity does overlap with that of your students, use your knowledge and skills of the curriculum and your knowledge and skills from your shared cultural background to your students' advantage by amplifying the assets of your shared culture (which is typically the standard curriculum), as well as the cultural assets of nondominant groups that are not represented in the curriculum. Help your students humanize themselves and others. Do it all within appreciative and humble approach. In all, considering your differences and humanity, humanization of Others is the minimum that each person deserves.

References

Aspen Institute. (2015, June 28). *Physical literacy in the United States: A model, strategic plan, and call to action.* Project Play.

Azeen, G. (2022, June 10). *Report reveals sharp rise in transgender people in the U.S.* The New York Times. https://nytimes/2022/06/10/science/transgender-teenagers-national-survery.html

Centers for Disease Control and Prevention. (2022). *Classroom physical activity.* Retrieved June 7, 2022, from https://www.cdc.gov/healthyschools/physicalactivity/classroom-pa.htm

Cervantes, C. M., & Clark, L. (2019). Cultural humility in physical education-teacher education: A missing piece in developing a new generation of socially just physical education teachers. *Quest, 72*(1), 57–71.

Garrahy, D. (2001). To Integrate or Not to Integrate? That is the Question. *Strategies, 14*(4), 23–25.

Isenberg, B., & Jaffe, M. (1984). *Albert the running bear's exercise book.* Clarion Books.

National Physical Activity Plan Alliance (2018). *The United States Report Card on Physical Activity for Children and Youth.*

Terrill, M., & Correa, M. (2014, June 12). Project Humanities hosts free workshop on privilege. *ASU News.* https://news.asu.edu/content/project-humanities-hosts-free-workshop-privilege

U.S. Department of Health and Human Services (2018). *Physical activity guidelines for Americans* (2nd ed.).

Walton-Fisette, J. L. (2019). Physical education is a social justice issue. In *Teaching about social justice issues in physical education.* (ix). Information Age.

APPENDIX

Funds of Knowledge

FOK Class Demographic Sheet

Grade____Teacher____

Funds of Knowledge: The competencies students embody that can directly or indirectly connect to formal classroom learning. It encompasses the knowledge, skills, and experiences acquired through historical and cultural interactions of an individual in their community, family life and culture.

Student #	**Gender**	**Race/ Ethnicity**[1]	**SES**[2]	**Home Language**	SPED[3]	**Funds of Knowledge** [4] Family values & tradition, caregiving, household chores, skills, knowledges, responsibilities, insights, experiences, family occupations, etc	**Challenging Circumstances** that *may* affect focus & learning
	What to reflect in the curriculum and be mindful to not act upon implicit biases			*What to consider & accommodate*		*What to celebrate & incorporate*	*What to consider and accommodate in teaching*
1.	F	Black	UM	Haitian Creole	Visual/spatial deficit	Of Haitian descent, strong faith, reading, recycles, loves historical fiction, running, speaks conversational Spanish	Recent immigrant, Learning English
2.	M	Other	LI	English		Mixed African American and Vietnamese, travels to Hanoi every summer, sketching, loves basketball	
3.	F	Black	LI	AAVE		African American, cooks well, recycles, social media, yoga	
4.	F	Latinx	LI	English		Peruvian, learning violin, loves sandboarding, yoga	Highly mobile
5.	M	Black	LI	French		Of Togolese descent, enjoys afro-beat music, loves math, has a YouTube channel	
6.	M	Latinx	LM	Portuguese		Brazilian, Afro Latino, meal prep, loves *America's Got Talent*, social media,	
7.	M	Latinx	M	English		Guatemalan, aspiring meteorologist, has a YouTube channel, likes long drives, yoga	Older sibling is undocumented
8.	M	Asian	LM	English	ADHD	Mainland China, calligraphy, painting cherry blossoms and other watercolors	From Wuhan
9.	F	Asian	LI	Hindi		Indian, wants to be a botanist, recycles, plays cricket, cooks well, social media, yoga	
10.	F	Middle Eastern	LI	English		Egyptian, Islam, dancing, hip-hop music, social media, Eid al-Fitr, and Eid al-Adha	Fasting at times
11.	M	Turkish	M	Turkish	Processing delays	Aspiring economist, loves musicals and sing-a-longs, loves the beach and nature walks, Eid al-Fitr and Eid al-Adha, Islam	Fasting at times
12.	M	Black	LI	English		Loves K-pop, Kemetic history, sketching, hip hop music, boxing, social media,	Mother, a boxer, recently passed away
13.	M	White	LI	English		Likes sketching, great story writer, loves theater, loves baseball & football, loves pizza	Parents divorcing
14.	F	White	UM	English	Dyscalculia	Elder care, hip hop music, likes hiking, likes teas, traveled to 6 countries in Europe	
15.	F	Native American	LI	Muscogee		Creek nation, social media, likes teas, loves autobiographies, types 40 wpm, recycles	

1. Race/Ethnicity: Asian (A), Latinx (L), White(W), Black (B), Native American (NA), Middle eastern (ME), Other (O)
2. Socioeconomic Status: Lower Income/Under-resourced (LI); Lower Middle (LM); Middle (M); Upper Middle (UM); Upper (U)
3. Language: Hmong, Somali, Tagalog, Swahili, Ewe, Portuguese, Yoruba, Creole
4. SPED Classification: Autism, Deafness, Visual Impairment, Speech Impairment, Intellectual Disability Emotional Disturbance, Etc.

About the Authors

Tameka Ardrey is the founder of Bridging the Gap Early Education Consulting and is currently the Birth-Kindergarten Teacher Education program coordinator at Georgia Southern University. She has authored several publications addressing issues of cultural diversity and social inequities within the early education field. Additionally, Dr. Ardrey has had the privilege of sharing her work through presentations and speaking engagements both nationally and internationally.

Katie Lynn Brkich is a Professor of Elementary Science Education at Georgia Southern University and is the chair of the Master's of Elementary Education Program. Her published scholarship includes studies on place-based P-5 science education, the impact of Contextually Mitigating Factors (CMFs) in science education attainment for non-majority populations, and science teacher education promoting equity, diversity, and social justice outcomes.

Ariel Cornett is an Assistant Professor of Elementary Social Studies at Georgia Southern University. She teaches undergraduate and graduate elementary social studies methods courses. Her research interests focus on the place-based teaching and learning of social studies in elementary classrooms and communities. Currently, she serves on the board of directors for the Georgia Council for History Education (GCHE). Prior to her career in higher education, she taught kindergarten, first grade, and third grade in a Virginia public school system.

Deborah A. Garrahy, Ph.D., is a Full Professor in the Physical Education-Teacher Education Program at Illinois State University and was the Director of ISU's Lauby Teacher Education Center, which serves 4,000 education majors. During this time, she oversaw ISU's successful 2019 accreditation review through the Council for the Accreditation of Educator Preparation. Prior to teaching at the University level, Dr. Garrahy was a licensed Adapted Physical Education and General Physical Education Teacher in Ohio Public Schools.

Alesia Mickle Moldavan, Ph.D., is an Assistant Professor of Mathematics and Science Education in the College of Education at Georgia Southern University. She teaches elementary mathematics and science methods courses for preservice and in-service teachers. Her research interests include equitable teaching practices, culturally responsive pedagogy, and the use of digital technology in teacher education. Her work develops innovative curricula in teacher education that promotes cultural awareness and justice-oriented advocacy in global contexts.

LaPortia Mosley, M.Ed., is a Double Eagle alumna and an elementary education instructor in the Department of Elementary and Special Education at Georgia Southern University. Mosley earned a bachelor's and master's in elementary education from Georgia Southern and holds a Gifted and ESOL endorsement. Mosley has taught in both special education and elementary education classrooms across Southeast Georgia. Her research interests include preservice teacher education/preparation, elementary ESOL education, and instructional technology tools.

Erin Piedmont is an Assistant Professor of Elementary Social Studies at Georgia Southern University. She teaches undergraduate and graduate-level social studies methods courses. Erin's teaching and research interests stem from her commitment to preparing preservice and in-service teachers for anti-oppressive social studies pedagogy. Her work currently explores how particular pedagogical approaches in social studies methods courses foster the sociopolitical and critical consciousness of teacher candidates.

Alexandra J. Reyes, Ph.D., is an Associate Professor in the College of Education at Georgia Southern University. Dr. Reyes prepares pre- and in-service educators to work with culturally and linguistically diverse students, and to integrate arts and literature across the curriculum. Her scholarship focuses on how the intersections of language, culture, and identity inform learning experiences for marginalized communities across contexts, as well as the power of arts-integrated pedagogies and methodologies to lower barriers for members of these communities.

Sam Rhodes, Ph.D., is an Assistant Professor of Elementary Mathematics Education at Georgia Southern University. His research examines cognitive, metacognitive, and affective factors that influence student success in mathematical problem solving.

Chelda Smith Kondo, Ph.D., (she/her/hers) identifies as a cisgender, able-bodied, Americanized Haitian womxn. Chelda is an Associate Professor specializing in Culturally Sustaining Pedagogy at the University of St. Thomas (UST). Prior to joining UST, she served as an Associate Professor of Critical Multicultural Education at Georgia Southern University, where she was also director of the Elementary Education Master of Arts in Teaching, a social justice education and initial licensure program that she co-founded. Her scholarly articles have been published in leading education and interdisciplinary journals (i.e., Teachers College Record, Anthropology & Education Quarterly, Equity & Excellence in Education). Her scholarship has been honored for excellence in three different subfields: intersectional justice in education, qualitative research, and culturally relevant pedagogy. Chelda currently sits on the governing board of InterAction Inc, a non-profit committed to activating and advancing Young People of Color (YPOC) and their counter-narratives to build a more just, inclusive, and equitable society. In 2021–2022, Chelda was a visiting scholar at the Opportunity & Inclusive Growth Institute (OIGI) at the Federal Reserve Bank of Minneapolis.

Montana Smithey is a previous elementary classroom teacher and earned her PhD from the University of North Carolina Greensboro in Teacher Education and Development. She is currently an Assistant Professor of Elementary Mathematics Education at Georgia Southern University and works to learn from and support preservice and in-service teachers. Her research interests include mathematics anxiety, teaching that is responsive to children's mathematical thinking, and using social justice within children's literature as an avenue to teach mathematics.

Kara M. Taylor, Ph.D., is a black womxn, mother, wife, sister, friend, and activist. She is currently a clinical assistant professor at Indiana University Purdue University Indianapolis. She teaches literacy methods in the Urban Teacher Education program. She leverages her former experiences as an elementary school teacher to explore the healing and emancipatory power of literacy through the courses she teach along with her research. She is dedicated towards seeking equity for marginalized communities in everything she does.

Anne Valauri is an Assistant Professor of Elementary and Special Education at Georgia Southern University. Her research interests include humanizing and decolonizing family engagement, particularly with multilingual immigrant families. Before coming to Georgia Southern, she spent several years as a teacher/researcher at an early childhood center in the U.S. Midwest with a large immigrant population of diverse regional origin and also taught several years in a bilingual Head Start classroom.

Laura Vines – I grew up in a small rural town in Georgia with incredibly hard-working parents who stressed independence and development of the individual. I don't know if my mindset is a product of my upbringing, my region, my generation (X), or just plain stubbornness, but I hate being "put in a box." I am complex, still evolving, still incomplete, but often feel as an outsider or observer. I think this mindset is what originally drew me to science. In fact, prior to becoming an educator, I was a research scientist.

Index